AF541202

ISI, Indian Mujahideen and Global Terror

ISI, Indian Mujahideen
AND
GLOBAL TERROR

Brig. (Retd.) S. P. Lohia

NEHA PUBLISHERS & DISTRIBUTORS
DELHI

Publisher
NEHA PUBLISHERS & DISTRIBUTORS
4832/24,Prahlad Lane,S-207 Ansari
Road, Daryaganj, Delhi-110002
Ph.: 43570976, 23278261
Email: nehapubdistributors@gmail.com

Edition: 2015

ISBN: 978-93-80318-63-9

Laser Typesetting
JEE-VEE Graphics, Delhi

Price: 1195/-

Printed
Vikas Computers, Delhi

Preface

The Directorate for Inter-Service Intelligence [ISI] was formed in 1948 by the British Army Officer Major General William Cawthorne, then serving as the new state of Pakistan's Army Deputy Chief of Staff. The ISI was established within the Pakistan Army to supplement the existing Military Intelligence [MI] as a means to address the lack of inter-service intelligence co-operation which had proven so disastrous for Pakistan in the 1947 Indo-Pak war. Trained from its early days by UK's Military Intelligence, and a little later by the CIA and, for a short spell, the French SDECE, the ISI originally had no role beyond that of military intelligence-gathering except in relation to the disputed region in Pakistan Administered Kashmir and the Northern areas of Gilgit and Baltistan.

Indian Mujahideen (IM) is a terrorist group based in India. The group has carried out several attacks against civilian targets in India. The emails sent by Indian Mujahideen claimed that they were responsible for the following terror incidents. One warning email was received 5 minutes before the first blast in Ahmedabad. Another was received soon after the first blast of Delhi bombings. The timing makes it impossible for any other groups to have sent the two emails.

A study of the modus operandi of the IM has shown that the role of educated and technologically advanced youth in masterminding and executing terror attacks is of utmost importance. Such subversive elements have been indoctrinated with assorted ideologies like the Wahhabi and Deobandi schools of thought, to give legitimacy to their version of terror in the name of Islam. Drawing their own interpretations of the Quran, there has been a rapid spread of 'radical' teaching in the mushrooming *madrasas*. During the recent times there has been a sudden surge in the formation of such destructive organisations throughout India. One such organisation is the Students Islamic Movement of India (SIMI), which gave birth to the IM.

This book is a modest attempt to discuss all these issues.

—Editor

Preface

Contents

Preface (*v*)

1. The ISI and the War on Terrorism 1
2. The Pakistani ISI Directorate's Sponsorship of Terrorism 41
3. Democratic Control of Intelligence Agencies in Transitional Democracies 80
4. Indian Mujahideen 123
5. Attacks Claimed by Indian Mujahideen 182
6. Threat of Indian Mujahideen 232
7. Pakistan, the Radicalization of the Jihadist Progress and the Challenge to China 253
8. The Indian Mujahideen and the Islamist Terror Matrix 270

Bibliography 286

Index 287

Contents

1

The ISI and the War on Terrorism

INTRODUCTION

For the West there is arguably at present no more important intelligence organisation than Pakistan's Directorate of Inter-Service Intelligence [ISI], yet after decades of close co-operation the ISI remains an enigma. Is it the indispensable ally of the West as the Pakistan President insists? Or is it something else: an organisation that foments terrorism, that operates against Western interests, and that functions as an obstacle to, rather than the means for, progress in the War on Terrorism?

Of course, this is to pose a slightly false dichotomy: the ISI need not be a trusted ally to remain important to the West. The real question is whether there is sufficient overlap between Western interests and the activities of the ISI to merit the trust and the investment the West, primarily the USA, makes in the ISI indirectly through the support of the military government of Pakistan and directly to the organisation itself? This briefing is an attempt to respond to this question.

The Directorate for Inter-Service Intelligence [ISI] was formed in 1948 by the British Army Officer Major General William Cawthorne, then serving as the new state of Pakistan's Army Deputy Chief of Staff. The ISI was established within the Pakistan Army to supplement the existing Military Intelligence [MI] as a means to address the lack of inter-service intelligence co-operation which had proven so disastrous for Pakistan in the 1947 Indo-Pak war. Trained from its early days by UK's Military Intelligence, and a little later by the CIA and, for a short spell, the French SDECE, the ISI originally had no role beyond that of military intelligence-gathering except in relation to the disputed region in Pakistan Administered Kashmir and the Northern areas of Gilgit and Baltistan.

The assumption of martial law in Pakistan for this first time in 1958 under Lt Gen Ayub Khan brought the ISI into the political realm. It was tasked by Ayub with three roles which continue to define it: (a) to safeguard Pakistan's interests, (b) to monitor political opposition, and (c) to sustain military rule in Pakistan. It is clear from these functions that the ISI from 1958, if not before, viewed its *raison d'etre* first and foremost in terms of the Pakistan military rather than in relation to any broader concept of the defence and security of the nation-state or of the people of Pakistan. Moreover, Ayub Khan's formulation gave the ISI primacy amongst the other intelligence agencies in Pakistan – the MI and the civilian Intelligence Bureau [IB] – because it combined in the one agency the dual roles of internal and external intelligence. Unlike the UK's MI5 and MI6 or the US's FBI and CIA, the ISI faces no equivalent turf-war with a powerful internal rival, and is thus able to integrate the internal and external facets of its work with profound implications for the way it operates and the power it is able to exercise within Pakistan and outside it.

THE ISI AND AFGHANISTAN

The Soviet invasion of Afghanistan in December 1979 transformed the ISI. The decision by the United States to support Afghan forces in a guerrilla campaign against the Soviet Union placed Pakistan on the frontline as the base from which the US would mount its campaign. The crucial development for the ISI was the decision by the US, through the CIA, to use Pakistan's ISI as the instrument of support for the Afghan rebels. The ISI already had deep inroads into Afghanistan and laid down strict conditions, which the CIA accepted, that the ISI would control almost all aspects of how the guerrilla war was fought and supported. The

ISI insisted that it would retain control over contacts with Afghan rebels, that no Americans [CIA included] would cross the Afghan border from Pakistan, that movements of weapons within Pakistan and their disbursement to Afghan groups would be handled exclusively by the ISI, and that all the training of Afghan rebels would be handled by the ISI. The willingness of the CIA to agree these terms, at least for the early years of the war, enabled the ISI to hijack US money and arms for its own purposes in Afghanistan and for Pakistan interests more broadly. It was the scale of these flows of money and materiel, and the operational space they afforded, which were to transform the ISI.

By 1984, three years after serious money began to flow from Washington, the US was supporting the Afghan rebels with at least $200 million dollars annually, almost all of it handed over to the ISI. Moreover, this figure was matched by Saudi funding also channelled directly to the ISI through the General Intelligence Department [GID], the external intelligence arm of Saudi Arabia. These immense funds were in turn supplemented by money raised by the ISI from drug and arms smuggling and crime. Neither the CIA nor the GID had clear and tight oversight of what the ISI [and by extension the Pakistan military government] was doing with the money or the arms. It has since become clear that the ISI siphoned off hundreds of millions of dollars for its own purposes as well as millions of small arms.

Equally importantly the ISI was free to use the money and materiel to pursue Pakistan's distinct objectives in Afghanistan. For Islamabad a stable and friendly Afghanistan has always been a central plank of Pakistan's security, and its obverse – an unstable or, worse, pro-Indian Afghanistan-one of its key fears. Policy from the outset was thus centred on engineering the dominance and success of pro-Pakistan forces in Afghanistan in anticipation of the withdrawal of the Soviet army and the fall of the communist Afghan government. This meant a policy centred on Pashtun groups in Afghanistan, with which the Pakistan military government and ISI had strong and close links, but it also meant a focus on those Pashtun groups which were not sympathetic to ideas of Pashtun unity and self-determination. Thus it was that the ISI began to organise amongst the millions of Afghan refugees fleeing into Pakistan and amongst the groups inside Afghanistan to ensure that pro-Pakistan groups, specifically those which shared Islamabad's and Riyadh's Sunni Islamism, were empowered relative to the panoply of Afghan tribal groups united temporarily against the Soviet Union.

To further support the war the ISI created a string of training camps and *deeni madaris* [religious schools] along the Afghan-Pakistan border, many with Saudi funding, to turn out religiously motivated students, in what later became characterised as an "assembly line of gun-fodder" for the mujahidin. The students, in the resonant words of one informed author, were "crafted for one function alone – to kill the infidel communists or die trying and to view either outcome as the ultimate victory". Moreover, to ensure a sustained throughput of students the ISI came up with idea of reaching out to radical Muslims across the Islamic world and inviting them to come for training, paid for largely by the Saudis and CIA, in the Madaris and training camps of Pakistan. This is the moment at which Pakistan began to promote the idea of pan-Islamic Jihad for its own geostrategic in Thousands of young men from across the Islamic world, and from Muslim communities in the non-Islamic world, made their way through the camps. As is now well known these men were to be an important element in the emergence of Al-Qaeda and of the Taliban in the 1990s, both of which therefore were from their inception tied deeply to the ISI. They were also to become part of the fabric from which was woven the global Jihad from Algeria and Bosnia to Chechnya and the UK.

By the end of the 1980s the ISI's policy of promoting Islamist clients in Afghanistan and the flow of Saudi and Arab money to Islamist factions, had "effectively eliminated all the secular, leftist and royalist political parties that had formed when Afghan refugees fled communist rule". Afghanistan was subsequently plunged into civil war as the Soviet client regime of Najibullah clung to power in the context of rising internecine conflict between mujahidin and warlord factions. Most perniciously the United States scaled down its involvement in the region leaving Pakistan and the ISI to handle the conflict and instability in Afghanistan with an all but free hand.

The Turbulence of the 1990s

The death of Pakistan's President-General Zia ul-Haq in a mysterious plane crash on 17th August 198820 led to a resumption of civilian rule in Pakistan under first Benazir Bhutto [Prime Minister 1988-90 and 1993-96] and then Nawaz Sharif [Prime Minister 1990-93 and 1997-1999]. Bhutto had been subject to ISI intimidation for years. The ISI worked assiduously against the PPP she had taken over from her father and murdered her brother Shah Nawaz Bhutto in 1985 in an attempt to dissuade her from returning to Pakistan to contest elections. The ISI is also strongly suspected to have had a role in the murder of a second brother Murtaza Bhutto in 1996.

This then was the turbulent political background against which the ISI engineered two overlapping – and deeply interlinked – Islamist projects: the one an attempt to finally wrest the disputed territory of Jammu and Kashmir from India, the other to orchestrate the rise to power in Afghanistan of a pro-Pakistani Pashtun Islamist student-led movement, the Taliban.

From the late 1980s the ISI launched a much more assertive strategy to destabilise Jammu and Kashmir. The pertinent elements of this plan were four fold: (a) to divert arms and ammunition from the Afghan conflict – including many of those siphoned off during the Afghan War by the ISI – and use the weapons to empower favoured J&K separatist groups. (b) to expand the number of Madaris and training camps inside Pakistan Administered Kashmir to boost the number of trained and indoctrinated fighters who could be infiltrated into Indian controlled territory; (c) to transit Afghan and international Muslim fighters from the Afghan conflict to the new pan-Islamist "Holy War" in Jammu and Kashmir, and (d) to create new militant organisations which could become the vehicles for ISI control of the separatist insurgency. The latter included Lashkar-e-Taiba [formed in 1990], Harakat ul-Ansar [formed in 1993] and Jaish-e-Mohammed [formed in 1994]. All of these groups comprised majority proportions of non-Kashmiri fighters drawn from Afghanistan and Pakistan as well as Arabs and other Muslims radicals.

The effect of these policies was to sharply escalate the violence in Indian Administered Kashmir throughout the 1990s, a spiral of violence reinforced by the repressive tactics of India's counter-insurgency, which in total cost more than 50,000 lives. Equally perniciously the non-Kashmiri fighters – strongly backed by Saudi money-brought with them an extremist form of Wahhabi Islamism which displaced the historically tolerant Sufi-influenced "Kashmiriat" Islam of the region's indigenous Muslim peoples.

In Afghanistan, guided by Pakistan's Interior Minister Naseerullah Babar and with the assent of Benazir Bhutto, the ISI began to funnel arms and ammunition to the Taliban, to provide the Taliban with access to huge weapons stores kept in Afghanistan after the Soviet war, to provide intelligence and specialised training, and to expand the size of the Taliban with Afghan, Pakistani and foreign radical Muslims still transiting Pakistani and Afghan Madaris and training camps. Moreover the ISI promoted Mullah Mohammed Omar as the Taliban leader believing he was their man and would remain under their influence. Within two years, and with widespread Afghan support, the Taliban had risen to power defeating or displacing Afghanistan's other tribal and warlord groups.

It is widely commented that the Taliban were empowered by the ISI but not created by them. In fact the ISI were very much the fathers and supportive parents of the Taliban, if not perhaps the mothers and midwives. It was the ISI from the late 1970s which, with Saudi money and in cooperation with Pakistani Islamist parties, had organised the building of large numbers of Madaris and training camps around Peshawar, Quetta and Karachi, through which tens of thousands of Afghan and Pakistani students passed for the war in Afghanistan, including many displaced from Kandahar. It was here that the future Taliban militia were schooled in austere Deobandi/Wahhabi Islam, and it was through these Madaris and camps, with the support of the ISI, that the footsoldiers of the Taliban – Afghan and non-Afghan-continued to pour throughout the 1990s. As the Taliban took Kabul in 1996 Pakistan was the first and one of only three countries to offer diplomatic recognition to the new regime and the Taliban has continued to benefit from close ISI support, including military training, through all their excesses, through September 11th 2001, and up to the present time.

The closeness of relations between the ISI and the Taliban, and the closeness of relations between the Taliban and Al-Qaeda necessarily raises the issue of the nature of relations between the ISI and Al-Qaeda. The link between the ISI and Osama Bin Laden goes back more than 25 years. The wealthy Saudi Bin Laden with strong links to the Saudi royal family and Saudi intelligence almost inevitably had good contacts with the ISI. Bin Laden had emerged as a significant, if marginal, foreign fighter for the ISI during the Afghan war, more because his wealth could be used deniably by the ISI than because of his military prowess on the battlefield. By most accounts Al-Qaeda was formed sometime between May and August 1988 [with many of the foundational meetings taking place in Pakistan] as the Soviets began their withdrawal from Afghanistan, as a means of continuing the Jihad against the global enemies of Islam. It is clear at this time that Bin Laden enjoyed the protection of the ISI and that the ISI sought to co-opt Bin Laden for two projects: the overthrow of Najibullah in Kabul and the dismissal of Benazir Bhutto in Islamabad, both of whom were seen as the enemies of Islam by Bin Laden and by the ISI. Bin Laden's absence from Afghanistan for the four years between 1992 and 1996 meant he had no direct role in the rise of the Taleban, and indeed was unfamiliar with them when he returned to Afghanistan in May 1996. It was the ISI that reportedly facilitated Bin Laden's initial meetings with the Taleban which were successful enough to see him move to Kandahar as the winter of 1996.

Under the protection of the ISI and the Taliban Osama Bin Laden began to expand the activities of Al-Qaeda for global Jihad. Focussed on its regional agenda – Kashmir, the support of the Taliban, and a growing determination to stake a strong hand in the oil-rich southern Caucus – the ISI colluded with Bin Laden to establish further training camps inside Afghanistan, and to facilitate the spread of Bin Laden's influence in existing camps on both sides of the border, in order to host, indoctrinate and train foreign fighters who could reinforce Kashmiri separatist/terrorist groups like Lashkar-e-Taiba, support the Taliban, and promote a pro-Pakistan Islamist agenda from Chechnya, through Uzbekistan, to China.

The critical insight is that even after General Pervez Musharraf came to power by military coup in October 1999, the degree of overlap between the pan-Islamist agenda of Pakistan, exercised through its ISI, and Al-Qaeda was deep and extensive. Pakistan was the hub of a radiating network of Islamist groups and organisations which by 2000 were asserting a pro-Pakistan agenda across the region taking in Afghanistan, the Southern Caucus, the west of China, Kashmir, and across South Asia in Bangladesh, Nepal, Sri Lanka and inside India itself, and which extended beyond the sub-continent to reach even North Africa.

THE ISI AFTER 9/11

For Pakistan and the ISI the consequences of the attacks of 9/11 were almost incalculable. Pakistan was co-opted by the United States as a necessary if uncertain partner for the "War on Terrorism" and as an indispensable forward base for the overthrow of the Taliban which – once the Taliban refused to hand the Al-Qaeda leadership over – became a *sine qua none* for the destruction of Al-Qaeda. The military government of Pervez Musharraf was given no choice other than to assist the United States and was offered lavish rewards of aid, debt write-off and the lifting of the Pressler sanctions and the additional sanctions imposed after the Pakistan nuclear weapons tests in 199833. In almost all other respects the consequences of the 9/11 attacks have been catastrophic for Pakistan.

The ISI and the Pakistan Army was asked to hunt down Al-Qaeda operatives in Pakistan and help hunt them down in Afghanistan. The way the ISI has responded has been shaped by two sets of tensions: the first the tensions between the need for Musharraf to demonstrate fidelity to the US in the pursuit of Al-Qaeda and Musharraf's sensitivity to the widespread support for Al-Qaeda and the Taliban across Pakistan, a support evinced by a large proportion of the people, by Islamist political parties, and by elements within Pakistan's Army and ISI. The second the tensions between US objectives in relation to Al-Qaeda and in terms of the region more broadly, and Pakistan's objectives in the region as a whole. These tensions explain the ambiguity of the ISI actions since 9/11.

Notwithstanding these complexities there is no question that the ISI was essential to the US and the West in the early phase of the War on Terrorism. The ISI helped the US to arrest many hundreds of suspected Al-Qaeda and Taliban members, amongst them many leading Al-Qaeda figures. These included Abu Zubaydah [captured 28th March 2002 in Faisalabad], Khlaid Sheikh Mohammed [captured 1 March 2003 in Rawalpindi], Ahmed Ghailani [captured 26 May 2004 in Gujerat], Amjad Farooqi [killed 26th September 2004 in Nawabshah] and Abu Faraj Al-Libbi [captured 2 May 2005 at Mardan near Peshawar]. The case of Khalid Sheikh Mohammed, the alleged mastermind of the 9/11 attacks in particularly instructive. Sheikh Mohammed was tipped off and narrowly escaped arrest in Karachi in September 2002 and was finally arrested in Rawalpindi, the garrison headquarters town of the Pakistan military. He was captured in the "safe house" of a serving military officer with close family links to the Islamist political party Jamaat-I-Islami, part of the MMA coalition that was in political partnership with the Musharraf government until late 2007 having previously been kept, moved and protected by a network of Pakistan military officers linked only by their Islamist beliefs.

The ISI has also been of some help to the West in unravelling some of the details of international terrorist operations or in helping foil international terrorist operations, a large number of which have had their roots in Pakistan. Of particular importance in this respect have been the investigations into the 9/11 attacks, and into the 7/7 London bombings, and the ISI's role in foiling the alleged summer 2006 plot to simultaneously blow up airliners leaving London Heathrow for the United State Law enforcement and intelligence service critics in the US and UK however point to systematic problems with the ISI's role in these operations, in particular that:

- the ISI tends to act on US and/or UK intelligence but not to be proactive in bringing its own intelligence to the West;
- the ISI is unhelpful in relation to specific investigations – most notably of 7/7 and 21/7 – where the trail in Pakistan seems to have gone cold;
- the ISI has restricted or denied the US/UK access to many alleged terrorists as well as to many of its own operatives and assets;
- the ISI manipulates intelligence for its own internal and geopolitical reasons, and misdirects US and UK intelligence services.

The crucial point is not that the ISI is aiding Al-Qaeda directly – though some of its operatives may be – but rather that Pakistan's geopolitical interests, and in particular the ISI's promotion of pan-Islamist Jihad makes it an unreliable ally for the West and plays into Al-Qaeda's hands.

In addition the ISI's support for Sunni Islamism in Pakistan adds another layer of complexity to the West's problems in Pakistan. Despite his moderate credentials Musharraf has eschewed the more Western-orientated political parties of the PPP and PML-N. Instead, as Islamist forces in Pakistan rose in the wake of 9/1147, Musharraf made common cause with a group of Islamist parties under the banner of the MMA [Muttadida Majlis-e-Amal] to sustain his position in power. As a result the ISI has been working assiduously to support the MMA and undermine pro-Western non-Islamist political parties in Pakistan and those working to restore democracy and the rule of law from outside. One consequence of this has been the rise to power by the MMA in the North West Frontier Province [NWFP] and in Balochistan, Pakistan's two most volatile and lawless provinces and each a base for the Taliban.

In addition, the ISI have taken the opportunity provided by the CIA's bounty on suspected Al-Qaeda and other terrorist group members to arrest, torture, and in dozens of cases, "disappear" domestic enemies of the regime. In sum the ISI continues to work systematically for the exclusion of pro-Western political parties, the intimidation and elimination of political rivals and those struggling to build civil society, and in support of alliances with Sunni Islamist groups. This has shifted the centre of gravity in Pakistan's polity in the direction of the Islamists, a point made the more grave by a growing concern that these forces may now be slipping out of the control of the ISI and the Pakistan government.

Conclusion

As ISI successes against Al-Qaeda have declined since 2002/3 and the hunt for the Al-Qaeda leadership has petered out, and as the number of Al-Qaeda directed or aided operations emanating from Pakistan continues to rise, the ambiguous role of the ISI in the War on Terrorism has become a mounting problem from the West. So too has the role of the ISI in subverting democracy and civil society in Pakistan, as this denies the people of Pakistan a legitimate outlet for their grievances, stifles the development of democracy, and leaves much of the political space open to colonisation by Islamists. Reflecting these major setbacks for the war on terrorism a western rethink of its intelligence strategy in Pakistan is now urgently overdue.

THE ROLE OF THE CIA-ISI TERROR NETWORK

Recent terror attacks in New Delhi on September 13, 2008, raise the questions of who was responsible and for what reason these attacks occurred. Terror attacks in India are not a new phenomenon, however, in their recent past, they can be largely attributed to the actions, finances, training and resources of one organization: The Pakistani Inter-Services Intelligence (ISI). These new bombings bare the same relationship with the ISI as has occurred in the past, and so it must be asked: what is the purpose of the ISI both in Central Asia as well as South Asia?

The ISI appears to play the role of a force for the destabilization of Central Asia, India and the Middle East. It acts as a Central Asian base of operations for the CIA and British Intelligence to carry out Anglo-American imperial aims.

India will be the main focus of this report, due to the escalation of organized terror and violence against it in the past few years. As India is one of the fastest-growing economies in the world, after China, its northern neighbor which also borders Central Asian countries, its place in the New World Order is yet to be set in stone. Do western, and particularly Anglo-American elites allow India to grow as China, all the while attempting to co-opt their banking system to the western banking elite, thus, making them controllable? Or, will India be destabilized and dismantled, as is the plan with the Middle East and Central Asia, in order to redraw borders to suit geopolitical imperial ambitions, creating a network of manageable territories feeding the Metropoles of the New World Order, specifically New York (Wall Street) and London (The City of London)?

THE SEPTEMBER 13, 2008 NEW DELHI BOMBINGS: 9/13/08

The Bombings

On September 13, 2008, five blasts ripped through New Delhi within 45 minutes of each other, killing 21 people and injuring roughly 100 more. The Indian Mujahedin claimed responsibility for the bombings, sending emails to major Indian news organizations. In July, bombings took place in the western state of Gujarat, which killed 45 people, and in May in the city of Jaipur, which killed 61 people. The Indian Mujahedin also claimed responsibility for those attacks. This new wave of attacks across Indian cities was intended to "sow panic, inflict civilian casualties and, according to Indian officials, inflame tensions between Hindus and Muslims."

National elections are also approaching in India, giving the opposition Bharatiya Janata Party the opportunity to criticize "the coalition government led by the Congress Party for its inability to prevent bombings like those of Saturday," making it a "major point of vulnerability for the incumbent administration."

What is the Indian Mujahedin?

According to Indian police, the Indian Mujahedin (IM) is "an offshoot of the banned Students' Islamic Movement of India (SIMI)." In fact, it is "the hardline faction of Students Islamic Movement of India (SIMI) that broke away in 2005 to protest against the diffidence of the moderate faction about declaring a full-scale war on India." Reports also link the IM with the banned organizations, Harkat-ul-Jihad-e-Islami and Harkat-ul-Mujahedeen.

The Students Islamic Movement of India (SIMI) has reported ties with the Pakistani ISI, in having had cadres of its members being trained by the ISI to launch terror attacks in India. The ISI is also reported to have maintained contacts with SIMI in relation to their operatives traveling around the Middle East, specifically Saudi Arabia, to engage in fund raising. SIMI's reorganization was also aided by the ISI, which led to the branching out of the hardline element, the Indian Mujahedin.

Harkat-ul-Jihad-e-Islami also has extensive ties with the ISI, as the group carried out terror attacks in Hyderabad in 2007, "at the instance of Pakistan's Inter Services Intelligence." Many members of the Harkat-ul-Jihad-e-Islami were trained at ISI camps in Pakistan, and it "receives patronage and support from Pakistan's Inter-Services Intelligence." Significantly, "the group's anti-India operations are planned by the ISI, mostly from the Bangladeshi capital Dhaka."

Harkat-ul-Mujahedeen, the third terror network with extensive ties to the Indian Mujahedin, used to be known as the Harkat ul-Ansar. Harkat ul-Ansar was created by then-Pakistani General and future President Musharraf in the early 1990s, and was active in recruiting 200 Pakistanis to be trained by the ISI and sent to fight a Jihad in Bosnia, "with the full knowledge and complicity of the British and American intelligence agencies." This group also has links to those individuals associated with financing 9/11, as well as being involved with the London 7/7/bombings.

So all three terrorist groups associated with creating and having links with the Indian Mujahedin (IM) have extensive ties with the Pakistani ISI. Since these three organizations created the IM, it is essentially a creation of the ISI itself.

Who Benefits?

Two days before the bombings took place, the *Times of India* ran a story discussing US defense corporations seeking major contracts in India, including "the single largest one-time military contract in history," India's buying 126 multi-role combat aircraft

(MRCA). The deal is said to be worth $10 billion, "which would not be concluded in the term of this government but by the next government." Two major US companies vying for this contract are defense giants Boeing and Lockheed Martin. India's Defense Minister A.K. Antony said that his recent meetings with US Defense Secretary Robert Gates and other Washington figures were primarily focused on "Pakistan's rapid descent into chaos and the stepped up terrorist activity by renegade elements in the country, including provocations on the border and in Kashmir."

Two days later, the attacks within India would confirm the need for a built up defense and military establishment within India. Contracts are sure to be signed.

The bombings also occurred at a time that "India is resisting renewed pressure from the West to send its troops into Afghanistan to boost the coalition troops there." More troops are needed in Afghanistan as the Taliban experience a resurgence, armed and financed by Pakistan's ISI.

However, as the *Times of India* notes, "India is not about to enter this particular cauldron because its troops would fan the flames in a way that no others would do. They would draw fire from Pakistanis and India would be sucked into a battle, which would have huge implications for its internal security." Perhaps this is the idea?

The attacks also occurred just as "the US Congress is considering the approval of the US-India civil nuclear deal and days before [Indian] Prime Minister Manmohan Singh visits Washington."

THE ISI-CIA ISLAMIC TERROR NETWORKS

The Mujahideen

The ISI has long established ties with terrorist networks in the region. The ISI was used as a conduit by the CIA in 1979 to finance and arm the Afghan Mujahideen in Afghanistan in the Afghan-Soviet War of 1979 to 1989. The Mujahideen then branched off, with the active financing and support of the ISI, into both Al-Qaeda and the Taliban.

During the 1980s, many "officers from the ISI's Covert Action Division received training in the US and many covert action experts of the CIA were attached to the ISI to guide it in its operations against the Soviet troops by using the Afghan Mujahideen, Islamic fundamentalists of Pakistan and Arab volunteers." Further, the "CIA, through the ISI, promoted the smuggling of heroin into Afghanistan in order to make the Soviet troops heroin addicts. Once the Soviet troops were withdrawn in 1988, these heroin smugglers started smuggling the drugs to the West, with the complicity of the ISI."

Al-Qaeda and Yugoslavia

The ISI not only has had close ties to Al-Qaeda, but also to guerillas fighting in the disputed territory of Kashmir between India and Pakistan. The ISI's connections with Al-Qaeda were so extensive, that even on the night before 9/11, Osama bin Laden was in a hospital in Pakistan protected by Pakistani military and intelligence.

The ISI also supported the wars in Bosnia, Kosovo and Macedonia throughout the 1990s, by training and sending militant Islamists into the regions to sow chaos and exacerbate ethnic tensions, leading to the break-up of Yugoslavia. All this was done with the tacit approval, support and complicity of British and American intelligence. The ISI financed its covert terrorist support through the global drug trade, especially important in Afghanistan. The ISI also supported terrorist groups in Chechnya.

The LeT

The Lashkar e Toiba (LeT) terrorist organization also works very closely with the ISI, and they work together in a "coordinated effort" in orchestrating terror attacks in Kashmir. The LeT is "funded, armed and trained by the Inter-Services Intelligence," and is linked up with Al-Qaeda, and is "the most visible manifestation" of Al-Qaeda in India. The LeT "receives considerable financial, material and other forms of assistance from the Pakistan government, routed primarily through the ISI. The ISI is the main source of LeT's funding. Saudi Arabia also provides funds." The

LeT also played a part in the ISI organized "Bosnian campaign against the Serbs," which was directed above the ISI by the CIA and British intelligence.

The ISI and 9/11

The ISI may also have played a roll in 9/11 itself, as its General was in Washington in the lead up to and during the 9/11 attacks, meeting with top intelligence, State Department and Congressional officials, including CIA Director George Tenet, Deputy Secretary of State Richard Armitage, Secretary of State Colin Powell, Senator Bob Graham, Representative Porter Goss, who would go on to become CIA director, and Joseph Biden, who is now Barack Obama's running mate.

The ISI's General, while meeting with all these top US officials in foreign affairs and intelligence, also happened to be the money man behind 9/11, having wired $100,000 to the lead 9/11 hijacker, Mohammed Atta.

The Liquid Bomb Plot

In August 2006 in the UK, there was a massive roundup of terrorism suspects as the British and Pakistani authorities revealed that they uncovered and prevented a massive terrorist plot to blow up several transatlantic airliners with liquid explosives. This plot is the reason for which people can no longer carry a bottle of water or any liquids through security at airports. However, following the roundups, Pakistan arrested the "lead suspect" who was said to have masterminded the whole operation, Rashid Rauf. Over a year later, Rashid Rauf escaped from Pakistani police custody, however, as it turned out, he was kidnapped by the ISI to prevent him being extradited to the UK.

As Craig Murray, former British Ambassador to Uzbekistan, wrote shortly after the plot was 'foiled', "According to John Loftus, a former Justice Department prosecutor, [bomb plot suspects] Omar Bakri and Abu Hamza, as well as the suspected mastermind of the London bombings Haroon Aswat, were all recruited by MI6 in the mid-1990s to draft up British Muslims to fight in Kosovo. American and French security sources corroborate the revelation."

Covert War Against Iran

It was revealed by the *London Telegraph* in 2007 that the US, through the CIA, was funding and arming terrorist organizations to "sow chaos" inside Iran. *ABC News* reported just over a month later that the terrorist group was a Pakistani militant group named Jundullah, which is based in the Baluchistan region of Pakistan, just across the border from Iran. Jundullah also has very close ties with Al-Qaeda. Although the US funds this Al-Qaeda-linked group, the funding is indirect, as it travels through Pakistan's ISI.

So clearly, the ISI has some troubling connections to Al-Qaeda, various other Islamic extremist groups, and British and American intelligence. Where the ISI is operational, so too, are Anglo-American ambitions.

THE 1993 BOMBAY BOMBINGS: 3/12/93

On March 12, 1993, Bombay (now called Mumbai) experienced 13 explosions in a coordinated attack, of which the most significant target was the Bombay Stock Exchange, which killed roughly 50 people. The total number of dead was 257, with roughly 1,400 other injured. Dawood Ibrahim was believed to have coordinated the attacks. Ibrahim is known for extensive ties to Osama bin Laden and Al-Qaeda, has financed operations of the Lashkar e Toiba (LeT), and was believed to be hiding out in Pakistan. The 1993 Bombay bombings were "organised by Dawood Ibrahim under pressure from the Inter-Services Intelligence of Pakistan." In 2007, the ISI was reported to have taken Ibrahim and his top lieutenant into custody from the Pakistan-Afghan border.

THE 2006 MUMBAI BOMBINGS: 7/11/06

On July 11, 2006, Mumbai experienced another major terrorist attack, as seven bombs went off within 11 minutes of one another on trains. The total deaths reached 209 with roughly 700 others injured.

The blame for the bombings was placed on the Lashkar-e-Toiba (LeT) and local Students Islamic Movement of India (SIMI), which are closely interlinked with each other and have direct links with the ISI. A few months later, following an investigation, Mumbai police "blamed Pakistan's intelligence agency ISI for masterminding the explosions which were executed by activists of the banned Lashkar-e-Toiba and SIMI." The Mumbai Police Commissioner said that, "the attacks were planned by ISI in Pakistan and carried out by Pakistan-based militant group LeT with the help of banned Students Islamic Movement of India (SIMI)." India even shared evidence of Pakistani ISI involvement in the attacks with the United States.

The bombings led to a postponement of India-Pakistan peace talks, which were set to take place the following week. The Indian Prime Minister had said that, "a peace process with Pakistan was threatened if Islamabad did not curb 'terrorist' violence directed at India." Again, perhaps a peace in the region is not in the interests of the Anglo-Americans.

THE 2008 INDIAN EMBASSY BOMBING IN KABUL: 7/7/08

On July 7, 2008, the Indian Embassy in Kabul, Afghanistan was bombed, killing 58 people and wounding 141. Two days after, it was reported that, "The Afghanistan government and Indian Intelligence Agencies have confirmed that some elements within the ISI in collaboration with the Taliban/Al Qaeda planned and executed the attack on the Indian embassy." Further, "the ISI Station Head in Kabul, is collaborating with the Taliban to destabilise India's strategic presence in Afghanistan."

The day after the attack, the Afghan Interior Ministry said that, " was carried out in co-ordination and consultation with an active intelligence service in the region," and as the*Financial Times* reported, "Western diplomats in Islamabad warned that the Kabul bombing was likely to increase the distrust between Pakistan and Afghanistan and undermine Pakistan's relations with India, despite recent signs that a peace process between Islamabad and New Delhi was making some headway."

It was also reported that the Afghan Interior Ministry stated that, "Militants who carried out this week's suicide bomb attack on the Indian embassy in the Afghan capital received their training at camps in Pakistan."

Just weeks earlier, on June 25, 2008, "An Afghan official accused Pakistan's premier spy agency on Wednesday of organizing a recent assassination attempt on Afghan President Hamid Karzai," and that they were "sure and confident" of an ISI connection.

On July 13, "Pakistan's Inter-Services Intelligence agency (ISI) [had] been blamed by India for the bomb attack on Kabul's Indian embassy." On July 10, "The United States has said there was no evidence suggesting involvement of foreign agents in the suicide bombing on the Indian Embassy in Afghanistan."

However, on August 1, the *New York Times* reported that, "American intelligence agencies have concluded that members of Pakistan's powerful spy service helped plan the deadly July 7 bombing of India's embassy in Kabul," and that, "The conclusion was based on intercepted communications between Pakistani intelligence officers and militants who carried out the attack."

Interestingly, "American officials said that the communications were intercepted before the July 7 bombing, and that the C.I.A. emissary, Stephen R. Kappes, the agency's deputy director, had been ordered to Islamabad, Pakistan's capital, even before the attack."

Further, "a top Central Intelligence Agency official traveled to Pakistan this month to confront senior Pakistani officials with information about support provided by members of the ISI to militant groups."

However, given that this is not new information, and that CIA collaboration with these efforts has been widely documented, what was the real purpose of this top CIA emissary going to Islamabad?

Two days after the *New York Times* report surfaced, it was reported that, "The United States has accused Pakistan's main spy agency of deliberately undermining Nato efforts in Afghanistan by helping the Taliban and Al-Qaeda militants they are supposed to be fighting." In January, the Bush administration "sent two senior intelligence officials to Pakistan" over "concerns" that the ISI was supporting militants, and further, "Mike Mc-Connell, the director of national intelligence, and [CIA director] Hayden asked

Musharraf to allow the CIA greater freedom to operate in the tribal areas." President Bush also "warned of retaliation if it continues."

Who Benefits?

In 2006, it was reported that as Hamid Karzai, President of Afghanistan, was trying to balance a relationship with Pakistan and India, "Islamabad might be feeling squeezed and do its best to undermine the renewed Afghan-Indian partnership — at great cost to Afghanistan."

As *Time Magazine* reported on the day of the Embassy bombing, "The bombing is likely to have regional ramifications, both for India's relations with the neighborhood and those of every other country supporting Afghan President Hamid Karzai." Further, "India and Pakistan have been vying for influence in Kabul for decades, and India — which for years backed the opposition Northern Alliance against the Pakistan-backed Taliban regime — came out on top after the U.S.-led invasion scattered the Taliban and installed President Karzai in power." India has also pledged $850 million in reconstruction aid for Afghanistan.

As the UK *Times* explained, India is "the only regional power committed to a new democratic Afghanistan. It was no accident that India shouldered part of the cost of the parliamentary and presidential elections. Nor should one ignore the symbolic value of the fact that India is building the new Palace of Democracy to house the Afghan parliament." Further, "The only power likely to offer Afghanistan long-term support is India. Helping Afghanistan would weaken radical Islamism and prevent Pakistan acquiring a hinterland through Afghanistan in Muslim Central Asia."

Historically, the Taliban were financed and armed by the Pakistani ISI, while India had backed the Northern Alliance during the 1990s. After the 2001 invasion and occupation of Afghanistan, the Northern Alliance was put back into power as the Taliban were deposed. This would explain why the ISI and Pakistan has again become the main supporter of the Taliban. However, in most discussion on Pakistan funding the revival of the Taliban, what is left ignored is the ISI's continued connections to British and American intelligence. For example, with the London 7/7 bombings, the mastermind was an MI6 asset and he had, along with several of the suspected bombers, connections to the Pakistani ISI.

Interestingly, keeping in mind the ISI's help in the resurgence of the Taliban, in February of 2008, it was reported that, "Britain planned to build a Taliban training camp for 2,000 fighters in southern Afghanistan, as part of a top-secret deal to make them swap sides." Further, "Afghan government officials insist it was bankrolled by the British. UK diplomats, the UN, Western officials and senior Afghan officials have all confirmed the outline of the plan, which they agree is entirely British-led, but all refused to talk about it on the record."

Conclusion

Ultimately, the benefactors of the Indian Embassy bombing in Kabul and other bombings, such as the recent New Delhi bombing in India, is not Pakistan, but is the Anglo-Americans. Pakistan ultimately will collapse as a result of these actions being taken. The ISI has long been referred to as Pakistan's "secret government" or "shadow state." It's long-standing ties and reliance upon American and British intelligence have not let up, therefore actions taken by the ISI should be viewed in the context of being a Central Asian outpost of Anglo-American covert intelligence operations. This connection between American and British intelligence and the ISI is also corroborated by their continued cooperation in the covert opium trade in Afghanistan, whose profits are funneled into the banks of Wall Street and the City of London.

The goal in Pakistan is not to maintain stability, just as this is not the goal throughout the region of the Middle East and Central Asia. Recent events in Pakistan, such as the assassination of Benazir Bhutto, which has been linked to the ISI, should be viewed in the context as an active Anglo-American strategy of breaking up Pakistan, which will spread chaos through the region.

Pakistan's position as a strategic focal point cannot be underestimated. It borders India, Afghanistan, China and Iran. Destabilizing and ultimately breaking Pakistan up into several countries or regions will naturally spread chaos and destabilization into neighbouring countries. This is also true of Iraq on the other side of Iran, as the Anglo-American have undertaken, primarily through Iraq, a strategy of balkanizing the entire Middle East in a new imperial project.

One of the main targets in this project is Iran, for which the US and Britain have engaged in massive acts of terror and orchestrating large battles and conflicts from within the already-failed state of Iraq. The Anglo-American role as terrorist supporters and as covertly orchestrating terror attacks within Iraq is amply documented. To imagine that these same Anglo-American intelligence and covert networks are not using their long-time conduit, the ISI, for the same purposes in Central Asia, is a stretch of the imagination and logic. It is not merely the Middle East that is the target, but Central Asia, specifically for its geographical relationship to the rising giants such as India and China. This also follows in line with Anglo-American strategies in destabilizing the Central European region, specifically the former Yugoslavia, and more recently, Georgia, largely in an effort to target Russia.

What we are seeing with Pakistan and India is an effort to drive the region into chaos. The US allowing blame to be placed on the Pakistani ISI for the Embassy bombings in Kabul has provided an excuse and basis for US military intervention in Pakistan, which has already begun, and which threatens to plunge the region into total war and crisis. But then again, that's the idea.

THE ISI AND TERRORISM: BEHIND THE ACCUSATIONS

Pakistan's military intelligence agency, the Inter-Services Intelligence (ISI), has long faced accusations of meddling in the affairs of its neighbors. A range of officials inside and outside Pakistan have stepped up suggestions of links between the ISI and terrorist groups in recent years. In fall 2006, a leaked report by a British Defense Ministry think tank charged, "Indirectly Pakistan (through the ISI) has been supporting terrorism and extremism—whether in London on 7/7 [the July 2005 attacks on London's transit system], or in Afghanistan, or Iraq." In June 2008, Afghan officials accused Pakistan's intelligence service of plotting a failed assassination attempt on President Hamid Karzai; shortly thereafter, they implied the ISI's involvement in a July 2008 attack on the Indian embassy. Indian officials also blamed the ISI for the bombing of the Indian embassy. Pakistani officials have denied such a connection.

Numerous U.S. officials have also accused the ISI of supporting terrorist groups, even as the Pakistani government seeks increased aid from Washington with assurances of fighting militants. In a May 2009 interview with CBS' *60 Minutes*, U.S. Defense Secretary Robert Gates said "to a certain extent, they play both sides." Gates and others suggest the ISI maintains links with groups like the Afghan Taliban as a "strategic hedge" to help Islamabad gain influence in Kabul once U.S. troops exit the region. These allegations surfaced yet again in July 2010 when WikiLeaks.org made public (*NYT*) a trove of U.S. intelligence records on the war in Afghanistan. The documents described ISI's links to militant groups fighting U.S. and international forces in Afghanistan. In April 2011 during a visit to Pakistan, U.S. Chairman of the Joint Chiefs of Staff Admiral Mike Mullen pointed to ISI's links with one such group, the Haqqani network. The May 1, 2011, killing of America's most wanted terrorist Osama bin Laden in a Pakistani military town not far from Islamabad raised new questions over army and ISI support for the al-Qaeda leader and the legitimacy of their counterterrorism efforts. Pakistan's government has repeatedly denied allegations of supporting terrorism, citing as evidence its cooperation in the U.S.-led battle against extremists in which it has taken significant losses both politically and on the battlefield.

Supporting Terrorism?

"The ISI probably would not define what they've done in the past as 'terrorism,'" saysWilliam Milam, former U.S. ambassador to Pakistan. Nevertheless, experts say the ISI has supported a number of militant groups in the disputed Kashmir region between Pakistan and India, some of which are on the U.S. State Department's Foreign Terrorist Organizations list. While Pakistan has a formidable military presence near the Indian border, some experts believe the relationship between the military and some Kashmiri groups has greatly changed with the rise of militancy within Pakistan. Shuja Nawaz, author of*Crossed Swords: Pakistan, its Army, and the Wars Within,* says the ISI "has certainly lost control" of Kashmiri militant groups. According to Nawaz, some of the groups trained by the ISI to fuel insurgency in Kashmir have been implicated in bombings and attacks within Pakistan, therefore making them army targets.

"I do not accept the thesis that the ISI is a rogue organization." —William Milam, former U.S. ambassador to Pakistan.

On Pakistan's western border with Afghanistan, the ISI supported the Taliban up to September 11, 2001, though Pakistani officials deny any current support for the group. Pakistan's government was also one of three countries, along with the United Arab Emirates and Saudi Arabia, that recognized the Taliban government in Afghanistan. The ISI's first major involvement in Afghanistan came after the Soviet invasion in 1979, when it partnered with the CIA to provide weapons, money, intelligence, and training to the mujahadeen fighting the Red Army. At the time, some voices within the United States questioned the degree to which Pakistani intelligence favored extremist and anti-American fighters. Following the Soviet withdrawal, the ISI continued its involvement in Afghanistan, first supporting resistance fighters opposed to Moscow's puppet government, and later the Taliban.

Pakistan stands accused of allowing that support to continue. Afghan President Hamid Karzai has repeatedly said Pakistan trains militants and sends them across the border. In May 2006, the British chief of staff for southern Afghanistan told the *Guardian,* "The thinking piece of the Taliban is out of Quetta in Pakistan. It's the major headquarters." Speaking at the Council on Foreign Relations in September 2006, then-president Pervez Musharraf responded to such accusations, saying, "It is the most ridiculous thought that the Taliban headquarters can be in Quetta." Nevertheless, experts generally suspect Pakistan still provides some support to the Taliban, though probably not to the extent it did in the past. "If they're giving them support, it's access back and forth [to Afghanistan] and the ability to find safe haven," says Kathy Gannon, who covered the region for decades for the Associated Press. Gannon adds that the Afghan Taliban needs

Pakistan even less as a safe haven now "because [it has] gained control of more territory inside Afghanistan."

Many in the Pakistani government, including slain former prime minister Benazir Bhutto, have called the intelligence agency "a state within a state," working beyond the government's control and pursuing its own foreign policy. But Nawaz says the intelligence agency does not function independently. "It aligns itself to the power centre," and does what the government or the army asks it to do, says Nawaz.

CONTROL OVER THE ISI

Constitutionally, the agency is accountable to the prime minister, says Hassan Abbas, research fellow at Harvard's Kennedy School of Government. But most officers in the ISI are from the army, so that is where their loyalties and interests lie, he says. Experts say until the end of 2007, as army chief and president, Musharraf exercised firm control over the intelligence agency. But experts say it is not clear how much control Pakistan's civilian government—led by Bhutto's widower, President Asif Ali Zardari—has over the agency. In July 2008, the Pakistani government announced the ISI will be brought under the control of the interior ministry, but revoked its decision (BBC) within hours. Bruce Riedel, an expert on South Asia at the Brookings Institution, says the civilian leadership has "virtually no control" (PDF) over the army and the ISI. In September 2008, army chief Ashfaq Parvez Kiyani replaced the ISI chief picked by former president Musharraf with Lt. Gen. Ahmed Shuja Pasha. Until then, Pasha headed military operations against militants in the tribal areas. Some experts said the move signaled that Kiyani was consolidating his control over the intelligence agency by appointing his man at the top. In November 2008, the government disbanded ISI's political wing, which politicians say was responsible for interfering in domestic politics. Some experts saw it as a move by the army, which faced much criticism when Musharraf was at the helm, to distance itself from politics.

"I do not accept the thesis that the ISI is a rogue organization," Milam says. "It's a disciplined army unit that does what it's told, though it may push the envelope sometimes." With a reported staff of ten thousand, ISI is hardly monolithic: "Like in any secret service, there are rogue elements," says Frederic Grare, a South Asia expert and visiting scholar at the Carnegie Endowment for International Peace. He points out that many of the ISI's agents have ethnic and cultural ties to Afghan insurgents, and naturally sympathize with them. Marvin G. Weinbaum, an expert on Afghanistan and Pakistan at the Middle East Institute, says Pakistan has sent "retired" ISI agents on missions the government could not officially endorse.

Resistance in FATA

Pakistan's tribal areas along the Afghan border have emerged as safe havens for terrorists. Experts say because of their links to the Taliban and other militant groups, the ISI has some influence in the region.

But with the mushrooming of armed groups in the tribal agencies, it is hard to say which ones the agency controls. Also, there appears to be divisions within the ISI. While some within the intelligence agency continue to sympathize with the militant groups, Harvard's Abbas says others realize they cannot follow a policy contradictory to that of the army, which is directly involved in counterterrorism operations in the area.

Bruce Riedel, an expert on South Asia at the Brookings Institution, says the civilian leadership has "virtually no control" over the army and the ISI.

Mixed Record on Counterterrorism

Pakistan has arrested scores of al-Qaeda affiliates, including Khalid Sheikh Mohammed, the alleged mastermind of the 9/11 attacks. The ISI and the Pakistani military have worked effectively with the United States to pursue the remnants of al-Qaeda. Following 9/11, Pakistan also stationed eighty thousand troops in the troubled province of Waziristan near the Afghan border. Hundreds of Pakistani soldiers died there in resulting clashes with militants, which, as Musharraf told a CFR meeting in September 2006, "broke the al-Qaeda network's back in Pakistan."

But Musharraf did crack down on terrorist groups selectively, as this Backgrounder points out. Weinbaum in 2006 said the Pakistani military has largely ignored Taliban fighters on its soil. "There are extremist groups that are beyond the pale with which the ISI has no influence at all," he says. "Those are the ones they go after." In 2008, Ashley J. Tellis, senior associate at the Carnegie Endowment for International Peace, wrote (PDF) in *TheWashington Quarterly* that Musharraf tightened pressure on groups whose objectives were out of sync with the military's perception of Pakistan's national interest.

THE TALIBAN AS A STRATEGIC ASSET

Pakistan does not enjoy good relations with the current leadership of Afghanistan, partly because of rhetorical clashes with Afghan President Hamid Karzai, and partly because Karzai has forged strong ties with India. But there have been increased efforts by the United States to close this gap.

The Obama administration's regional strategy unveiled in March 2009 focused on creating new diplomatic mechanisms; a trilateral summit of the leaders of the United States, Pakistan, and Afghanistan has been one such step toward helping reduce the level of distrust that runs among all three countries. But lingering suspicions about ISI's support for the Taliban continue to pose problems. In an October 2006 interview, Musharraf said some retired ISI operatives could be abetting the Taliban insurgency in Afghanistan, but he denied any active links. Zardari, too, denies any ISI links with the Taliban or al-Qaeda. In a May 2009 interview with CNN, he remarked all intelligence agencies have their sources in militant organizations but that does not translate to support. "Does that mean CIA has direct links with al-Qaeda? No, they have their sources. We have our sources. Everybody has sources."

Some experts say Pakistan wants to see a stable, friendlier government emerge in Afghanistan. Though the insurgency certainly doesn't serve this goal, increased Taliban influence, especially in the government, might. Supporting the Taliban also allows Pakistan to hedge its bets should the NATO coalition pull out of Afghanistan. In a February 2008interview with CFR.org,

Tellis said the Pakistani intelligence services continue to support the Taliban because they see the Taliban leadership "as a strategic asset," a reliable back-up force in case things go sour in Afghanistan.

Not everyone agrees with this analysis. According to Weinbaum, Pakistan has two policies. One is an official policy of promoting stability in Afghanistan; the other is an unofficial policy of supporting jihadis in order to appease political forces within Pakistan. "The second [policy] undermines the first one," he says. Nawaz says there is ambivalence within the army regarding support for the Taliban. "They'd rather not deal with the Afghan Taliban as an adversary," he says.

Allegations of Terrorist Attacks

Indian officials implicated the ISI for the November 2008 terrorist attacks in Mumbai that killed nearly two hundred people. India's foreign ministry said the ISI had links (Reuters)to the planners of the attacks, the banned militant group Lashkar-e-Taiba, which New Delhi blames for the assault. Islamabad denies allegations of any official involvement, but acknowledged in February 2009 that the attack was launched and partly planned (AP)from Pakistan. The Pakistani government has also detained several Islamist leaders, some of them named by India as planners of the Mumbai assault. Gannon says this is an unusual step by Pakistan, which never got enough credit in India because the country was in the middle of a national election. "I don't see any evidence" to believe that the ISI was behind the Mumbai attack, she says. However, she doubts the agency has severed all its ties with groups like Lashkar-e-Taiba which it supported to fight in Indian-administered Kashmir.Indian officials also claim to have evidence that the ISI planned the July 2006 bombing of the Mumbai commuter trains, but these charges seem unlikely to some observers of the long, difficult India-Pakistan relationship. The two nations have a history of finger-pointing, and while some of the allegations hold water, there is a tendency to exaggerate.

Following the release of the British report regarding its July 7, 2005, bombings of London's mass transit system—which London insists is not a statement of policy—Weinbaum said it makes "too broad a statement." Though Pakistan does offer safe haven to Kashmiri groups, and perhaps some Taliban fighters, the suggestion that the ISI is responsible for the 7/7 bombings is "a real stretch," Gannon says.

DE-CLASSIFIED OPERATIONS OF INTER-SERVICES INTELLIGENCE

In the 1950s, the ISI's Covert Action Division was used in assisting the insurgents in India's North-East and its role was expanded in the late 1960s to assist the Sikh Home Rule Movement of London-based Charan Singh Panchi, which was subsequently transformed into the Khalistan Movement, headed by Jagjit Singh Chauhan in which many other members of the Sikh diaspora in Europe, USA and Canada joined and then demanded the separate country of Khalistan. CIA and ISI worked in tandem during the Nixon Administration in assisting the Khalistan movement in Punjab.

ISI decided to spy on the residence of Colonel Hussain Imam Mabruk who was a Military Attaché to the Embassy of Libya in Islamabad as he had made some inflammatory statements towards the military regime of Zia-ul-Haq. The spying paid off as he was seen talking with two Pakistani gentlemen who entered and left the compound suspiciously. The ISI monitored the two men and were later identified as Pakistani exiles that hated the current military regime and were Bhutto loyalists. They had received terrorist training in Libya and were ready to embark on a terrorist campaign in Pakistan to force the Army to step down from power. All members of the conspiracy were apprehended before any damage could be done.

ISI foiled an attempt by the French Ambassador to Pakistan, Le Gourrierce and his First Secretary, Jean Forlot who were on a surveillance mission to Kahuta nuclear complex on June 26, 1979. Both were intercepted and their cameras and other sensitive equipment were confiscated. Intercepted documents later on showed that the two were recruited by the CIA.

After the failure of Operation Eagle Claw, the U.S. media outlets such as Newsweek and Time reported that CIA agents stationed in Tehran had obtained information in regards to the location of the hostages, in-house information from a Pakistani cook who used to work for the U.S. Embassy. ISI successfully gathered evidence, and intercepted communication documents and showed it to the Iranian Chief of J-2 which cleared the cook. The Iranian chief of intelligence said, "We know, the Big Satan is a big liar."

ISI successfully intercepted two American private weapons dealers during the Soviet-Afghan war of the 1980's. One American diplomat (his name has not been de-classified) who lived in the F-7/4 sector of Islamabad was spotted by an ISI agent in a seedy part of Rawalpindi by his Car's diplomatic plates. He was bugged and trailed and was found to be in contact with various tribal groups supplying them with weapons for their fight with the Soviet Army in Afghanistan. Another was Eugene Clegg, a teacher in the American International School who also indulged in weapons trade. All of them were put out of business.

ISI had placed a mole in the Soviet Embassy in Islamabad. The mole reported that the Third Secretary in the Soviet Embassy was after information in regards to the Karakurum Highway and was obtaining it from a middle level employee, Mr. Ejaz, of the Northern Motor Transport Company. ISI contacted Mr. Ejaz who then confessed that a few months ago the Soviet diplomat approached him and threatened his family unless he divulged sensitive information in regards to the highway such as alignment of the road, location of bridges, the number of Chinese personnel working on the Highway, etc. The ISI instead of confronting the Soviet diplomat chose to feed him with false information. This continued until the Soviet diplomat was satisfied that Mr. Ejaz had been bled white of all the information and then dropped him as a source.

ISI was very worried that among the large influx of Afghan refugees that come into Pakistan due to the Soviet-Afghan war were members of KHAD (Afghan Intelligence). In order to gather information on these spies, the ISI successfully convinced Mansoor Ahmed who was the Charge-de-Affairs of the Afghan Embassy in Islamabad to turn his back on the Soviet backed Afghan government. He and his family were secretly escorted out of their residence and were given safe passage on a London bound British Airways flight in exchange for classified information in regards to Afghan agents in Pakistan. The Soviet and Afghan diplomats tried their best to find the family but were unsuccessful.

A routine background checks on various staff members working for the Indian embassy raised suspicions on an Indian woman who worked as a school teacher in an Indian School in Islamabad. Her enthusiastic and too friendly attitude gave her up. She was in reality was an agent working for RAW. ISI monitored her movements to a hotel in Islamabad where she rendezvoused with a local Pakistani man who worked as an engineer for Pakistan Atomic Energy Commission. ISI then confronted her and were then able to turn her into a double agent spying on the Indian Embassy in Islamabad.

ISI became aware of a plot to assassinate the President of Pakistan, Zia-ul-Haq and then launch a bloody coup to depose the current government and install an extreme Islamic government in its place. The attempted assassination and coup was to occur on March 23, 1980 during the annual March 23 Pakistan day parade. The masterminds behind the coup were high ranking Military and Intelligence officers and were led by Major General Tajammal Hussain Malik, his son, Captain Naveed and his nephew Major Riaz, a former Military Intelligence officer. ISI decided against arresting these men outright because they did not know how deep this conspiracy went and kept these men under strict surveillance. As the date of the annual parade approached, ISI was satisfied that it had identified the major players in this conspiracy and then arrested these men along with quite a few high ranking military officers.

Ilam Din also known as Ilmo was an infamous Indian spy working from Pakistan. He had eluded being captured many times but on March 23 at 3 A.M., Ilmo and two other Indian spies were apprehended by Pakistani Rangers as they were illegally crossing into Pakistan from India. Their mission was to spy and report back on the new military equipment that Pakistan will be showing in their annual March 23 Pakistan day parade. Ilmo after being thoroughly interrogated was then forced by the ISI to send false information to his RAW handlers in India. This process continued and many more Indian spies in Pakistan were flushed out such as Roop Lal.

ISI uncovered a secret deal in which naval base facilities were granted by Indian Prime Minister Indira Gandhi to the USSR in Vizag and the Andaman & Nicobar Island and the alleged attachment of KGB advisers to the then Lieutenant General Sunderji who was the commander of Operation Bluestar in the Golden Temple in Amritsar in June 1984.

ISI, CIA and Mossad carried out a covert transfer of Soviet made PLO and Lebanese weapons captured by the Israelis during the Israeli invasion of Lebanon in June 1982 and their subsequent transfer to Pakistan and then into Afghanistan. All knowledge of this weapon transfer was kept secret and was only made public recently.

ISI played a central role in the U.S.-backed guerrilla war to oust the Soviet Army from Afghanistan in the 1980s. That Central Intelligence Agency (CIA)-backed effort flooded Pakistan with weapons and with Afghan, Pakistani and Arab "mujahideen", who were motivated to fight as a united force protecting fellow Muslims in Soviet occupied Afghanistan. The CIA relied on the ISI to train fighters, distribute arms, and channel money. The ISI trained about 83,000 Afghan mujahideen between 1983 and 1997, and dispatched them to Afghanistan.

CIA through the ISI promoted the smuggling of heroin into Afghanistan in order to turn the Soviet troops into heroin addicts and thus greatly reducing their fighting potential.

Major General Sultan Habib who was an operative of the ISI's Joint Intelligence Miscellaneous department successfully procured nuclear material while being posted as the Defense Attaché in the Pakistani Embassy in Moscow from 1991 to 1993 and concurrently obtaining other materials from Central Asian Republics, Poland and the former Czechoslovakia. After Moscow, Major General Habib then coordinated shipping of missiles from North Korea and the training of Pakistani experts in the missile production. These two acts greatly enhanced Pakistan's Nuclear weapons program and their missile delivery systems.

ISI engineered the takeover of Afghanistan by the hard-line Islamic Taliban regime after the fall of the Communist government in Kabul in 1992.

Altaf Hussain, was tasked by the ISI to start the political movement Muhajir Qaumi Movement, political party which represented the Muhajir (Immigrants from India during the partition of 1947) population in [[Karachi] to counter Pakistan Peoples Party. However, later MQM started a terror campaign by bombing, random murders and political assassinations to force the Pakistani government into creating an independent country for the Pakistan's Muhajir population. Hussain who had the backing of India and was living in exile in London, England and out of the reach of the Pakistani Justice but nevertheless, the ISI systematically dismantled his terror campaign and MQM has since supposedly renounced its militant ways.

ISI played a major role by informing British agencies in advance about terrorist plan to simultaneously blow up 10 airplanes over the Atlantic using liquid explosives in August 2006.

Failures

The 1965 war in Kashmir provoked a major crisis in intelligence. When the war started, there was a complete collapse of the operations of all the intelligence agencies, which had been largely devoted to domestic investigative work such as tapping telephone conversations and chasing political suspects.

The ISI, after the commencement of the 1965 Indo-Pakistan war, was apparently unable to locate an Indian armored division due to its preoccupation with political affairs. Ayub Khan set up a committee headed by General Yahya Khan to examine the working of the agencies.

In 1981, a Libyan Security company called Al Murtaza Associates sends recruiters to Pakistan to entice former soldiers and servicemen for high paying security jobs in Libya. In reality, Libya was recruiting mercenaries to fight with Chad and Egypt as it had border disputes with both nations. Only later did the ISI become aware of the plot and the whole scheme was stopped, but nearly 2,700 Pakistanis had already left for those jobs.

The PAF Field Intelligence Unit at their base in Karachi in July 1980 captured an Indian agent. He was interrogated and revealed that a large network of Indian spies were functioning in Karachi. The agent claimed that these spies, in addition to espionage, had also assassinated a few armed personnel.

He also said the leader of the spy ring was being headed by the food and beverages manager at the Intercontinental Hotel in Karachi and a number of serving Air Force officers and ratings were on his payroll. The ISI decided to survey the manager to see who he was in contact with, but then President of Pakistan Zia-ul Haq superseded and wanted the manager and anyone else involved in the case arrested immediately. It was later proven that the manager was completely innocent.

ISI failed to perform a proper background check on the British company which supplied the Pakistan Army with its Arctic-weather gear. When Pakistan attempted to secure the top of the Siachen Glacier in 1984, it placed a large order for Arctic-weather gear with the same company that also supplied the Indian Army with its gear.

Indians were easily alerted to the large Pakistani purchase and deduced that this large purchase could be used to equip troops to capture the glacier. India then mounted an operation (Operation Meghdoot) and secured the top of the glacier before Pakistan.

ISI failed to calculate the international reaction to the Kargil operation in summer of 1999. Subsequent heavy pressure by foreign countries such as USA forced the Pakistani-backed forces to withdraw from Kargil.

NEW DEVELOPMENTS OF INTER-SERVICES INTELLIGENCE

In late 2001, as al-Qaida fugitives fled from Afghanistan into Pakistan, Musharraf ordered that the agencies show full cooperation to the FBI, CIA and other US security agencies. In return, the Americans would give them equipment, expertise and money.

Suddenly, Pakistan's agencies had sophisticated devices to trace mobile phones, bug houses and telephone calls, and monitor large volumes of email traffic. "Whatever it took to improve the

Pakistanis' technical ability to find al-Qaida fighters, we were there to help them," says Michael Scheuer, a former head of the CIA's Osama bin Laden unit. An official with an American organisation says he once received a startling demonstration of the ISI's new capabilities. Driving down a street inside a van with ISI operatives, he could monitor phone conversations taking place in every house they passed. "It was very impressive, and really quite spooky,".

SOME OTHER INFORMATION ABOUT ISI

Departments

Joint Intelligence X: JIX is the coordinator of all the other departments in the ISI. Intelligence and information gathered from the other departments are sent to JIX which prepares and processes the information and from which prepares reports which are presented.

Joint Intelligence Bureau: JIB is the largest part of the ISI and was perhaps the most powerful component of the ISI in the late 1980s. It's main area of work is to gather intelligence on political parties. It also has three sub-sections which include operations in India, conducting anti-terrorism operations and providing security to VIPs.

Joint Counter Intelligence Bureau: JCIB is Pakistan's version of the NOC's of the CIA. Pakistani diplomats who conduct intelligence gathering operations report directly to this department. The area in which most of this kind of operations are conducted are in the Middle East, South Asia, China, Afghanistan and the Central Asian republics.

It is alleged that the ISI has expanded the range of the diplomats to conduct intelligence gathering operations in Europe, Africa and South America as well.

Joint Intelligence North: JIN is exclusively responsible for the Jammu and Kashmir region and in particular the Indian troop movement along the LOC (Line of Control). However, due to recent peace overtures between India and Pakistan, the size of this department is being reduced.

Joint Intelligence Miscellaneous: JIM is responsible for conducting espionage, offensive spy missions, surveillance and any other activities during war time.

Joint Signal Intelligence Bureau: JSIB has three Deputy Directors who are each charged with wireless communication intercepts, Monitoring enemy agents and other assets and conducting reconnaissance operations such as photographs. Most of the work force in this department are recruited from the Military College of Signals Academy and others come from the Army Signal Corps.

Joint Intelligence Technical: JIT is responsible for developing gadgets, monitoring equipment, explosives and even has known to have a chemical warfare section. Other than that, not much is known about this department.

Recruitment and Training

Both civilians and members of the armed forces can join the ISI. However for civilians, recruitment is advertised and is jointly handled by the Federal Public Services Commission (FPSC) and civilian ISI agents are considered employees of the Ministry of Defense. The FPSC conducts various examinations testing the candidate's knowledge of current affairs, English and various analytical abilities. Based on the results, the candidates are shortlisted by FPSC and the shortlist is sent to the ISI which conducts the initial background checks. The selected candidates are then invited for an interview which is conducted by a committee comprising FPSC and ISI officials.

Those candidates who passed the interview then have to go through rigorous fitness, medical and psychological evaluations. Once the candidate clears these evaluations, the ISI performs a very thorough background check on the candidate before being offered to join the ISI. Security clearance is granted once the candidate accepts the offer. Recruited agents then go to the Inter-Services Intelligence School for basic training following which they are employed on an initial one year probationary period. However, civilian operatives are not allowed to rise above the equivalent of the rank of Major and are mostly assigned to JIX,

JIB and JCIB departments and the rest of the departments are solely headed by the armed forces but there have been rare cases in which civilians have been assigned to those departments.

For the armed forces, officers have to apply for admission into the Inter-Services Intelligence School. After finishing the intelligence course, they can apply to be posted in Field Intelligence Units or in the directorate of Military/Air/Naval intelligence. Then they wait and hope that their performance is good enough to be invited to the ISI for a temporary posting. Based on their performance in the military and the temporary posting with ISI, they are then offered a more permanent position.

Senior ISI officers with ranks of Major and above are only assigned to the ISI for no more than 2-3 years to curtail the attempt to abuse their power. Almost all of the Director-Generals of the ISI have never served in the organization before being appointed by the Military commanders to lead it. ISI also monitors former, current and retired military officers who at one point or another held sensitive positions and had access to classified data.

Controversies

Critics of the ISI say that it has become a state within a state, answerable neither to the leadership of the army, nor to the President or the Prime Minister. The ISI has been deeply involved in domestic politics of Pakistan since the late 1950s. The 1990 elections for example were widely believed to have been rigged by the ISI in favor of the Islami Jamhoori Ittehad (IJI) party, a conglomerate of nine mainly rightist parties by the ISI under Lt. General Hameed Gul, to ensure the defeat of Bhutto's Pakistan People's Party (PPP) in the polls. Gul has denied that the vote was rigged. In September-October 1989, two ISI officers launched Operation Midnight Jackals in a bid to sway PPP members of the National Assembly to back a vote of no confidence against the Bhutto government.

ISI's Internal Political Division has been accused by various members of the Pakistan People's Party in assassinating Shah Nawaz Bhutto, one of the two brothers of Benazir Bhutto, through poisoning in the French Riviera in the middle of 1985 in an attempt to intimidate her into not returning to Pakistan for directing the movement against Zia's Military government, but no proof has been found implicating the ISI

The ISI was also involved in a massive corruption scandal dubbed "Mehrangate," in which top ISI and Army brass were given large sums of money by Yunus Habib (the owner of Mehran Bank) to deposit ISI's foreign exchange reserves in Mehran Bank. This was against government policy, as such banking which involves government institutions can only be done through state-owned financial institutions and not private banks. When the new director of the ISI was appointed and then proceeded to withdraw the money from Mehran Bank and back into state-owned financial institutions, the money had been used up in financing Habib's "extra-curricular" activities. On April 20, 1994, Habib was arrested and the scandal became public.

India has blamed the ISI for training, arming and giving logistics to the militants who are fighting the Indian security forces in Indian occupied Kashmir. FAS reports that the Inter-Service Intelligence, is the main supplier of funds and arms to the militant groups. The British Government had stated there is a 'clear link' between Pakistan's Inter-Services Intelligence and three major militant outfits The Guardian newspaper had uncovered evidence that Pakistani militants were openly raising funds and training new recruits and that the ISI's Kashmir cell was instrumental in funding and controlling these outfits. India also accused ISI of masterminding the 1993 Mumbai bombings, with backing from Dawood Ibrahim's D-Company. Aside from Kashmir, India accuses the ISI of running training camps near the border of Bangladesh in late 1990s where India claims the ISI trains members of various separatist groups from the northeastern Indian states. The ISI has denied these accusations.

In January 1993, the United States placed Pakistan on the watch list of such countries which were suspected of sponsoring international terrorism. This decision was made in part because the current head of the ISI in 1993, Lt. Gen. Nasir, had become a stumbling block in American efforts to buy back hundreds of shoulder-fired, surface-to-air FIM-92 Stinger missiles from the

Afghan Mujahideen and was assisting organizations such as Harkat ul-Ansar, which had been branded as a terrorist organization by the US. Once Nasir's tenure as ISI chief ended, the US removed Pakistan from the terrorism watch list. The ISI is also suspected to have been involved with the hijackers of the 9/11 terrorist attacks, having paid the ringleader Mohammad Atta. After 9/11, ISI was purged of members who did not support President Pervez Musharraf's stance towards the Taliban and Al Qaeda.

In the BBC Newsnight Programme on 27 September 2006, a research paper prepared for the Ministry of Defence (United Kingdom), was quoted linking the ISI with support for the Taliban and other terrorist acts in the west. The report states, "The US/ UK cannot begin to turn the tide until they identify the real enemies from attacking ideas tactically-and seek to put in place a more just vision. This will require Pakistan to move away from Army rule and for the ISI to be dismantled and more significantly something to be put in its place." This was denied by President Musharraf, "I totally, 200% reject it. I reject it from anybody-MoD or anyone who tells me to dismantle ISI. The Council on Foreign Relations, a US foreign policy think tank published an article casting doubt on some of the accusations, 'Though Pakistan does offer safe haven to Kashmiri groups, and perhaps some Taliban fighters, the suggestion that the ISI is responsible for the 7/7 bombings of London's mass transit system is "a real stretch," [Kathy] Gannon says'. However, a later report by the same think tank, The Council on Foreign Relations, stated there was probably support for terrorism from rogue elements of the ISI. The head of the British think tank himself rebutted Newsnight's claims in an interview to Newsnight and said that the programme has misportrayed research notes as an official document. The whole media scandal lasted for about a week and led to nowhere.

Amnesty International publish a report on 29 September 2006 accusing Pakistan of detaining hundreds of alleged terror suspects without legal process. The group says some were tortured or otherwise ill-treated, others were sold to the US military, and others have vanished without trace. "Journalists and human rights activists have told Amnesty International that most terror suspects deemed important by Pakistani intelligence were held in "safe houses" run by "the agencies" – Pakistan's intelligence agencies including the Inter-Services Intelligence (ISI) and Military Intelligence (MI). 'In many cases, U.S. agents paid a bounty of $5,000 (2,667 UK pounds) to those, usually intelligence agents, who simply declared people terrorists, seized them and handed them over for interrogation with no legal process, Amnesty said. "Enforced disappearances were almost unheard of in Pakistan before the start of the U.S-led war on terror — now they are a growing phenomenon, spreading beyond terror suspects," Amnesty researcher Angelika Pathak said.' Gen Musharraf strongly denied the allegations that some alleged terror suspects had vanished without trace, "I don't want even to reply to that, it is a nonsense, I don't believe it, I don't trust it". 'Gen Musharraf has boasted of the arrests as proof of his commitment to the fight against al-Qaida. In his new memoirs, In the Line of Fire, he claims that the CIA has paid Pakistan hundreds of millions of dollars in bounty payments for the capture of 369 al-Qaida suspects since 2001.'

Some members of the American media and political establishment have questioned Pakistan's commitment in combating the Taliban and Al Qaeda remnants in border areas. In response, Pakistan has pointed to the deployment of nearly 80,000 troops in the border areas and the arrests of more than 700 Al Qaeda members carried out by mostly ISI members, the most high profile ones including 9/11 mastermind Khalid Sheikh Mohammed, as proof that the ISI was serious in its commitment to fighting the War on Terrorism. However, the recent deal with the rebels to end the Waziristan War has been seen by many observers as a defeat for Pakistan that has strengthened Taliban powerbase in Waziristan. Moreover, NATO's top commanders have criticized ISI's continued role in supplying weapons and providing sanctuary to the terrorists but have approved the deal.

2

The Pakistani ISI Directorate's Sponsorship of Terrorism

During the Spanish Civil War in the 1930s, a Nationalist General named Emilio Mola Vidal, marched his army on the city of Madrid. He announced that four columns of his force would be supported by a covert 'fifth column' comprised of militant supporters. This fifth column was defined as a "clandestine group or faction of subversive agents who attempt to undermine a nation's solidarity by any means at their disposal. Their principal tactic would be the infiltration of sympathizers into the entire fabric of the nation under attack and, particularly, Holt and Gray into positions of policy decision and national defense" (Britannica). Within Pakistan a fifth column has been operating for decades; permeating through all echelons of the Pakistani government and clandestinely sowing the seeds of terror through unsavory organizations across the globe.

Nine years after the attacks of September 11, 2001, the global war on terrorism has claimed the lives of thousands of combatants and cost the international community over $1 trillion dollars. It has reached every corner of the globe, from the cities of Europe and Africa to the Pacific islands and border areas of South America. The United States (U.S.)-led war on terrorism has set the precedent that state sponsors of extremism and terrorism are intolerable enemies of the international community. After close to a decade of increased intelligence gathering, counter-terrorism efforts, and military operations across the globe-the world is still left with extremely real and tangible threats. Pakistan has become an essential ally to counterterrorist operations in Southwest Asia, providing airspace, logistical access and supply routes for coalition personnel. For the international community, Pakistan has become a centerpiece and critical node for defeating Islamic extremism and countering future attacks against worldwide interests. Yet, within the ranks of Pakistan's military, society, and population lives a widespread web of terrorism, fundamentalism, extremism, and Islamic Jihad, promoted and fostered by a shadowy intelligence organization.

The Pakistani state has been left at an impasse: appeasing the extremist divisions of its population to prevent domestic upheaval and also cooperating with the international community's efforts to defeat transnational terrorism and violent fundamentalism. "The Pakistani Inter- Services Intelligence Directorate (ISI) serves as the state's foreign intelligence and counterintelligence organization- but is also deeply embedded in domestic politics and foreign policy initiatives. The ISI...has often been called a 'rogue' agency or a 'state within a state'... but it operates at the behest of the government, civil and military" (Nawaz xli). Truly, the ISI has become the fifth column of Pakistan's military. The agency specializes in utilizing terrorist organizations as proxies for Pakistani foreign policy, covert action abroad, and controlling domestic politics. The ISI is deeply entrenched in the Pakistani state as well as within unsavory networks spanning the globe. "For more than two decades the ISI [has] sponsored Islamic militancy to carry out its secret wars" (Hussain 12). Pakistan's Inter Services Intelligence Directorate is a clandestine sponsor of worldwide extremism and transnational terrorism. The fragile nature of military centric politics, deeply entrenched religious foundations, and a nuclear arsenal in Pakistan makes the ISI the foremost terrorist threat and non-state sponsor of terrorism in the international community.

ORIGINS OF A PAKISTANI SPY AGENCY

The Islamic Republic of Pakistan, or Pakistan, achieved its initial independence in 1947 when the British divided the colonized Indian sub-continent based on religious lines. Pakistan was centered on the religion of Islam, drawing geographically separated regions out of Muslim population centers in the West (West Pakistan) and the eastern portion of Bengal (East Pakistan).

The Indian state catered to the Hindu faith and resided between the two newly formed Pakistani provinces. The British divisions forced the relocation of millions of people on all sides, creating poverty, destruction, and casualties in its wake. "Partitions along ethnic lines usually result in The Pakistani Inter-Service Intelligence Directorate's Sponsorship of Terrorism mutually inflicted violence, but the politicians of that time had no understanding of the magnitude of what they had prepared" (Ali 30). After the dust and blood had settled, the world embraced a newly emerged Muslim state, drawn from loosely constructed boundaries and ethnic divisions.

A structural contradiction lay at the heart of the new country. "Religious affinity was the only rationale for uniting West Pakistan and its Muslim majority provinces – Punjab, Sind, Baluchistan, and North-West Frontier – with East Pakistan, which was the Muslim majority slice of Bengal". The new state was led initially by the Governor-General Mohammad Ali Jinnah and Prime Minister Liaquat Ali Khan, who sought cooperative relations between the newly divided Hindu and Muslim states, but was challenged over the contested territory of Kashmir. A poorly established border between India and Pakistan left Kashmir contested between both nations, as well as the Chinese. The disputes over the small region resulted in the 1947 Indo- Pakistani war and the birth of the modern day ISI. The ISI stemmed from the Pakistani desire to streamline intelligence collection and dissemination between its military branches in the time of conflict. After the 1947 Indo- Pakistani war over Kashmir, the ISI was created as a separate entity from the intelligence bureau (IB) to meet this function and expand Pakistan's collection capabilities. "The agency was initially charged with performing all intelligence tasks at home and abroad... its scope of operation extended to all areas related to national security" (Hussain 13). Originally, the role of the ISI was crafted to focus the efforts of the agency on foreign intelligence collection and the dissemination of national security concerns.

However, in the 1970s, the ISI's responsibility took a new shape as it was given additional responsibilities including the oversight of domestic politics.

"Ironically, it was a civilian leader, Zulfikar Ali Bhutto who created the ISI's internal wing which played a critical role in the ousting of his government a few years later. [The ISI] was to cast a heavy shadow over the country's politics in later years" . Beginning with Bhutto's creation of the internal wing, set to monitor domestic security threats and political trends, the ISI began to take on the shape of a 'big brother' entity.

However, the seeds of militancy, religious fundamentalism, and clandestine terrorist support were planted when Bhutto appointed General Zia al-Haq as the army chief in 1976. General Zia was a devout Muslim, and Bhutto thought he would never betray his trust (Coll). "Once elevated to the top position, the General did not take much time to develop secret contacts with hard-line religious groups and conspired with them to overthrow his benefactor".

In 1977, General Zia al-Haq took the seat of power from Bhutto, with strong support from the ISI and religious groups, and immediately began to instill Islamist fundamentalism and teachings throughout the Pakistani military. Jamaat-i-Islami (JI), the largest Islamic political party, gained strength and momentum and fostered extremist leadership within the military ranks under Zia's guidance. "The main objective of the JI was to penetrate the army and use it to seize state power. The practice introduced by General Zia of sending combat officers to universities in Pakistan, in which the JI often had pervasive influence facilitated the party's [Islamic] objective" (Hussain 20). The ISI began to take shape as a mediator, facilitator, representative, and liaison for militant Islam, extremism, and Pakistani covert action.

During the Cold War, Pakistan proved to be a strategic ally for the U.S. due to its geographic location and inherent rivalry with India which drove an automatic anti-Soviet stance. The ISI was leveraged by Western intelligence services, including the Central Intelligence Holt and Gray Agency (CIA), to undermine Soviet action in the region and provide an outlet for the sharing of intelligence between Pakistan and the U.S. When the Soviet Union invaded Afghanistan in the 1980s the CIA and ISI embarked on one of the largest covert campaigns in history: financing and arming the Mujahedin, comprised of Islamic extremists, for their efforts in Afghanistan. "Zia did not allow the CIA or any other foreign intelligence agency to aid the Mujahedin directly, enter Afghanistan, or plan the Mujahedin's battles and strategy. That became the prerogative of the ISI, which, with its newfound wealth and American patronage, had become a state within a state, employing thousands of officers in order to run what was now also Pakistan's Afghan war" (Rashid 10).

While increased funding and motivation from the West poured through the ranks of the ISI to bolster the capabilities of the Mujahedin in Afghanistan, Zia mandated strict Islamic and religious training and indoctrination for the military and agency. "The ISI's training of guerrillas was integrated with the teaching of Islam. The prominent theme was that Islam was a complete socio-political ideology under threat from atheistic communists. The Afghan war produced a new radical Islamic movement" (Hussain 17).

Simultaneously, Zia took steps to turn Pakistan into an Islamic state, obedient to a strict interpretation of Sharia law (Islamic law), and used the ISI as the face of enforcement and religious cultivation. [Military] units were required to take non-combatant mullahs with them to the front line. Soldiers were encouraged to attend 'Tablighi' [(Deobandi movement within Pakistan)] gatherings. The purpose was to indoctrinate cadets and young officers with an obscurantist interpretation of Islam. Many of those cadets later rose to positions of power and took control of sensitive institutions, including ISI.

The Afghan war created a leviathan and powerful intelligence agency in the ISI while Zia mandated Islamic fundamentalism and Deobandism (a strict interpretation of the Hanafi school of Sunni Islam) into their shadowy ranks. With aid from the U.S. and a pivotal and violent struggle against the Soviets in Afghanistan, the ISI cultivated a relationship with extremists from across the globe, including al-Qaeda. While being forced to adhere to fundamental Islam from the Pakistani state, the ISI itself became recognized in the international system and feared within domestic society. Throughout the 1990s, the ISI maintained its relationship with extremist networks and militants that it had established during the Afghan war to utilize in its campaign against Indian forces in Kashmir.

The ISI had become a state-mandated and Western-built sponsor of contemporary and fundamental terrorism.

An Unsavory Past

Many high-profile terrorist incidents, ranging from the September 11, 2001 attacks on New York and Washington to the July 7, 2004 subway bombings in London to the November 2008 assault on Mumbai, have had direct connections to individuals and groups operating in Pakistan (Ganguly and Kapur 47). The sponsorship and recruitment of terrorist and guerilla movements against the Soviets in Afghanistan is paramount when examining historic ties between terrorism and the ISI.

However, the agency also took part in, and was responsible for, numerous international operations and violent acts across the globe. The instilled radicalization from Zia and the campaigns in Afghanistan and Kashmir vetted and emboldened the ISI. Yet the The Pakistani Inter-Service Intelligence Directorate's Sponsorship of Terrorism agency's clandestine operations and sponsorship for violence and Islamic extremism abroad generated the attention of the international community.

The most notable and dangerous connection to transnational terrorism is the ISI's cooperation and support for al-Qaeda (AQ) and its leader, Osama bin-Laden. During the 1980s, militants poured into Pakistan from the Muslim world, including Palestinian teacher and preacher Abdullah Azzam, who had taught in Jordan and Saudi Arabia, preaching Muslims' duty to wage Jihad.

One of his students was Osama bin-Laden. Azzam created Maktab al-Khidmat (Services Office or MK) in Peshawar to recruit Arabs and raise funds. Bin Laden, with ISI ties, was a key MK organizer. Under bin Laden, MK transformed into al-Qaeda. ISI Directory General Akhtar Abdul Ramna personally met with him many times, providing money and intelligence. (Roberts 105)

AQ and the ISI enjoyed a close relationship in the 1980s when Muslims from across the globe shared bases of operations in the Northwest Frontier Province (NWFP) and Federally Administered Tribal Areas (FATA).

The tribal regions, governed strictly by Pashtun tribal codes, were considered a safe haven for militants, foreign fighters, and terrorists. Following the Afghan war, the U.S. essentially lost interest in the region, cutting ties with the Islamic militants who fought across the border and also losing influence over the large population of refugees created by the fighting. The refugee population was a virtual breeding ground for Islamic extremism, spearheaded by the ISI and its network of madrassas. "The Taliban (the word literally means 'students') were children of the Afghan refugees and poor Pathan families 'educated' in the madrassas in the 1980s" (Ali 136).

The same Taliban controlled and supported by the ISI harbored today's most wanted terrorist: Osama bin-Laden. Pakistani President Pervez Musharraf observed: We helped created [sic] the mujahedin, fired them with religious zeal in seminaries, armed them, paid them, fed them, and sent them to Jihad against the Soviet Union in Afghanistan. We did not stop to think how we would divert them to productive life after the Jihad was won. This mistake cost Afghanistan and Pakistan more dearly than any other country. Neither did the United States realize what a rich, educated person like Osama bin Laden might later do with the organization that we all had enabled him to establish. (Roberts 106) Leading up to the attacks of September 11, the ISI had a working relationship with Osama bin-Laden and his militant network and had a supportive and controlling relationship with the Taliban, which was then firmly in control of Afghanistan. "In 1996, Osama bin Laden settled in Afghanistan. He met an ISI representative, who proposed an alliance between bin- Laden's network and the Taliban, which won the Afghan civil war in 1996, achieving ISI's aim of a sympathetic government in Kabul" (106). Following the Afghan war, the ISI directly sponsored, controlled, and orchestrated the Taliban's movement into Afghanistan. They brokered a relationship between al-Qaeda, Osama bin-Laden, and the Taliban and sponsored the terrorist state which had been established. "In 1997, the ISI asked Saudi intelligence for permission to sponsor bin-Laden"...only four short years before the deadliest terrorist attack the international community had ever experienced.

Aside from the strong influence and sponsorship of terrorism exemplified in Afghanistan, the Taliban, and al-Qaeda, the ISI has also focused a great deal of effort on fostering terrorist organizations in the Kashmir region. Kashmir sits at the top of Pakistan, bordering both India and China. All three nations dispute the territory as falling under their sovereign control. Historically, the region has been a catalyst for three wars and repeated military exchanges involving guerilla action, artillery fire, and high-altitude fighting.

The ISI has actively sought to enhance, finance, and promote terrorist organizations which serve to undermine the Indian influence in Kashmir. "In 1990, ISI operated 30 training camps for Kashmiri militants. By 2002, there were 128 ISI-sponsored camps training militants to fight in Kashmir. Approximately, 1,000 members of Harakat-ul-Mujahideen [(HUM)], Jaishe- Muhammad (JEM), and Lashkar-e-Taiba (LET) received training each year" . The lessons learned by the ISI, including its strategy of low-intensity conflict in Afghanistan were applied in the Kashmiri campaign. The ISI served as Pakistan's liaison and training force for HUM, JEM, and LET, equipping and planning operations against Indian targets. Aside from attempting to seed Islamic extremism into the Kashmiri movement, the ISI also sought to preoccupy Indian forces in Kashmir, limiting India's ability to utilize them elsewhere and undermining their control of the military (Weaver). The ISI enabled HUM, JEM, and LET, hardline Islamic groups, to lead the terrorist action in Kashmir, and change the complexion of the struggle (Hussain 25).

Many of those Islamic groups expanded their terrorist operations outside of Kashmir and into neighboring India. In 2008, the city of Mumbai fell under siege at the hands of heavilyarmed LET militants. Using assault rifles and explosives, a handful of LET terrorists killed almost 200 people on Indian soil. "Indian officials implicated the ISI [for the attack]. India's foreign ministry said the ISI had links to the planners of the attacks, the banned militant group [LET], which New Delhi [blamed] for the assault" (Bajoria 2009). The men were later found to be controlled by operators within Pakistan using cellular phones. While Pakistan has denied all of the Indian allegations that the ISI was involved, it is likely that the ISI's connection with LET remains strong, even following the attacks in Mumbai.

Outside of the Southwest Asian sphere of influence the ISI, has maintained an active influence over the operations of terrorist organizations and guerilla movements, most notably with the expansion of ISI operations and sponsorship overseas under the leadership of General Javid Nasir. "A member of the proselytizing Tablighi Jamaat, Nasir had become a devout Muslim with a flowing white beard. And he had no intelligence background" (Nawaz 452). After his appointment to lead the ISI, Nasir oversaw covert action across the international community.

The ISI's involvement was not limited to India, however. Under General Nasir's instructions, the ISI violated the UN embargo on supplying arms to the warring parties in Bosnia-Herzegovina and airlifted heavy weapons and missiles for the Bosnian Muslims. In 1993, several Arab countries, including Egypt, Tunisia, and Algeria, had complained about General Nasir extending support to radical Islamic movements in their countries. (Hussain 27) After Zia's extremist indoctrination and Nasir's expansion of the ISI, the agency continued to expand its influence across borders and among terrorist organizations worldwide. The ISI's track record for sponsorship of terrorist organizations is extensive and stretched far beyond the conflicts in Afghanistan and Kashmir. The links it established to al-Qaeda and other global Islamic movements during the Soviet-Afghan war enabled its actions in other nation states. "At least two former ISI chiefs, General Hamid Gul and General Javid Nasir, remained actively involved with Islamic radical movements. Both promoted pan-Islamism and strove for an Islamic revolution that would free Pakistan from perceived western, and particularly American, cultural and political influences" . Those relationships and motivations within the ISI remain strong today and continue to threaten the stability and counter terrorist goals of the international community.

Both Sides of the Fence?

The attacks of September 11, 2001 and the U.S. response in Afghanistan changed the nature of the game for Pakistan and the ISI. President George Bush enacted a policy of preemption, mandating the international community cooperate or stand in his way. In October 2001, the U.S. began conventional military strikes in Afghanistan. Before those air strikes began, the ISI and the state of Pakistan was presented a list of demands from the U.S. government, outlining their future role in the emerging global war on terrorism. Ultimately, Pakistan had little choice if it wished to remain in Washington's good graces and off of the list of state sponsors of terror. Pakistan agreed to the terms. However, since the attacks of September 11, the ISI has sought to undermine the U.S. relationship with Pakistan and remove the Pakistani state out from under Western control. Quite literally, the ISI has been playing both sides of the field: cooperating with the U.S. when convenient and beneficial for the agency, but continually supporting terrorist organizations and cross-border operations against North Atlantic Treaty Organization (NATO) forces in Afghanistan.

In 2009, Admiral Michael Mullen, the U.S. Chairman of the Joint Chiefs of Staff (CJCS), traveled with CIA officers to Islamabad to present intelligence to ISI officers, linking them to militant groups in Afghanistan. Mullen was interviewed by PBS correspondent Martin Stewart and expressed his concerns over the ISI's links to terrorist organizations and militants. Rehman Malik, the Interior Minister of Pakistan, was asked the following:

Martin Smith: The Defense Intelligence Agency, the CIA, U.S. military and Afghan intelligence all points to ISI and Pakistani cooperation and support for segments of the Taliban. Are they all lying?

Rehman Malik: I think it's outdated intelligence. They must be talking of the past. We are cooperating. ("Frontline: Obama's War")

Many members of the Pakistani state, including top government officials are influenced by the ISI and maintain professional, yet clandestine, relationships with militant leaders in the tribal areas of Pakistan. These relationships are evident when examining the past record of Pakistani and ISI cooperation with CIA, FBI, and U.S. Special Forces in capture/kill operations, counterterrorist operations, and investigative ventures within Pakistan.

In 2002 an investigative journalist for the Wall Street Journal named Daniel Pearl was abducted by Pakistani militants and brutally beheaded. Pearl was investigating the links between the ISI and terrorist organizations in Pakistan when he was abducted outside of Islamabad. "After one of his assassins surrendered to his ISI 'handler,' authorities waited a week before notifying the United States, highlighting the ISI support for regional and Kashmiri militant groups. The incident called attention to the possible involvement of ISI, or its client JEM, in Pearl's abduction and murder, raising questions of [the Pakistani state's] control over ISI" (Roberts 109).

In 2006 Rashid Rauf was captured in Northwestern Pakistan on suspected ties to al- Qaeda and specifically a plot involving the bombing of multiple international airliners. Rauf was identified as a financier and logistical node for al-Qaeda operations. The CIA and British intelligence were eager to interrogate and extract intelligence from Rauf, who would have undoubtedly proven lucrative for information on al-Qaeda and future operations. However, before his trial and his likely extradition from Pakistan, Rauf escaped. "On the way back to jail from a court hearing...his police drivers apparently stopped their van and visited McDonald's for a bite to eat, allowing Rauf to enter a mosque to pray. They never saw him again" (Moreton and Buncombe).

It is apparent that the ISI and Pakistan are willing to only cooperate with counterterrorism operations superficially, only to appease the international community. There have been a number of successful operations to capture terrorists within Pakistan, and with Pakistani assistance. Yet none of these operations were triggered by actions on the part of the ISI or Pakistani military.

In March 2002, Abu Zubaydah, a senior al-Qaeda member, was captured in Faisalabad. Ramzi bin al-Shibh, a deputy leader of the task force that coordinated the September 11 attacks, was captured in Karachi in September 2002. And in March 2003, another task force leader, Kahlid Sheikh Mohammad, was picked up in

Rawalpindi. Other prominent captures include those of communications expert Naeem Noor Khan, Ahmed Khalfan Ghailani (linked to the 1998 U.S. embassy bombings in Africa), and Abu Farj al-Libi, believed to be the head of al-Qaeda operations in Pakistan. (Friedman and Bokhari 2005)

The involvement of the ISI in capturing terrorists within Pakistan is a front, motivated by the agency's resolve to appear cooperative in international counter-terrorism operations. After a decade-long manhunt for al-Qaeda leadership, largely living within Pakistan, the ISI and Pakistani state has little to show. This lack of success presents alarming questions and highlights the ISI's capability to operate on both sides of the fence:

How is it that al-Qaeda's mostly Arab leadership is able to evade detection in a country with very few Arabs? More important, how can a foreign non-state actor evade detection, when he is known to be in a certain region, with massive global search and destroy operations hunting him, unless he is granted succor and protection from some members of the local security and intelligence organizations closest to the front? (Friedman and Bokhari 2005)

The international community is unable to rely on or trust the ISI to operate independently to track down terrorists or militants. The same militants and terrorist leaders the international community wishes to bring to justice are invited to drink tea with ISI officers. Given the track record of the ISI, and the agency's haphazard and selective participation in counter-terrorist operations, the international community must assume that the ISI is more of a hindrance than an ally.

THE ISI AND PAKISTAN'S NUCLEAR SECURITY

The current war in Afghanistan has highlighted the challenges faced by the international community in containing Islamic extremism in Pakistan and stopping the proxy relationship between the Taliban and ISI. While succeeding in Afghanistan is critical for contemporary American foreign policy, the largest security threat lies in the export of Islamic extremism from Pakistan and the security of Pakistan's nuclear weapons. The ISI has proven it is willing and able to provide aid to terrorist organizations and orchestrate their actions abroad. Its shadowy network has penetrated all ranks of the Pakistani government and military. The presence of al- Qaeda and terrorist organizations within close proximity to potentially insecure Pakistani nuclear weapons presents the foremost threat of nuclear terrorism to the international community. "Little is known in open sources about Pakistan's nuclear [arsenal]. Current estimates suggest that Pakistan has approximately 60 nuclear weapons, stored in at least six locations throughout the country" (Jagadish 206). Pakistan's security protocols surrounding its nuclear arsenal include separation of components, three-person review, cryptologic launch codes, and underground facilities ("Pakistan Nuclear Weapons"). Islamic extremists [or foreign terrorist organizations] desiring to steal a Pakistani nuclear weapon must have sufficient intelligence [and technical competence] to differentiate between storage sites that house shields and storage sites that house fissile cores" . The security practices surrounding Pakistan's nuclear facilities demands that any successful terrorist attempt at acquiring a nuclear weapon would necessitate the cooperation and involvement of the ISI or senior level Pakistani officials.

The world was shaken at the discovery of Pakistan's founding scientist for nuclear technology Abdul Qadeer Khan's nuclear proliferation network, spanning from Libya to North Korea. Khan was the leading scientist for nuclear weapons and a top advisor and technical expert for the Pakistani state. "Although there is no evidence suggesting that Khan sold nuclear technology to Islamic extremists, some authors note that Khan was able to bypass the weak Pakistani export controls with the full knowledge of the Pakistani government and operate a private-sector nuclear bazaar offering all the necessary equipment to create a nuclear device".

Following the discovery of A.Q. Khan's proliferation network, the Pakistani state is widely believed to have implemented further nuclear protection policies. Most notably is the establishment of a lengthy security clearance and investigation process for all individuals working in sensitive positions or in nuclear facilities. However, the Pakistani ISI remains vitally embedded in the clearance process. "Clearance investigations are reportedly conducted by approximately 8,000 personnel from four agencies, including the [Strategic Planning Directorate], the ISI, the Intelligence Bureau, and Military Intelligence" . The ISI undoubtedly has a presence in all three of the other agencies and intelligence divisions responsible for granting access to Pakistan's weapons.

Terrorist organizations with past links to ISI have already expressed interest in acquiring nuclear weapons, including Osama bin-Laden and his al-Qaeda network. Islamists seem to have become concentrated in two areas of senior Pakistani leadership, however, the ISI and...the Pakistani nuclear weapons program. The original emphasis on building an "Islamic bomb" and resentment against the US for sanctions against Pakistan's nuclear program (at a time when India's was more discreet, before the 1998 tests by both countries) may have helped draw radicals into the nuclear program. Clearly that remains a cause for concern, as senior Pakistani scientists have been interrogated by the government over their visits to Afghanistan. ("The Pakistani Conundrum")

The Bulletin of Atomic Scientists in 2009 stated:

In an effort to develop access to nuclear technologies, [al-Qaeda] tried, reportedly without success, to discreetly contact the rogue nuclear supplier network run by...A.Q. Khan. Al Qaeda had a bit more success consulting with another Pakistani 'WMD for hire' network called Ummah Tameer-e-Nau, which offered its services to bin-Laden before 9/11. (Mowatt-Larssen 65)

Scientists with access to the nuclear weapons program within Pakistan offered their expertise to bin-Laden before he demonstrated his capability to inflict massive casualties on the American homeland. The iconic status bin-Laden achieved following the 9/11 attacks coupled with the anti-American sentiment within the ISI and many regions of Pakistan is extremely concerning for the future threat of nuclear terrorism.

Unique Among State Sponsors

Across the international system many state sponsors of terrorism exist and foster relationships of violence and extremism. All of these proxies and sponsors of terrorism represent dangers to the international community. Iran's support of Hamas is a well-known and established proxy relationship with a terrorist organization. Syria's support and control of Hezbollah is a further example of notable state sponsorship. However, in relation to the funding, capabilities, and elements of Islamic extremism in the Pakistani ISI, these examples are marginalized. A comparison of the nature, environment, and capabilities of each relationship establishes the ISI as the most dangerous sponsor of terrorism in the international system.

Iran is arguably the most active state sponsor of terrorism on the globe. It has consistently engaged in supporting insurgencies targeting Western forces in Iraq and has historically financed and operated proxy organizations targeting Israel. Specifically, the Iranian Quds Force, which is reminiscent of the Pakistani ISI but more focused on special operations, is a leader of sponsoring terrorist organizations throughout the Middle East. "[A U.S. congressional report last year] said the Quds Force trained the Taliban on small unit tactics, small arms, explosives, and indirect fire weapons" (Porter). "Iran continues to top the list of state sponsors of terrorism, where it has been since 1984. The list is now down to four since the removal last year of North Korea. Iran is joined by Syria (added in 1979), Cuba (1982) and Sudan (1993).

Designation carries sanctions, including bans on arms-related sales" (Goodenough). While Iran may continue to be the most active sponsor of terrorism, the world has seen Pakistan evade the U.S. state sponsor of terrorism list and has allowed its ISI to clandestinely support the most dangerous terrorist organizations, including al-Qaeda. The ISI evades this list of state sponsors because it's characterized as a non-state actor or a "state within a state." The number of terrorist attacks in each region exemplifies the increasing danger of ISI-supported groups within Pakistan. Between 2007 and 2008 terrorist incidents in Iraq fell from 6,210 attacks to 3,258. However, in those same years in Pakistan, terrorist incidents climbed by 890 incidents, from 1,340 to 2,239 (Goodenough). The same congressional report which outlined Iran as the most active sponsor of terrorism also alluded to the difference of threats posed by alThe Qaeda to that of regional terror sponsors such as Iran. "Al-Qaeda and related networks, while losing ground, continued to pose "the greatest terrorist threat to the United States and its partners in 2008" (Goodenough). The ISI eludes the international list for "state" sponsors of terror, but actively grants refuge to the world's deadliest transnational terrorist threats in an unstable, mostly lawless region with close proximity to nuclear weapons.

"The [above mentioned congressional] report said al-Qaeda and allies had moved into "the remote areas of the Pakistani frontier, where they have used this terrain as a safe haven to hide, train terrorists, communicate with the followers, plot attacks and send fighters to support the insurgency in Afghanistan" (Goodenough). Asif Ali Zardari, the current President of Pakistan turns a blind eye to a wide range of the ISI's action and sponsorship activities in the FATA. In many cases, Pakistan has been unable to penetrate the tribal regions of the Northwest Frontier Province. However, the ISI moves freely and provides security and cooperation to the Taliban, al-Qaeda, LET and other militant organizations. "The growing influence of militant Islam, particularly in the strategically located North West Frontier Province and the western province of Balochistan is ominous. The militants, who fashion themselves on the legacy of Afghanistan's ousted Taliban regime have already established rigid Islamic rule in the Waziristan tribal region" (Hussain 190). While Iran finances and funds Hamas, the ISI supports and defends a figurative "playground" for al-Qaeda and Islamic extremists. The ISI represents a larger threat to the international community because of its ability to operate freely within Pakistan, Pakistan's nuclear capability, and the danger of those two paths converging.

FUTURE ENGAGEMENT WITH THE ISI

When interviewed about the relationship between the West and Pakistan and the ongoing conflict in Afghanistan, the bestselling author Steven Coll stated:

This could not be a more complicated war. If you think about it, the United States is essentially waging a war against its own ally. The Taliban are a proxy of the government of Pakistan [orchestrated by the ISI]. We are an ally of the government of Pakistan. We are fighting the Taliban. In the end, the Taliban will be defeated strategically when the government of Pakistan makes a strategic decision that its future does not lie in partnership with Islamic extremists. (2009)

Coll pinpoints the root of current and future problems in dealing with the ISI and their clandestine terrorist support networks. In 2009, the U.S. provided close to $6.5 billion dollars in aid to the Pakistani government; $300 million of that was dedicated to military spending (Mohammad). The West is figuratively caught between a rock and a hard place. It requires the assistance of Pakistan to successfully prosecute counter-terrorism campaigns in Southwest Asia. Yet, the ISI has infiltrated all ranks of Pakistan's military structure and leverages sympathizers and supporters throughout the Pakistani population.

A large amount of that military aid is falling into the hands of the sponsors of the exact networks the West is attempting to defeat. On February 16, 2010 the Taliban's second in command, Mullah Baradar, was captured in a raid conducted jointly by the ISI and the U.S. Western leaders hoped that this would be a catalyst for strengthening the cooperation between the ISI and Western intelligence agencies and serve as an indication that the ISI would begin dismissing its historical involvement with militants. However, after a close examination into the raid, the New York Times provided: Relations between the intelligence services, [CIA and ISI], of the United States and Pakistan have long been marred by suspicions that Pakistan has sheltered the Afghan Taliban. The Pakistanis have long denied it. New details of the raid indicate that the arrest of the No. 2 Taliban leader was not necessarily the result of a new determination by Pakistan to go after the Taliban, or a bid to improve its strategic position in the region. Rather, it may be something more prosaic: "a lucky accident..." (Shane and Schmitt) Upon Baradar's capture, ISI officers delayed allowing U.S. intelligence officers to question him and were hesitant in sharing news and information about his detention with the Pakistani press (in fear of casting themselves in a pro-Western light).

The ISI will continue to act out of its own interest. It has grown in size from its inception and now forms a state within the Pakistani state. While it serves as an intelligence agency of the Pakistani government, the Pakistani government is largely unable to control its actions or relationships with terrorist organizations, both domestic and abroad. Ongoing operations to defeat extremists and terrorists places the ISI at a crossroads with Western intelligence agencies and irregular warfare personnel. Without a complete transformation of the ISI's motivations, allegiances, extremist slant, and structure, it will continue to exist as more of an enemy to the West than an ally.

Conclusion

The historic actions of the ISI in sponsoring organizations like al-Qaeda, JEM, LET and HUM, as well as their utilization of the Taliban as a proxy for foreign policy, signals that the ISI is a significant state sponsor of terrorism. "Since Pakistan has terrorism, nuclear weapons, religious extremism, economic instability, and political volatility, easy [foreign policy] answers provide little guidance in a dangerous, fluid environment. If, due to ISI sins of omission or commission, terrorists acquire Pakistani nuclear weapons and there is a nuclear incident or nuclear war, the consequences will be unthinkable" (Roberts 109). These variables set the ISI's sponsorship apart from other international sponsors and make it definitively the most dangerous.

A careful policy of continued engagement with the ISI and accountability of Western funding to Pakistan will be essential to secure future stability in the region.

The ISI will continue to be a clandestine sponsor of worldwide extremism and transnational terrorism. The fragile nature of Pakistani politics, the existence of deeply entrenched Islamic foundations, and insecurity surrounding the Pakistani nuclear arsenal make the ISI the foremost terrorist threat and non-state sponsor of terrorism in the international community. The ISI masquerades as a controllable tool of the Pakistani government while covertly supporting enemies of the international community – conclusively acting as a threat to international stability and as a fifth column within the Pakistani state.

PERSPECTIVES PAKISTAN: INTER SERVICES INTELLIGENCE DIRECTORATE

The ISI was set up in 1948, shortly after the first war with India, to strengthensharing of intelligence between the army, navy and air force. It was headed first byMaj Gen R. Cawthorne, one of the last British officers to leave Pakistan. He continued at the helm of ISI till 1956. Thereafter, for almost three years, it remained headless as Pakistan faced constitutional turmoil leading finally to Ayub Khan's first martiallaw take-over. Ayub appointed Brig Riaz Hussain as ISI chief and he continued up to1966. He was replaced by Brigadier, later Maj Gen Mohd Akbar Khan, who continuedas head of ISI till the calamitous break up of the country in1971.

During this period, about 80 per cent of ISI personnel were on deputation from the three defence services along with a small cadre of civilian deputationists from the police. There are no accurate figures about its overall strength but present estimates assess that its total personnel strength ranges, between 7,000 and10,000.

Its organisation and existence was designed as an adjunct of the army. Thelocation of its field offices was near the Field Intelligence Units (FIU) of the army inborder areas, thus sharing the army's obsession about the threat from India. The earliest known organisational format of ISI was structured in 'Joint Intelligence' terms, along with Military Intelligence (MI):

The ISI Headquarters was referred to as JIX, whereas field deployments could be in JIN (North-commonly known to Kashmiri and other militants operating againstIndia – Ironically speaking, 'Jin" – in local Urdu parlance denotes equivalent of 'demon' or 'a genie', which ISI/army leadership has been reluctant to, or finds it difficult today, to put back in the bottle). There were also other sections designatedas-JIM (Middle East/Muslim countries, JCIB (Joint Counter Intelligence Bureau) and JIB (Joint Int – Technical-which included also the technical and signalsintelligence wings). These have now been modernised and several specialised wings or units have been added.

This close identification of ISI with MI also perhaps saw the genesis of a personnellocation policy or convention followed even now, wherein officers serving in the MIor as the chief of military intelligence at a lower rank (Major General) were later invested with higher responsibility (in rank of Lieutenant General) in ISI.(Hamid Gul, Asad Durrani, Ehsan ul Haq). In one of the major India-related operational initiatives undertaken by ISI during this period was when contacts were firstestablished, in London with Naga National Council leader, Phizo. He was later taken to Karachi.

The ISI also had a foretaste of dabbling in internal political affairs during theAhmediya community's persecution in the early fifties, and then again, in Gen Yahya Khan's time, when the state signally failed to tackle emerging Bengali dissentwhich soon boiled over into a separatist irridenta. ISI spawned Razakar, Al Badr outfits in East Pakistan in an effort to scuttle the Awami League's agitation for a separate Bengali nation. Despite these moves, the ISI's inability to anticipate events leading to this break up of the country signified a major failure in its track record, which left a deep scar in the mind set of officers and ranks of its personnel in the years to come.

CHANGES BETWEEN 1971-1979

The Bhutto Years

Even as he struggled to contain the negative impact of Chief Justice Hamoodur Rehman's report on the Dhaka debacle, the initial period of Zulfiqar Ali Bhutto's prime ministership was plagued by an uneasy relationship with the servicestop brass, including the new army chief, Gen Gul Hassan. The latter was seen as obstructionist and soon replaced by the overly obsequious Tikka Khan.

In domestic politics too, Bhutto's penchant for not relying too long on chosen favourites and pick up new 'blue eyed boys' only to dump them soon enough did not auger well for institutions to develop or prosper. Though a 'Political Cell' was set up within ISI at this time, Bhutto did not trust middle level army officers and preferred to rely more on the civilian set up under the Intelligence

Bureau. The way he dealt with the Baluchistan situation indirectly helped to bring the army back into the political arena, a development that would haunt Bhutto later.

Attock Conspiracy Case

Younger army officers, in particular were alienated by Bhutto's dictatorial style. Military intelligence and ISI were able to penetrate one such group of disgruntled army officers of the rank of major, and lieutenant colonel. This was the Attock Conspiracy trial which was headed by then Major General Zia ul Haq. Though harshsentences were given to the conspirators, they became heroes in the eyes of their younger colleagues. The army's unhappiness against Bhutto was heightened.

However, the Attock process helped consolidate Zia's rise to power, despite anadverse army record. He came closer to Bhutto. In March, 1976 Bhutto made himarmy chief superseding six generals senior to him. Bhutto created new securityorganisations personally loyal to him – like the Federal Security Force (FSF) whichwas headed by police officers of dubious record like Haq Nawaz Tiwana and MasoodMehmud, the Federal Investigation Agency (FIA) and the Airport Security Force(ASF). He brought in police officers who were loyal to him-such as former IGPs,Saeed Ahmed Khan and Rao Rashid in advisory capacity at various levels. In effect,Bhutto tried to set up a system of intelligence gathering and control parallel to thatof the Pakistan army and ISI. This system of personalised reporting did not helphim much during in the aftermath of the rigging allegations in the 1977 elections.

Zia Years

Lt Gen Ghulam Jilani Khan was appointed ISI chief by Gen Yahya Khan in 1971 butcontinued under three masters-Bhutto. He remained at the helm of ISI till 1978. It is believed, Jilani kept Zia informed of Bhutto's moves in the fateful days afterthe July 1977 elections. Zia rewarded him by first making him defence secretaryand later Punjab governor. (March,1980-Dec1985). He was credited with involvingthe ISI more directly in internal affairs, which helped Zia to curb initial dissentagainst his martial Law take-over, and later in helping select amenable politicianslike Junejo, and the Sharif family (whose iron foundry nationalised by Bhuttoin 1973 was de-nationalised by Zia and given back to them), including a youngNawaz (more a cricketer then!) to sugar coat Zia's gradual revival of politicalactivities in the mid/late 1980s. Nawaz was first made finance minister, later chief minister of Punjab.

Defence services officers in this early phase, did not particularly aspire to a careerin the ISI. The general view among services was to regard it as a 'backwater' for sidelined officers who were posted on rotation or deemed unfit for operational action or duty, or on health or some other grounds. Most of the officers posted on rotation were reluctant to go there and tried to finish their stints early and move back to the regular stream. Even those who returned were seen as 'unreliable' by their military colleagues and shunned by peers in the services' social network, which was so strong.

1979-1988

All this changed rather dramatically after the Soviet occupation of Afghanistan.The ISI was used as the main conduit for organising Afghan resistance and fordistribution of arms and financial largesse provided by the Americans andSaudi intelligence.

AFGHAN OPERATIONS

The ISI organised the fund flows and intensified its political control over the seven main Afghan Islamist resistance groups fighting against the Russians. This was done by the then ISI chief Lt. Gen Akhtar Abdul Rehman, after some initial setbacks in which three Pakistani army officers were found guilty of misappropriating funds along with a few Mujahideen commanders(the so-called 'Quetta incident' after which the first brigadier in charge of the ISI's Afghan bureau was replaced). They were sacked and the responsibility of organizing this chain was given to Brig Mohd Yousaf.

Later, these arrangements were overseen both by CIA director Casey and the SaudiIntelligence chief, Prince Turki bin Faisal. The Saudi intelligence's link up with theISI was a significant landmark as hitherto, their contacts had remained confined tothe Pakistani civilian intelligence organization, the Intelligence Bureau (IB). This link was established before the CIA came in, in full earnest, to back the Afghan resistance effort from Pakistan.

As this chart shows, the main distribution points for arms and cash flows to the Afghan Mujahideen were the ISI's field bureaus at Peshawar and Quetta. This was the time when the Afghan resistance leaders were able to build luxurious homes for themselves, mainly in the University Town area of Peshawar. Under the ISI's stewardship, they also recruited Afghan refugees and Pashtuns from selected mosques and madrassas in the NWFP, notably the Akora Khattak madrassa of Maulana Samiul Haq and the Pashtunabad madrassa on the outskirts of Quetta. These madrassas would later (1994-95) be used to nurture the Taliban.

By 1987, the four main Islamic fundamentalist Afghan mujahideen outfits — Hizbe-Islami headed by Gulbadin Hikmatyar, Jamiat-e-Islami headed by Burhanuddin Rabbani (Ahmed Shah Massoud was then a follower of Rabbani), Ittehad-e Islami of Abdul Rasool Sayyaf and Hizb-e-Islami of Yunus Khalis were getting almost 70 per cent of all the aid. Whenever complaints of misappropriation of aid were received the ISI instituted a pattern of directly contacting the field commanders to close these loopholes. Several bases were opened along the major borderroutes between Pakistan and Afghanistan across the two provinces of NWFP and Baluchistan which were closely supervised by ISI officers. This experience and exposure was to stand the ISI in good stead during the resurgence of the Taliban resistance in the next decades.

REPLICATION IN KASHMIR

After the successful image fillip brought about by its Afghan operations, this same pattern of organisation could be replicated by the ISI to aid and abet Kashmiri resistance fighters from late 1989 onwards, till well into the 1990s. The alienationin the state had been brewing and the Jamaat–e-Islami, Hind, inside Kashmir was getting help from its Pakistani ideological counterpart, Jamaat–e-Islami to fund mosques and Islamic teachings of aggressive, fundamentalist intent far removed from the ethos of a more tolerant

Islam and 'Kashmiriyat' prevalent inside Jammu &Kashmir. The allegations of rigging in the state elections of 1987 compounded these errors. Activists like Syed Salahuddin were till then seeking political platforms buthe went across to Pakistan Occupied Kashmir at this stage.

Replication-ISI Kashmir Cell

The JIN (Joint Intelligence North) played a crucial role in co-ordinating theseoperations in the decade of the 1990s, acquiring almost 'mystical' salience as handlers of Kashmiri militants, both of indigenous and trans-border origin. The word 'JIN' was frequently bandied in code communications intercepted by Indian security agencies-it seemed to indicate super human powers akin to the 'genie' of Alladin's lamp, which ironically grew larger than life in later years of the Tehrik e Taliban militancy Pakistan started assisting Amanullah Khan's Jammu & Kashmir Liberation Front (JKLF) at first but not finding all its mass based supporters totally amenable to political and military dictation, soon switched its support to more obscurantist forces. The Jamaat–e-Islami's Indian counterpart in J&K and its militant frontorganisation, Hizbul Mujahideen was used. Other outfits also joined later, to form the United Jehad Council.

ISI'S INVOLVEMENT IN SIKH MILITANCY

Even before shifting its focus to Jammu & Kashmir, the ISI started supporting the post 'Blue Star' (1984) Sikh insurgency in India. This was accomplished by taking advantage of the visits of prominent Sikh diaspora leaders to the holy shrines located inside Pakistan. Ganga Singh Dhillon was patronised by Zia acolyte, Chaudhry Zahoor Elahi and his protege (Ch. Shujaat Hussain and Pervez Elahi) during his annual visits to Lahore during the early 80s. The ISI then took over logistic arrangements for their stay and monitored their activities, interaction with visiting Sikh jathas from India.

Hard core Sikh militants like Wassan Singh Zafarwal, Daljit Singh Bitto and Paramjit Panjwar were provided refuge in safe houses near the Dera Saheb Gurudwara in Lahore. The International

Sikh Youth Federation (ISYF) and Babbar Khalsa units inUK, Germany and other parts of Europe as also their branches in USA and Canada started receiving generous financial assistance for anti-Indian activities abroad.

Their cadres were instigated to undertake de-stabilising militant actions inside India, including attempted assassinations of political leaders. Over the years, the organisational functions of ISI have developed or diversified according to the needof the hour.

Not all the posts of Deputy Directors General (DDG) appear to be filled up all the time. In the past ISI made do with two or three DDGs, offering one of the posts to eitherthe air force or navy, according to appropriate rank – air vice marshal/vice admiral– who would usually be entrusted with the liaison assignment dealing with foreignmilitary attaches. More important operational assignments remained under army officers. The post of DDG, Strategic Analysis has emerged as vital. He is sometimesused as the ISI's interface with the West, to project its 'moderate Islamic' face.

Protocol: Usually entrusted to equivalent rank officers from the navy or air force internal coordination: Euphemism for domestic political intelligence;

Comment: Vintage: 2009-2010;

Encircled portions represent operational units, not all of which are located in ISI Hqrs., Islamabad;

Section 28: Parts of Sec 28 or even Sec 21 – which has covert action tasks against India are located in Karachi; Sec 25: May have offices in Muzaffarabad, PoK.

Till recently, the Kashmir operations of the ISI were headed by Brig (retd.) Javeed Aziz Khan, an artillery regiment officer commissioned in the 40th Long Course (968)(he retired from army in 2003), who had served as defence attache in India (Oct 98-Oct 02). He was originally from the Rajput Sisodia clan of Udaipur, (India).His father was from Ludhiana and mother from Pakistani Punjab. He liked to use the nom de plume of 'Rathore'. He was replaced by Brig Sohail.

Some details of ISI's outstation operational units in Quetta & Peshawar are given below:

New Sections: 90 – for Covert Operations abroad; 92 – For non-embassyoperations; 94-Defence acquisitions: used to be clandestine – in Beijing and someWest European missions: Germany, France, Belgium & UK;

ISI has specialized detachments in sensitive Capital towns:

Details of its Internal Task wings are given below:

Details of other operational units known:

Comment: Vintage 2010;

Sec 29: Could be exclusively dealing with India directed Militant Groups;L Det: Lashkar e Toiba related? Or could be Lahore located operations; K Det: Kashmir related operations? Or could be Karachi located operations;

Comment: Vintage 2010;

CT: Counter Terrorism & International Liaison related work.

Some specialised units for analysis/psy operations appear to have been set up in recent years:

ISI Chiefs — A Chronology

Though remaining at all times under the hierarchical authority of the chief of armystaff (COAS), the ISI evolved through the personality traits of its various directors from time to time, some of whom enjoyed a special personal rapport with the army chief/ dictatorial head of the government at the time.

Akhtar Abdul Rehman (1980 –March 87)

Lt. Gen Akhtar Abdul Rehman was one of the most formidable ISI chiefs. After his stint in the ISI, Rehman was promoted as a four star general and appointed chairman, joint chiefs of staff committee in March 1987. He was regarded as a no-nonsense officer with a singular vision of fighting the Soviets and driving them out of Afghanistan. He brooked little interference – even from the Americans-in the internal operations of the ISI's Afghan cell.

Large sums of money were handled by the ISI at that time and audit controls werevirtually non-existent. Though no allegations of financial impropriety were voicedopenly against Rehman and then, as the halo of martyrdom attached to the manner of his demise, soon after he had been put on a lofty pedestal as a national hero, it is generally known that his sons inherited vast properties in Punjab, including a nascentindustrial empire which seems to have prospered overnight.

His elder son, HumayunAkhtar Rehman became a Member of the National Assembly, joining Nawaz Sharif's Muslim League. In 1999, he hitched his bandwagon with Gen Musharraf and became commerce minister in the cabinet of Prime Minister Shaukat Aziz.

Hamid Gul (Mar 1987 – Mar 1989)

Lt.Gen Hamid Gul is credited with establishing a better system of financial controls and audit within the ISI that accounted for the weapons and cash in the pipeline from the Saudis and Americans. He too did not welcome undue interference from the Americans on the conduct of operations in Afghanistan.

Once the financial and supply networks were set up it was the ISI, and not the army that took on the role of executing covert operations against the Soviets. This gave the ISI an autonomy and financial strength it had not possessed before. It has remained a powerful force ever since, so much so that some analysts sometimes posit the hypothesis that the ISI's "typical intelligence mentality" dominates over a more professional or military mindset within the army.

The Ojhri ammunition dump explosion in April, 1988 was a setback to the ISI'simage but Prime Minister Junejo was dumped by Zia before he could fix the blamefor mismanagement there on any army general or the ISI.

In the domestic context, Hamid Gul was to acquire notoriety for implementing the army high command's planto drum up political opposition against Benazir Bhutto's People's Party of Pakistan(PPP) in the November 1988 elections after Zia's death. The Islami Jamhoori Ittehad(IJI) was cobbled together, under the leadership of Nawaz Sharif.

Midnight Jackals

Another intelligence officer, Hamid Gul's deputy, Brig Imtiaz Ahmed 'Billa' (so calledbecause of his cat's eyes!) came into prominence during this period for trying to subvert PPP MNAs loyal to Benazir. He was helped in these nefarious doings by another army officer, Major Amir. Both these officers were later rewarded by Nawaz Sharif when he became prime minister.

ISI VERSUS POLITICAL EXECUTIVE

This was the first time the ISI, and by default, the army leadership openly came into conflict with the political leadership. Despite having agreed to take on a retiredgeneral to steward the foreign ministry, Lt.Gen (retd) Sahibzada Yaqub Khan (whohad, ironically, been a 'conscientious objector' against the army's brutal repressionin Bangladesh in 1971), Benazir decided to replace Hamid Gul as DG, ISI and bringin retired Lt.Gen Shamsur Rehman Kallue, as the new DG,ISI-May,1989.

It was rumoured that Gen Aslam Beg, who became army chief by default after the Zia plane crash in August 1988 never really liked the idea of Akhtar Abdul Rehmanand Hamid Gul wielding such immense powers. After the Jalalabad fiasco in May 1989, he supported Benazir's move to oust Hamid Gul from ISI by offering Gul, an armoured corps officer, the sop of a posting him to the prestigious II Corps, Multan Pakistan's second strike formation, traditionally entrusted with a defensive role in the south eastern front against India.

Baig never really liked Benazir Bhutto. Though he went along with the move to induct Kallue, as army chief he subsequently began manipulatign of ISI's internal political oversight wing, and its operations, mainly in Sindh-where the PPP's fragile alliance with the Muhajir Quami Movement (MQM) was destabilised from the very outset. Kallue did not have a clue about these moves. He could barely last till August 1990. Soon thereafter, Benazir herself was dismissed as PM by PresidentGhulam Ishaq Khan, using his extra-ordinary powers under Art. 58(2)(b) of the Constitution, brought in by Zia's 8th Amendment in 1985.

Mehrangate

Aslam Baig also got adverse notices, for channelising the money paid by abusinessman (Yunus Habib) for starting the IJI (Opposition common political front against Benazir's PPP) into his own private ' Think Tank' account (FRIENDSexposed in 'Mehrangate' scandal).

Asad Durrani (Aug '90-Mar '92)

The next ISI chief was Lt Gen Asad Durrani. He had been director general, military intelligence immediately prior to this posting and though he had not particularly distinguished himself professionally, he was able to develop good relations with Benazir Bhutto even though she was in the opposition by now. This earned him thedisapproval of subsequent army chiefs such as Gen Waheed Kakar but Asad Durraniwas rewarded during the second Benazir administration with ambassadorship to Germany, and also by Musharraf, who sent him as ambassador to Saudi Arabia. Hisdeployment to ISI in August 1990 when a caretaker administration was in-charge was because of the army chief's approval rather than that of the political executive.It also confirmed the convention of the DGMI moving to the ISI slot.

Asad Durrani remained as DG, ISI till March, 1992-when a politically resurgent Nawaz Sharif brought in his father's Tablighi Jamaat acolyte, Lt. Gen Javed Nasir as his replacement. Once again, this was a political appointment with which the army and the new army chief (Gen Asif Nawaz) were not fully happy. It sowed seeds of the army leadership's dislike of Nawaz Sharif, despite the latter enjoying the support of the predominantly Punjabi middle level officers and other ranks.

Javed Nasir (Mar '92-May '93)

Nasir's strong, almost fanatical pro-Islamic leanings were rather well known.He was the first ISI chief from the corps of engineers.He had no backgroundin intelligence work. A course-mate of Hamid Gul, he had become a devoutMuslim in 1986. He wore a flowing beard and did not look at women in public!He would turn his face away if a woman entered the room. He is known to havegiven militarily unsound advice on the repercussions of 'body bags' policies inIraq, when Americans were seeking the support of Muslim countries against the Iraqi invasion in Kuwait. While travelling with the Saudi Intelligence chief, Prince Turki on a Pakistani plane to Kabul after the fall of Najibullah's government,he uncharacteristically shouted an Islamic war cry to signal their 'triumphantentry' to Afghanistan!

As ISI chief, Javed Nasir was keen to find ways of supporting Islamic causesworldwide. He set up arrangements to arm and support Bosnian Muslims, incollaboration with Iran. He saw opportunities to hurt India, not only in Kashmir but in other regions as well. He is reported to have established contact withTamil extremists (LTTE) and set up a gun running operation with links to LTTE in Bangkok. He funded Arakenese Muslims (Rohingiyas)-who inhabit the areabordering Myanmar's frontier with Bangladesh, to help them in their struggle for an independent enclave.

A strange, almost non-military atmosphere developed at the ISI office during Javed Nasir's tenure. Bearded officers in 'shalwar kameez', many of them hitched up to their ankles (a signature practice of the Tablighi Jamaat) strolling about in office corridors. The 'strong room',which had currency stacked to the roof duringthe heyday of Afghan operations was now empty as 'adventurist' ISI officers had been allowed to take away suitcases filled with cash to the field, ostensibly for operations even in Central Asian countries.

There were neither any accounts nor any receipts for these money transfers. Most officers remained absent from office for long periods, especially during prayer hours and neither the government nor the ISI had any record of properties acquired or transactions conducted in its name. There was lack of command and control with a lot of junior officers directly interacting with the DG, violating the chain of command.

The Americans were aware of some of these hair brained operational initiativesand complained about the same to Nawaz Sharif but he initially disregardedthese reports. A US TV channel investigated the ISI's links, in the fundingactivities of the Jamaat ul Fuqra, a militant islamic outfit based in the US. Oneof its operatives, Mubarak Shah Gilani, was later found to be involved in theDaniel Pearl kidnapping (and subsequent murder).

Information about these dangerous and extensive activities of ISI was again conveyed to the Pakistani leaders through US back channels. Ultimately in May 1993, the new army chief, Gen Waheed (after Asif Nawaz's demise in office) was able to persuade Nawazto remove Javed Nasir and replace him with Lt Gen Javed Ashraf Qazi, once againa former DG, Military Intelligence.

Javed Ashraf Qazi (May 93-95)

Qazi was a quintessential army prototype. He would normally have had a shot at the chief's post but for an early detected heart condition, which made him accept the ISI charge. One of his first tasks was to restore military discipline and ethos in ISI. Serving army personnel were asked to wear military uniforms of appropriate rank while in office. The long absences for prayers were also gradually reduced.

Maverick operations in South East Asia (including the Bangkok gun running) werewound up and he began the process, of repatriating extremist elements from ISI, including Afghan war veterans back to the army or police, where, hopefully, they wouldnot be able to spread their militant gospel as easily. (Hopes now seen to be belied!)

To open up the ISI, Qazi started the practice of inviting foreign military attaches to visit forward operational areas, either on the Afghan front or on the eastern border with Kashmir.

Even in supporting the Kashmiri operations, a distinction started being made, of giving preference to outfits consisting of genuine Kashmirislike the Hizbul Mujahideen (this policy now stands reversed). He also reduced ISI's role in domestic politics.

Javed Ashraf Qazi's critics accuse him of eviscerating the operational heart of the ISI but both he and the army chief, Waheed understood the importance of avoidingd is approval of the United States. Qazi remained ISI chief till 1995 and later became minister for railways under Gen Musharraf.

Naseem Rana (1995-Oct '99)

Maj Gen Naseem Rana was ISI head between 1995 till October, 99. He was also the army chief's (Gen Karamat) appointee. He tried his best to play a mediatory role during PM Nawaz Sharif's confrontation with the higher judiciary under a Sindhi chief justice, Sajjad Ali Shah.

He is reported to have worked closely with the Americans in building up a joint commando force to search for Osama bin Laden. He went with Saudi intelligence chief, Prince Turki to meet Mullah Omar for the initial parleys on the possibility of giving up Osama.

Khwaja Ziauddin Butt (Oct '98 – Oct '99)

Ziauddin's appointment as ISI chief is one more example of a political decision, in October 1998, not supported by the then army chief (Karamat – who himself quit amonth later, following differences with Nawaz Sharif). Ziauddin had earlier servedon Aslam Baig's and Asif Nawaz's (while latter was a major general) personal staff. He was from the Engineers but had always been highly ambitious. A Kashmiri by biradari (sub caste) affiliation, he was qualified enough to ultimately aim for the chief's slot having already done a brief stint in Corps Command. However, he was junior to other generals in the queue for the army chief's post.

Ziauddin claims he met Mullah Omar twice and was almost able to persuade him to give up Osama bin Laden. Nawaz Sharif selected a new army chief after Karamatresigned, violating the army's seniority norms. Musharraf, a 'Mohajir' (originally arefugee who came from India) was chosen over two of his seniors – Ali Kuli Khan Khattak (a Pathan) and Khalid Nawaz (a Punjabi). One argument that weighed with Nawaz Sharif in making this choice was that Musharraf, not being a Punjabi would remain beholden to a Punjabi PM, popular with army Other Ranks (ORs). (This hope was belied). Musharraf was uncomfortable with Ziauddin as ISI chief from the outset and kept him out of the loop while planning the December 98-May99 Kargil offensive.

The October 1999 Coup

Musharraf was unhappy with Nawaz Sharif's choice of Ziauddin as DG, ISI and countered by bringing Lt Gen Mohd Aziz Khan, who was Deputy DG in ISI as Chief of General Staff (CGS), usually regarded as the next most important post in the army, after the COAS. As differences between Musharraf and Nawaz Sharif widenedand with the international disclosure of Pak Army's direct complicity in the Kargil misadventure, through the Musharraf-Gen Aziz (his Chief of General Staff then) tapes, a strange spectacle was witnessed – that of the Director General, Military Intelligence (Maj. Gen Nadeem Ejaz – Musharraf's man) taping conversations between the DG, ISI and the prime minister. This led to the unprecedented sackingof Lt Gen Tariq Pervaiz, GOC XII Corps, Quetta by Musharraf, on grounds of openly airing his dissent on the merits of the Kargil operation and alleged leaking ofminutes of a Corps Commanders' meeting to the prime minister. Matters soon cameto a head, with Nawaz appointing Ziauddin as his new army chief while Musharrafwas on a tour abroad (Sri Lanka, Maldives), the Army Chief requisition ingassistance from his Corps Commanders in Rawalpindi (Lt Gen Mehmud Ahmed) and Karachi (Lt Gen Usmani), to dishonor these orders and help effect yet anothercoup against an elected Political Executive (Oct 12, 1999)

Since then, all subsequent ISI chiefs have been appointees of the army chief. These include Lt. Gen Mehmud Ahmed (Oct '99-Oct-2001), Lt. Gen Ehsan ul Haq (Oct'01-Oct'04), Lt. Gen Ashfaq Pervez Kayani (Oct'04-Oct'07), Lt Gen Nadeem Taj(Oct'07-Oct'08) and Lt. Gen Ahmed Shuja Pasha (Oct'08-till date, on extension till March 2012).

Mehmud Ahmed (Oct '99-Oct 2001)

Educated at the prestigious Lawrence College, Murree, Mehmud Ahmed considered himself an intellectual. As a Brigadier in the War Staff College, heundertook a magnum opus study of the ' failed Akhnoor offensive' against India.(History of Indo-Pak War, 1965 – which the Pakistan army initially did not allowto be published, but it was released much later,in 2006). He too had served as DGMI in the mid-'90s, during Benazir Bhutto's second stint as PM-just beforeshe fell out with her own presidential appointee, late Farooq Leghari. Somesuspicion attached to rather indiscreet comments made by Mehmood Ahmedabout Benazir's corruption but the latter's complaint to Karamat in this regardwas apparently disregarded.

Mehmood Ahmed played a crucial role during the October 99 coup of Musharraf as Corps Commander of the Rawalpindi X Corps, ordering tanks out of the 111 Brigade (then commanded by Brig Salahuddin Satti) to surround the PM's house and the TV station where the new army chief Ziauddin was holed up.

Ironically enough, Mehmood Ahmed later fell out with Musharraf, shortly after 9/11. Musharraf has recently claimed, that Mehmud Ahmed wanted to be made army chief after Musharraf overthrew Nawaz Sharif.

Mehmud Ahmed is alleged to have given contrary advice to Mullah Omar during one of his mediation visits to Kabul just after 9/11, to stand up to the Americans. Unconfirmed rumours link him also to the terrorist, Omar Sheikh,-one of the hostages released from the IC 814 plane hijacking who was later implicated in the Daniel Pearl murder. Other rumours allege that Mehmud Ahmed was aware of Omar Sheikh's role in sending money to the 9/11 plotters in Europe.

After the Americans complained to Musharraf, Mehmud Ahmed was sacked as ISI chief and kept under house confinement in Lahore, before being rehabilitated in a Fauji Foundation assignment. By this time, he had turned religious, joined the Tablighi Jamaat as a full-fledged member and grown a flowing beard.

Ehsan ul Haq (Oct'01-Oct'04)

Ehsan ul Haq was commissioned in the Air Defence Corps in 1969 and is theonly officer to have risen so high from this unit. He was not generally considered to have any special ability but his meteoric rise is ascribed more to obsequious conduct and opportunism. A Pathan from Mardan, NWFP, he had done stints as DGMI and corps commander of XI corps, Peshawar (briefly, for 6 months only). Hehad experience in staff assignments — Brigade

Major, GSO-1 in Infantry Div Hqrs & in the Military Operations Directorate. He was considered anti-jehadi, liberal and pro-United States in views and remained loyal to Musharraf during his stint in the ISI. However, he was a hardliner with traditional Pak army views on the Kashmir issue. He was elevated to four star rank in the largely ceremonial post of chairman, Joint Chiefs of Staff Committee before he retired.

Ashfaq Pervez Kayani (Oct 04-Oct 07)

Commissioned in the Baloch Regiment on August 29, 1971, 59-year-old Kayani is from a traditional Punjabi army family. Kayani's father was a naib subedar (JCO) in the army. As major general, he was GOC. 12 Div Murree (Jan,99 – Oct,01) when Musharraf was corps commander,1 Corps, Mangla. He became director general, Military Operations (Oct-01-Sept-03), and then was GOC, X Corps, Rawalpindi for a year, before being appointed DG,ISI by Musharraf.

As DG, ISI he was involved in Musharraf's parleys with Benazir Bhutto while the latter was in exile in UAE. He was privy to the American link of these confabulations. He came to be well regarded by his Western interlocutors, notably Admiral Mullen. He remained loyal to Musharraf but underplayed this loyalty when the latter had to be eased out as president after restoration of Chief Justice Iftikhar Chaudhry.

Some of his peers in neighbouring countries considered him an introvert, a nervouschain smoker, who could buckle under pressure. However, as army chief, Kayani seems to have outgrown this image, at least till the Osama bin Laden debacle, whensome of these traits re-surfaced! Kayani is considered typically hardline and anti Indian, on the Kashmir issue and most other matters concerning India, including abetment of terrorist groups like the Lashkar-e-Toiba.

Nadeem Taj (Oct 07-Oct 08)

A Musharraf appointee to the DG, ISI's post after Kayani was elevated as army chief, Nadeem Taj is a Punjabi Arain (an influential sub caste in Punjabi politics). He was commissioned in the 11

Punjab Regiment in July 1972. He was military attache in Iraq in the early 90s and then in USA (1996-97). He is believed to have become anti-Shia while in Iraq.

Taj was military secretary to Musharraf at the time of the Oct 99 coup against Nawaz Sharif. He became DGMI in Dec 3. Later, he was sent to head the Pakistan Military Academy in Kakul. As DG, ISI he is known to have developed links with pro-Wahhabi Islamic fanatic elements. He became corps commander, 30 Corps, Gujranwala before his retirement in April, 2011.

Ahmad Shuja Pasha (Oct 08 – till date)

Commissioned in the Frontier Force Regiment (Fiffers) in April 1974 Pasha is a Pathan with a Punjabi wife. He is 58 years old (D.O.B-19.03.'52). He belongs to a prominent Quereshi family from Attock now settled in Wah. His father was the headmaster of a school in Wah (the Pak Ordnance Factory township). His elder brother was a brigadier. Pasha suffered a tragedy in personal life, when he lost his son in a car accident in Multan several years ago. He was chief of staff to GoC, 30 Corps, Gujranwala. As a major general he held charge of an Infantry Division in Sialkot, was an instructor in the Command & Staff College, Quetta before proceeding on an international peace-keeping assignment with the UN. He came back to become director general, Military Operations (April 06-Sept 08), holding this post during the Musharraf-Kayani transition before taking over as DG, ISI.

ISI'S ROLE IN DRUG SMUGGLING AND PUSHING IN OF COUNTERFEIT CURRENCY

The ISI has often been suspected of being involved in drug trafficking or of using drug trafficking networks of Afghan warlords or the Pashtun ' truck mafias' in Karachi to fill its coffers or divert unaccounted funds for operations but there is little specific evidence to substantiate these allegations.

The ISI has pushed counterfeit currency into India either through the Nepal route or by using the Indian or Pakistani diaspora residing in countries like Malaysia, whoare part of the criminal underworld with links to Dawood Ibrahim, long sheltered by the ISI in safe havens inside Pakistan.

ISI & Tribal Areas

Army officers in ISI believe they can selectively build bridges with some elements within the Tehrik e Taliban (TTP) by using traditional rivalries such as those between the Wazirs & Mehsuds, and the Shias and Sunni in Parachinar.

ISI & 'Rogue Elements'/Retired Officers

The ISI still employs retired army officers. Other 'rogue' elements also continue toassist in varying degrees and in operational roles. This recently became evident when two of its emissaries, both former employees-Squadron Leader KhalidKhwaja and Col Sultan Amir Tarar were killed, at different times, by the Punjab Allah Tigers and Hakimullah Mehsud with whom they were trying to negotiate for the release of a British journalist Asad Quereshi. While the journalist was released after payment of ransom, a ransom demand for the release of Col Imam could not be paid by his relatives. The ISI appears to have washed its hands off this operation mid-way, for reasons not well known so far.

There are other well known instances of re-employment of army officers in ISI. Brig Moslehuddin was entrusted with important psy-operations work in ISI after his stint as defence attache in Bangladesh, where he played a crucial role in activating anti-India terror modules using Pakistani LeT activists or Indian Muslims trained in Pakistan. Brig Javeed Khan'Rathore' continued to deal with Kashmir operations in ISI, after his stint in India as a defence attache.

Headley Interrogations

Evidence emerging from the David Coleman Headley and Dawood Gilani interrogations in the US to which an Indian team from NIA was given access revealed the role of ISI rogue elements which the ISI and the army leadership must have been fully aware of. The interrogation reports have also brought out how LeT used ex-service personnel with more than a passing familiarity and contacts within ISI, to provide specialised training in surveillance, photography and communication techniques before Headley was sent into India on several reconnaissance missions. LeT members were in regular touch with serving ISI officers to whom Headley handed over photographed material – tapes and cell phone pictures etc. Though confronted with this evidence in the Indian dossiers handed over to Pakistan, DG. ISI, Pasha has only acknowledged involvement of 'rogue elements', but not serving ISI personnel.

In recent times, ISI has supported the LeT's expansion into the provision of social services like flood relief. It is unlikely to abandon its reliance on such groups though greater care is being taken to camoflauge such links by progressive involvement of indigenous outfits like Indian mujahideen in terror modules directed against India.

ISI & FOMENTING OF GLOBAL TERROR

In the post 9/11 decade, ISI's involvement in fomenting terror modules in different parts of the world, using proxy outfits like the LeT or the HUJI has been exposed, be it through the arrest of Virgil Brigitte in Australia (2003) or the failed terror plots in the UK and the US in more recent times.

This global terrorist networks with linkages to ISI us shown in the diagram that follows. Outfits inside Pakistan which have had links with or were spawned by the ISI include the LeT, the Jaish e Mohd (JeM), Lashkar e Jhangvi (LeJ – more into sectarian terrorism), Harkat ul Mujahideen (HuM) which morphed into HUJI, and the Dawood underworld mafia. On the periphery ring are outfits with presence in countries like Bangladesh-the Ahle Hadis al Bangladesh (AHAB), HUJI-BD, Jamiyatul Mujahideen Bangladesh (JMB) and Jagrata Muslim Janata Bangladesh (JMJB). In recent years though, security agencies of the new government in Bangladesh havedone much to dismantle these outfits. Nevertheless, linkages persist between ISI and Pakistan based religious or ideologically motivated terrorism outfits like LeT, Jaish and HUJI in countries like Afghanistan. Modules have also been found in Europe or USA.

Decision makers in army/views and orientation of senior officers in Army/ISI on matters of geo-strategic import.

A career or a posting in the ISI has now emerged as a desirable option, with young officers of the rank of captain, major or colonel enjoying far greater power, perks and privileges in the ISI than many of their peers in more routine army field assignments. At any given time, the decision makers in the ISI are the army chief and the DG, ISI. At the second rung of ISI are major generals, one or the other of them could be personally close to the COAS, in which case they may be able influence policy decisions but this maybe the exception than the rule. As in the army itself, a collegiate or consensus decision making pattern is usually the norm and prevails in decision making and operational initiatives undertaken by ISI.

Army/ISI & Politicization

With regard to military-civilian interaction, all ISI officers believe in the primacy of the army and its status as the vanguard institution of state. There is a general contempt for all manner of politicians and political parties. This is compounded by the fact that there are no politicians of individually high popularity or charismain Pakistan at present.

Though the lustre attaching to ISI was somewhat tarnished by the US sealsmission to take out Osama bin Laden in Abbotabad in Ma,2011, as well asthe opprobrium following the Saleem Shehzad murder post the attack on theMehran Naval Base. But by and large, all army officers, especially those in ISI,even at middle or relatively junior levels believe that the army's dominant rolein taking vital foreign policy decisions has only been good for the country andcannot be questioned. They would not readily countenance any erosion in thisdominance, unless the army chief himself and the collegiate leadership group of Corps Commanders acquiesce in such a role re-definition. This is not likely to happen in the foreseeable future.

3

Democratic Control of Intelligence Agencies in Transitional Democracies

Common wisdom about Pakistan states that the polity is so weak and so corrupt, the military so entrenched in the political process and so essential for the country's unity and survival, and the intelligence agencies so strong that any change other than the marginal is simply impossible. Although exaggerated and sometimes debatable, each of these assertions contains an element of truth. The judiciary crisis—the refusal of one man, Chief Justice Iftikhar Muhammad Chaudhry, to legitimate the dictatorship—demonstrates the fragility of the entire edifice, however, and it opens a window of opportunity for structural changes deeper than the current redistribution of power.

Yet there is no magic formula to transform overnight an authoritarian régime into a full-fledged democracy nor to suddenly prevent intelligence agencies from targeting political opponents. Changes in the formal legal structures are only part of the answer if the law is to reduce the powers of the institutions that control the implementation mechanism. Reforms will bring about change only if they reflect the actual balance of power within the country.

Yet countries where the military has been as important an actor in political life as it is in Pakistan have managed to reduce the power of both the military institution and of the intelligence agencies. It may thus be useful to look at the democratic transition experienced by two other states—Indonesia and Chile—where the army enjoyed a similarly dominant position and where the intelligence agencies were an equally ruthless instrument of power. In Indonesia and Chile the establishment of democratic control over the intelligence agencies remains incomplete, imperfect, and in some respects flawed. Yet both countries have come a long way since the days of their dictatorships and, although there have been instances of abuse by the agencies, their behavior has improved significantly.

INTELLIGENCE REFORM IN INDONESIA

Indonesia has undergone significant reforms in its civil-military relations, especially since the late 1990s. The country's institutions are now reflecting the ascendance of civilian leadership although reforms need to be broadened and improved.

Civil-military relations and structure of the Indonesian intelligence agencies in Suharto's Indonesia. In Indonesia, the military enjoyed a dominant role after independence in 1945 but became the country's premier institution in 1966, when it assumed a central position. Even since the fall of Suharto in May 1998, a significant number of cabinet positions have been occupied by serving or retired generals, while active and retired officers have occupied seats in the People's Legislative Assembly (Dewan Perwakilan Rakyat) and the People's Consultative Assembly (Majelis Permusyawaratan Rakyat), the supreme governing body.

Besides its direct political influence at the national level, the military also maintained a regional and local infrastructure through territorial commands spread throughout the archipelago. This allowed the military to exert constant political pressure everywhere in the country. In strategic terms, the territorial commands were justified by an Indonesian defense doctrine based on withdrawal to the hinterland, during which the territorial forces would mobilize the population in a guerrilla resistance against any potential invader, as they had during the war of independence. In practice, however, the defense of the territory was a lesser concern than internal security and stability. But if the expansion of the territorial forces was inspired in the 1950s and 1960s by the strength of the

Communist Party of Indonesia (PKI) and a series of separatist movements, this mandate soon expanded to social control of the entire archipelago.

Damien Kingsbury notes, "Since the mid-1960s, Indonesia has been a state with military personnel, not a state with a military government." Even though Suharto sought to prevent the military from becoming an independent political actor, the military always enjoyed a considerable degree of administrative freedom. This freedom applied to the institution itself, in particular with regard to the appointments of lower-and middle-ranking officers. But its role extended far beyond a simple presence in the government, as asserted by its doctrine known as "dual function," in which the Indonesian military presented itself as both a defender of the state and "an active component of the social and political life of the state." As a defender of the state, the military's focus on actual or perceived internal threats rather than the stated invasion threat made it a highly political instrument. Its institutionalized social and political role, materialized by the insertion of officers into positions held in other countries by civilians as well as into key positions in the decision-making structures, was reinforced during most of the dictatorship by close ties between President Suharto and the leading generals.

Born out of a coup that led to the massacre of at least half a million people suspected of belonging to the PKI, the New Order regime of President Suharto first worked at consolidating itself. This consolidation provided an immediate argument in favor of a strong military, but it was further rationalized by the "geopolitical concern that communist infiltration during the cold war would escalate communist subversion," which also convinced officers of the prominent role of the defense forces in maintaining national integrity.

Suharto then intended to turn Indonesia into a centre of foreign investment, making economic and social development the nation's first priority and providing the military with a rationale that identified political stability as a precondition for development. The length of the initiative, measured in decades, ensured the prospect of long-term military control of politics. But if the country's development was the core ideological basis of the New Order regime, Suharto's concepts of a unitary state and a "greater Indonesia," which made the country the successor state of the Netherlands on all the area's territories previously occupied by the former colonial power, were also powerful arguments to convince the military to support the new regime.

In practice, this meant controlling labour organizations, political parties, Islamic movements, and separatist movements most active in East Timor, Aceh, and West Papua (Irian Jaya) but also in Maluku. Strong-arm tactics were routine. Suharto's control was asserted through intimidation, intelligence investigation of political opponents, and tight control over politics. Torture, extrajudicial killings, and illegal imprisonment became the norm in order to prevent the reemergence of the PKI in the first phase; and these methods were used against whoever looked like a threat to the regime or whose activity implied a risk of destabilization in part of the country in the second phase. In the second phase, the military regularly insisted that it had not achieved complete stability, thus reasserting the need for its constant intervention in politics. In this context, strong intelligence agencies and the regime itself were consubstantial.

The intelligence organizations that came to dominate Indonesia had been created before the New Order era, but Suharto gave them a new role and importance in the political system. Besides the armed forces and the national police, the intelligence service formed the third pillar of Indonesia's security apparatus, bringing the entire population under de facto surveillance. In the area of political control and repression, the activities of the intelligence organizations were more akin to the actions of a police force in a totalitarian state. They acted partly as a visible deterrent but also as an overt force for social control. Intelligence gathering itself had much more to do with the activities of individuals and groups for political purposes than with the gathering of information on the activities and interests of foreign governments, supposedly the raison d'être of intelligence agencies.

Although intelligence functions were performed by a plethora of organizations, two agencies clearly stood out: The Strategic

Intelligence Agency (Badan Intelijen Strategis [BAIS]), responsible for military and foreign intelligence, and the State Intelligence Coordinating Board (Badan Kordinasi Intelijen Negara [Bakin]).

BAIS, which operated domestically and abroad, was the most important military intelligence agency in Suharto's Indonesia and an internal part of the structure of the armed forces of Indonesia (known by the acronym TNI). Sitting atop the army's structure of intelligence, BAIS reported directly to the commander in chief, who decided what information should be forwarded to the president. BAIS was at the peak of the intelligence structures of the four separate services. BAIS was a "centralized operational intelligence gathering body, articulated with the operational resources of the Armed Forces Commander."

Under Suharto, BAIS was highly oriented toward political analysis, in line with the general concern of the armed forces for social engineering and social control. BAIS agents reached into every area of society, and the agency's permission was required for everything from appointment to high government office to admission to the military academy. The armed forces commander in chief was also chief of BAIS. Closely integrated with the army's Social and Political Affairs and Territorial Staff structure, and with the Social and Political and Special Directorates of the Department of the Interior and the office of the Deputy Attorney General (intelligence), BAIS operated on the entire archipelago, monitoring all social conditions considered significant. Its close relationship to the army's territorial presence, down to the village level, gave it an exceptional capacity for surveillance and intervention. The organization was known to "employ torture and abuse of legal rights on an administrative basis."

Bakin was established in 1967. It has been called a type of "military dominated secret police" although it was a nominally civilian organization. Although it employed civilians in its middle and lower ranks, all four senior deputies were active-duty or retired officers. The preeminent intelligence body of the regime, Bakin was known for its "black operations," but it lost some of its domestic operational role and authority to BAIS. It nevertheless played a key part in the maintenance of the system of surveillance and repression. Its primary targets were initially the political parties, the dissidents, and the Chinese community, especially those in the Chinese community thought to be planning a communist revival.

Both organizations staffed a third body, the Agency for the Coordination of Support for National Stability Development (Bakorstanas), led by the armed forces commander, which monitored political activities to prevent any political threats to the regime. Bakorstanas succeeded Kopkamtib, a body created to handle the massive arrests that followed the 1965 abortive coup, and it was used in effect to suppress political opposition through its authority to intervene "in the interest of political and social stability." Under an instrument called Litsus (search, scrutiny), it could inquire about anyone and could, for example, intervene in strikes and other labour actions or screen candidate lists at every level to determine whether candidates had been involved in the 1965 abortive coup or posed real or imagined security risks. After the fall of Suharto, Bakorstanas was disbanded, but its staff remained in their home agencies.

Of particular importance was also the political and social control of the population that was imposed by the territorial command structure. The army was and is organized in centralized and territorial commands. The territorial command, which employed about 140,000 personnel spread across the entire archipelago, complemented the civilian administration at each administrative level. It is subdivided into eleven regional commands, or Kodams, headed by major generals and subdivided into subregional commands, Korem, headed by colonels and based in the major towns of each region.

Army control was doubled by another intelligence network, not only at each administrative level, but also at the street level. Within the village itself, group or street chiefs reported to a higher echelon (*kepala/desa*), which reported to a higher echelon (*lurah*), then to the *camat, bupati,* and finally to the governor, who reported to the central government. This social control over every single aspect of individual life (including the most intimate) was independent of the intelligence agencies.

The territorial structure soon became the major instrument for keeping the Suharto regime in power. Territorial troops were used to monitor and control the activities of all nongovernmental organizations, political parties, student groups, religious organizations, and trade unions.

The institutionalized basis of the intelligence apparatus was in place as early as 1966, and it made a crucial contribution to the durability of the New Order regime. It included overt intelligence agencies, both civilian and military, as well as the intelligence bodies of the army, navy, air force, and police. Government departments such as the Department of Labour Affairs, the Ministry for the Reform of the State Apparatus, and the Attorney General's Department, also had intelligence divisions. Of particular importance was the Directorate for Social and Political Affairs of the Ministry of Interior. In addition, there were also coordination and command organs such as Kopkamtib and its successor, Bakorstanas, as well as ad hoc intelligence and combat sections of special military forces, "a varying cohort of looser and less bureaucratically standardized and legally authorized groupings of state officials, gangsters and hired goons, suborned or hired intellectuals and other such informers and enforcers."

Political background of the reforms. The reforms of the intelligence apparatus decided after the resignation of Suharto did not take place in isolation. They were part of a larger process of democratization and demilitarization of the state.

Indonesia's democratic transition was precipitated, however, by the consequences of the Asian financial crisis of July 1997. The depreciation of the Indonesian rupiah caused widespread defaults on loan payments and steep increases in the prices for basic goods. Riots, including student protests, multiplied throughout the archipelago. Students were at the forefront of the revolt, demanding first that the government address the crisis and later calling for Suharto's resignation, the end of the military's "dual function," and "full-fledged democratization."

The democratization process was also the result of the initiatives of reform-minded military officers who believed it was no longer tenable to maintain the old position of the military. Their ideas were formalized in a reform program called the New Paradigm, which constituted the framework through which the TNI was to achieve the separation of the armed forces from civilian and political functions. It included the separation of the police from the armed forces, the end of military involvement in local political affairs, the transformation of the Office of Social and Political Affairs into an Office of Territorial Affairs, the end of the social and political role of the armed forces in political affairs down to the local level, the end of the appointment of military officers to civilian positions in central and regional governments and the requirement that officers chose between military and civilian careers, the removal of the influence of the military from day-to-day politics, the reduction of the number of seats reserved for the armed forces in Parliament, and the neutrality of the military in politics. Despite the fact that the New Paradigm had been discussed long before the fall of Suharto, it was not until the resignation of the dictator that real public debate could begin.

The military itself was divided over the issue. Commander General Wiranto and Major General Yudhoyono, the chief of staff of sociopolitical affairs, convinced the aging dictator to step down, but they were up against hard-line elements of the armed forces such as Suharto's own son-in-law, Prabowo Subianto, and former armed forces commander Feisal Tanjung. They had tried to convince Suharto to declare martial law and were prepared to mobilize militant Islamic networks in Suharto's defense.

Suharto resigned from the presidency on May 21, 1998. His successor and former deputy, Jusuf Habibie, found himself under strong domestic and international pressure and felt he had little choice but to embark on a program of liberalization. Under pressure from Indonesian society, Wiranto and Major General Yudhoyono initiated a series of reforms that considerably reduced the role of the military in government along the lines of the New Paradigm. The reduction of military representation in Parliament, initiated reluctantly by Suharto, continued under Habibie.

The position taken by the military was met with considerable ambivalence. Most Indonesians resented the long history of atrocities perpetrated by the armed forces under Suharto as well as the deeply entrenched position of the military in the state's economy. However, the government's refusal to use force against popular protests granted Suharto some public approval and increased the personal popularity of some military leaders.

The armed forces leadership later acknowledged that its social and political role was too large in comparison with its defense responsibility. Active military officers serving in civilian positions had to choose between service with either the military or the civilian government.

Politically, the links with the government party, Golkar, were severed. The military presence in Parliament ended: until the mid-1990s, the military held 100 seats in Parliament, but this number decreased to 75 in the last years of the Suharto regime and was further reduced to 38 after his fall from power. The remaining presence of the military in Parliament was ended in 2004.

The degree to which the reforms succeeded in actually severing the link between the military and politics is often questioned. If the army has effectively given up all positions in Parliament and remained remarkably neutral in the elections (with the exception of East Timor in 1999), it has retained and extended its role in conflict areas, maintained its influence in local affairs, and is still a force to reckon with in day-to-day politics.

Nevertheless, the reforms constituted the background against which the redefinition of the intelligence agencies took place. They were perhaps less significant in their actual content than in symbolizing deeper societal and political change. As such, they signaled the beginning of a new era in which past quasi-totalitarian practices no longer had their place.

Institutional changes. A first important step in weakening the legal basis of the repressive interventions of the Indonesian intelligence system was the abolition of the 1963 Anti-Subversion Law by the Habibie administration in April 1999. Also during the Habibie administration, army special forces command officers who had committed crimes connected to the abduction and torture of political activists were prosecuted and convicted. The end of impunity constituted a major step in reducing the use of terror by state agents. The removal of the police force from the army command structure was also mandated during Habibie's tenure.

Still, the major institutional changes in the Indonesian intelligence apparatus took place during the presidency of Abdurrahman Wahid.

Committed to the principle of civilian supremacy and motivated by the need to secure his own position against military pressure, the new president limited considerably the capacity and freedom of action of the agencies, although it should be recognized that he had not come to power with a plan to reduce military power. In March 2000, in a move supposedly aimed at promoting civil society and human rights principles, President Wahid decided to disband Bakorstanas. Its intelligence functions were transferred to the Badan Intelijen Negara (BIN; the new state intelligence agency and the successor to Bakin), and the organization itself was liquidated. Some of Bakorstanas's personnel were reallocated to other military positions, but some were simply fired. As a consequence, procedures of "special investigation" that allowed extrajudicial action by Bakorstanas were also liquidated. Similarly, the Directorate of Social and Political Affairs of the Ministry of Interior was disbanded.

On April 17, 1990, Abdurrahman Wahid also abolished Presidential Decree No. 22. In practice, this meant that civil servants, politicians, and state officials, who previously had been screened to check whether any were members of the PKI or any other illegal organization or were linked through their relatives or by association, were no longer subject to such a screening procedure before assuming their new posts. Similarly, job seekers were no longer obliged to produce documents attesting to their good conduct. Most of the archives compiled by Bakorstanas were destroyed following its dissolution.

The civilian leadership also reasserted its power through the nominations at the head of the military. The upper echelons were replaced by more compliant officers. In addition, the minister for defense and security agreed to a request from the International Monetary Fund and the World Bank for an audit of the extrabudgetary funds of the military.

Organizational changes have remained limited although not negligible. During the Suharto era, BAIS, the military agency, was the more important of the two intelligence organizations. It exercised extensive vertical authority through the TNI, often bypassing the chain of command, although it lost some of its prerogatives and powers in 1994 when it was renamed, downsized from eight to five directorates, and no longer under the direct command of the armed forces commander in chief. Under the Wahid administration, BAIS regained its pre-1994 status and importance. The new structure has seven directorates and three operational units.

Since Suharto's time, however, the civilian BIN is officially preeminent although this is debatable in practice because BAIS is a much more professional organization. The Wahid administration not only changed its name from Bakin to BIN; it also increased its budget with the intention of emphasizing its operational function and diminishing the coordinating role that it had no longer really been exercising since the last years of the Suharto regime. This reflected the difficulties Abdurrahman Wahid was experiencing in obtaining intelligence material from BAIS and Bakin. The new president frequently complained of being deprived of intelligence from the state agencies. This lack of information was also a response to changing intelligence needs, as the failure to prevent the bombing of the Jakarta stock exchange demonstrated in 2000. Nevertheless, these changes primarily reflected the shift of emphasis from domestic to external threats and a new sense that foreign forces were at work to dismantle Indonesia.

Under Suharto, all intelligence agencies reported to the president, with the head of BIN nominally in charge of coordination among the agencies. This integration was, in fact, never totally realized. After the fall of Suharto, President Habibie created the National Defense Stabilization Council, which consisted of most of the important members of the cabinet in another guise, but he virtually abandoned any attempt at serious coordination. Today, BAIS reports to TNI headquarters while BIN and the police are "nondepartmental institutions," meaning that they do not belong to a ministry and, thus, report directly to the president. BIN's head is, moreover, the president's chief intelligence adviser. Parliament also has an oversight function over the agency.

Coordination deficiencies. The fact that two of the main intelligence organizations are under the direct responsibility of the president should have theoretically made the coordination between them easier. In practice, though, there is no executive authority to arbitrate between the agencies. Despite the restructuring of the intelligence apparatus, coordination has hardly improved.

Partly the result of a somewhat traditional interagency rivalry, the two agencies generate an unnecessary duplication of work and contribute to blurring the lines of authority and, consequently, a de facto autonomy of the agencies, which inevitably limits the effectiveness of any democratic oversight. Three agencies, BIN, BAIS, and the national police, are involved in collecting and analyzing information related to domestic security, meaning that in practice all three deal with terrorism in addition to their more specific assignments.

Parliamentary oversight of the intelligence system. Parliamentary oversight was also introduced by President Wahid. Three commissions are particularly relevant from the point of view of democratic control of the intelligence agencies: Commission I is in charge of defense, TNI, foreign affairs, and intelligence; Commission II deals with law enforcement; Commission III is in charge of police.

In practice, however, things are not as clearly defined as suggested by the commissions' attributions. Law enforcement comes, as indicated, under Commission II but if law enforcement implies the use of force, it falls under Commission III. In effect, the control exercised by each commission over the institutions each is charged with monitoring is nominal. Control is exercised through the budget and is indirect for BAIS, whose budget comes from the TNI. Control is direct for BIN, which receives its money directly from the state. Parliament can, of course, approve, reject, or curb the budget proposed by each institution, but there is no control on the way the budget is actually spent. More significant perhaps is the fact that, unlike civil society, parliamentarians seem to remain only marginally interested in the intelligence issue or are unwilling to antagonize the agencies.

Democracy, terrorism, and reform of the intelligence agencies in Indonesia. In Indonesia, as in most countries, the need to combat terrorism has created tension between the need to strengthen still very fragile democratic controls and the necessity for reinforcing the analytical and operational capacities of the intelligence agencies.

Wahid's successor, Megawati Sukarnoputri, had been strongly criticized for the lack of intelligence cooperation before and after the bombing in Bali in 2002. She immediately tried to restore the coordinating function of BIN. Similarly, she tried to reinforce the agency's operational functions, but subtle and cautious shifts in policy had been initiated even before the Bali bombing as the Indonesian authorities were becoming increasingly aware of an Islamic terrorist threat on their own soil.

Radical Islamist groups such as the Lashkar Jihad, whose leaders publicly promoted Jihad against Christians, enjoyed the support of some Indonesian power centers. Politicians long refused to acknowledge the reality of the problem. In 2001, when Philippine authorities arrested and tried Indonesians for alleged complicity in international terrorism, the response of part of the political class in Indonesia was to denounce the framing of its citizens. The claim by the head of BIN, Lieutenant General A. M. Hendropriyono, a former special forces officer, that foreigners had trained with Lashkar Jihad was met by similar reactions.

The tension between democratic control and operational capabilities became obvious and took a more serious turn when Hendropriyono tried to use the presidential instruction of October 2002 to have extensive police powers granted to BIN. The attempt was unsuccessful, but a draft intelligence law, in preparation since September 11, 2001, was leaked. The law, still pending in Parliament, was immediately attacked by human rights organizations for denying basic rights to detainees and violating Indonesian criminal law and international human rights law.

Among the major concerns were the vagueness of the legal standards, the lack of a provision defining a role for the judiciary in the oversight of BIN's activities, and the absence of clearly defined lines between criminal investigations and intelligence activities. The possibility for BIN to move into law enforcement and to arrest people for up to seven days and detain persons for up to thirty days without any judicial oversight or control, access to counsel, and the filing of criminal charges was seen as particularly threatening to civil liberties. The vague and broad definition of the notion of "threat to the nation" was also seen as using the law "to target peaceful political activists, opposition parties or groups, and indigenous groups."

Although the intelligence law is still pending, BIN expansion was authorized by Megawati Sukarnoputri in 2004. The transfer of some police intelligence functions to BIN after the September 2004 bombing of the Australian embassy in Jakarta raised concerns similar to those generated by the draft intelligence law.

The restructuring of BAIS, the military intelligence agency, was also subject to strong criticism although for different reasons. Opponents were notably uncomfortable with a greater military intelligence presence at a time of democratic change. Some blamed the agency for the increased conflict in Indonesia, accusing BAIS operatives of provoking unrest to underline (and resuscitate) the role that the military had long played in Indonesia's politics. BAIS reports on political, economic, social, cultural, security, and defense matters, both foreign and domestic, and there is suspicion that it may be pursuing its own agenda.

Richard Tanter, in his work on Suharto's intelligence apparatus, wrote that "the instruments of state surveillance are multiple, confused, and for much of the population, probably low level, passive and somewhat ineffective." The same comment could be made about today's intelligence services. The "totalitarian ambition" described by Tanter about an earlier time has indeed disappeared, and a progressive change in the role of the intelligence agencies has been observed, but the broader political changes within Indonesia are responsible for the changes within the intelligence agencies.

First, as observed by Damien Kingsbury, "since the fall of Suharto, internal intelligence activity has slowed in part because successive governments have been less paranoid and thus less concerned to exercise a tight grip on the political process." This change, in turn, has had a negative impact. The new situation of the intelligence system is characterized by a lesser, not a greater, degree of government control. The lack of bureaucratic strength—defined as the ability to develop coherent policies and then implement them as well as the near-absence of interdepartmental coordination—favors the compartmentalization of the intelligence function and real autonomy for each agency at the provincial and local levels, allowing agencies to define their roles themselves to a great extent.

Ten years after the change of regime, many important issues have not been tackled or have been addressed only marginally. The legal basis of the entire system is weak and sometimes nonexistent. Relations with Parliament and within the larger intelligence community—the lines of authority and the respective tasks of each agency—still have to be defined.

These issues have been partly corrected by the political dynamic of the democratic transition. The transition to a more traditional role for the intelligence agencies is also the result of the withdrawal of the military from politics and of a more politically pluralistic society. The climate of change in Indonesia has made traditional intelligence functions, as experienced by the population under the New Order regime, far less politically acceptable. As a consequence, the process has not resulted in a real assertion of control by civilian governments over the intelligence agencies.

The situation of the intelligence agencies is affected by the political culture of a country where government officials consider that all institutions are instruments of the development of the nation. The use of the intelligence agencies in such a context is therefore only as "democratic" as the country's leadership; it does not result from actual constitutional balances and checks.

The failure of the Yudhoyono administration to investigate and explain the murder of Munir Said Thalib, a human rights activist who was poisoned on a flight from Jakarta to Amsterdam in 2004, demonstrates that ten years after Suharto's downfall, the elected government still does not have full control over the intelligence agencies and that the agencies' involvement in politics is not really over. Munir's criticism of the agencies' human rights abuses in conflict zones such as Aceh, East Timor, and Papua had been viewed in Indonesia as one of the main reasons for Washington's decision to maintain its embargo on all military assistance, a policy the United States put in place after the Indonesian army backed violence that followed East Timor's vote for independence in 1999. Although the alleged murderer, Polycarpus Budi Priyanto, was jailed after the crime, he was acquitted by the Supreme Court in October 2006 for lack of evidence. The case was later reopened by the state prosecutor, who established a link between Priyanto and BIN, despite the latter's denials.

The case remains unsolved and is considered evidence of the Yudhoyono administration's inability to reform its agencies. BIN remains politicized, has successfully reactivated its local networks, and remains capable of conducting the type of black operations carried out under the previous regime. BIN now operates in a much more open, transparent, and pluralistic society—a society that is increasingly intolerant of violations of human and civil rights. This intolerance severely constrains BIN's nuisance capabilities and, although not absolute, is the best guarantee so far against a return to previous undemocratic practices.

INTELLIGENCE REFORM IN CHILE

Chile represents another interesting case. The centre-left coalition elected after the resignation of Augusto Pinochet not only had to disband the infamous National Centre for Intelligence (CNI) but also had to reassert control over the military's own intelligence agencies. This happened at a time when the civilian government, operating in a transition framework defined by the military, was still fragile and far from being totally emancipated from military patronage. Because the intelligence agencies had been the favorite instrument of political repression by the previous regime, intelligence reform was a key issue not only for civil-military relations but also for the credibility of the government.

The process that led to a gradual assertion of civilian predominance was, however, a tortuous and difficult one. After years of uneasy relations mixing confrontation and cooperation with the military, the new National Intelligence Agency (ANI) was created in 2004. The new organization did not totally challenge the autonomy of existing military intelligence organizations, however. At the end of the process, the military itself had changed and, although the polarization of the country has not completely disappeared, a return to the situation that prevailed during the dictatorship is no longer possible.

Civil-military relations and the structure of the Chilean intelligence agencies in Pinochet's Chile. On September 11, 1973, a military coup d'état ended democracy in Chile, killing the elected president, Salvador Allende, in the process. The following day, the four commanding generals of the armed forces and the police established a military junta. General Augusto Pinochet was designated president. The new government immediately intended to not only control and neutralize the opposition, which amounted to about 70 percent of the population, but also destroy it. Terror became the rule and arbitrary arrests, torture, and disappearances standard practice.

The creation of the Department of National Intelligence (Dirección de Inteligencia Nacional [DINA]) and the establishment of the state of terror were consubstantial. The clause creating the agency was part of a decree establishing a new institution, the National Prisoners' Service. DINA had the specific task of determining the degree of danger prisoners posed to the state and coordinating with the intelligence services of the armed forces, the police, and the political division of the national detective service. The department quickly became a state within the state.

Even before the 1973 coup, the Chilean military had a prominent role in intelligence and considered intelligence gathering to be "part of its organic role within society, since it believed constant vigilance was critical to maintaining a well-functioning body politic." It had been preceded by a spectacular development in intelligence services in all branches of national defense. As the human and material resources of the services grew, so did their rivalry. The Ministry of Interior was in charge of the civil police, while each branch of the Ministry of National Defense had its own police force, answerable only to its respective chief of staff. Six autonomous organizations worked with few connections among them. The army, air force, and navy each operated its own agency as well as the Directorate for Public Security and Information and the National Police and Investigations (the investigative arm of the police). The army's Dirección de Inteligencia del Ejército was the group most implicated in spying on civilians.

These forces were autonomous and difficult to control, leading to abuse and political irresponsibility by the state police. By mid-1974, it had become impossible to know the whereabouts of political prisoners and even the cause of their detention. A person detained, interrogated, and released by one police service could be immediately rearrested by another service.

After 1973, intelligence became the most important element of Pinochet's hold on power. He needed, however, to establish control over the intelligence services, which answered only to their own hierarchy and indulged in interservice rivalry at all levels. DINA was created in June 1974. It was a response to the need for a full-scale secret police service under Pinochet's personal command. It was independent of any military structure and tasked with coordinating the work of the other intelligence agencies. DINA put an end to the autonomy of the existing agencies and to the resulting interservice rivalry, and it became the backbone of the regime, the most influential organization at the national level. Personnel for DINA came from all branches of the National Defense Ministry and also included selected civilians. The army soon became predominant, however. DINA quickly became the main instrument of Pinochet's personal power—Pinochet himself, not the junta, directed intelligence activities.

Retired military officials explain that the creation of DINA was also a way for Pinochet, who was aware of the inevitability of a return to more normal relations between the military and society, to preserve the military institution. As a matter of fact, all three branches of the military involved in the political repression imposed by DINA and later CNI never returned to what can be termed "normal" military activities. Despite acknowledgement of the military's own responsibility in the repression, they insist that

DINA was not a military institution. DINA had five sections: Government Service, Internal, Economics, Psychological Warfare, and External. The two largest divisions, Government Service and Internal, concentrated their efforts on the bureaucracy and on Chilean citizens themselves. Telephones were tapped and mail was opened by the intelligence agencies, which also made arrests and conducted interrogations. The agency ran a network estimated to have employed 20,000 to 30,000 informants, half of whom held strategic positions in government offices throughout Chile. DINA also possessed extraterritorial capabilities that allowed the regime to pursue its opponents outside the country.

DINA was disbanded in August 1977, not because of any sudden concern for human rights but because of strong national and international pressure. A new agency, the CNI, replaced it until the end of the dictatorship. DINA formally depended on the junta, but the CNI was legally linked to the supreme government through the secretary of interior. CNI was, in fact, from the very beginning subordinated to the head of executive power, Augusto Pinochet. One after the other, DINA and the CNI became institutional figures of repression, responsible for torture and murder.

Political background of the reforms. The gradual and incomplete assertion of civilian control over the Chilean intelligence agencies cannot be understood without an examination of the evolution of civil-military relations in post-dictatorship Chile. Chile's transition to democracy, which took place under the rules established by the military dictatorship and the resignation of General Pinochet after he was defeated in the October 5, 1988, plebiscite, did not imply an immediate transition from military to civilian rule. As a matter of fact, Chile experienced not one but several transitions that followed different rhythms and time frames. The formal transition ended when General Pinochet handed over power to the newly elected president, Patricio Aylwin, but this did not mark the end of the economic, legal, and social transitions, nor the military one.

Changing the pattern of civil-military relations was a daunting task that required the transformation of the institutional framework to delineate the military's functional autonomy and its institutional involvement in domestic affairs. This was undertaken in a political context characterized by a strong alliance between the right-wing parties and the military. The transition itself had been designed by the outgoing administration. Rejecting opposition calls for a negotiated reform of the 1980 constitution, the Pinochet government unilaterally proposed a set of constitutional changes—in particular, limiting the executive's powers, appointing senators, and reforming the electoral law to favor the right-wing parties—that were ultimately approved with the support of the opposition in a plebiscite in July 1989.

These constitutional changes, especially the electoral law, had an impact not only on the transition itself but also on the very possibility of further changes of the constitution. The conditions existed for a transition—the end of the Cold War and the support of the broader population—but it was severely constrained from the beginning. Subordination of the military had always been an objective of the centre-left coalition but, in 1990, the military could remain a quasi-autonomous body because a substantial part of the polity, as expressed through the reformed electoral system, wanted it to retain its autonomy.

Successive presidents used different strategies to deal with the military. Although deprived of the legal tools to reduce military autonomy and lacking a sufficient political majority in the National Congress to introduce the necessary constitutional changes to accomplish this, President Aylwin placed the democratization of Chile's political structures and the goal of national reconciliation at the top of his agenda. He wanted to "reestablish a notion of the armed forces as an essentially obedient, non-deliberative, professional, hierarchical, and disciplined institution." He combined decisiveness with caution. If not confrontational, his strategy was at the very least noncooperative; and he used all legal and political means at his disposal—his veto power over promotions to freeze the careers of officers who had been involved in human rights violations and, more generally, specific gestures, norms of protocol, and symbols—to assert his authority.

Of particular importance was his willingness to demonstrate full political solidarity and support for his government officials in matters closely linked to military affairs. President Aylwin reiterated his confidence in his defense minister, Patricio Rojas, who was pressuring the military by postponing the signing of decrees that regulated internal military matters, whenever the army informally asked for Rojas's resignation. Aylwin's strategy was not without risks as it constantly placed the government in a dilemma: Should it reinforce civilian supremacy or provide political stability? On two occasions, related to a major corruption case in the army, the army resorted to intimidation, once by launching unannounced exercises throughout the country and the second time by declaring a state of alert for five days. The Aylwin administration bypassed such difficulties—and formal institutions such as the National Security Council (NSC) supposedly meant for dealing with national security issues—by developing and cultivating an informal network of military and civilian officials to resolve conflicts.

By contrast, the Eduardo Frei administration that followed the Aylwin administration did seek to promote civilian leadership through cooperation with the military. More business oriented than his predecessor and aware of his own political limitations, Frei focused on the country's modernization rather than change to the political system. He tried to establish a "non-traumatic relationship between the armed forces and some parties of the Concertación [the centre-left coalition in power] and particularly, the Christian Democrats." Issues such as constitutional reforms were downplayed. The NSC was no longer bypassed, while President Frei took care to nominate a minister of defense capable of generating confidence in the military.

This strategy failed, however, to prevent the resurgence of a crisis between the government and the military. It created tensions within the ruling coalitions, with some of Frei's partners objecting to his administration's program and gaining a greater say on issues such as human rights and institutional reforms, in turn generating new conflict with the military.

The most significant conflict was on the occasion of the sentencing of Manuel Contreras, former head of DINA and then CNI, to seven years in prison. Contreras had been one of the most reviled figures of the military regime. He and his second in command, Brigadier Pedro Espinoza, were sentenced to prison terms of seven and six years, respectively, by a Chilean court in 1993 for the 1976 assassination of Orlando Letelier in Washington, D.C. Chile's Supreme Court ultimately confirmed the sentence in May 1993 despite repeated attempts at intimidation by Pinochet, who reiterated the warning that he did not know what the reaction of the army would be. Contreras sought refuge in the south of the country; then he was moved with the assistance of the army to a military hospital in central Chile. Finally, both Espinoza and Contreras were jailed, and they completed their sentences despite demonstrations of solidarity by the military.

Manuel Contreras was released in 2001 only to be convicted again in 2002 of masterminding the forced disappearance of Socialist Party leader Victor Olea Alegra, and Contreras was given two life sentences in 2008 for the 1974 murders of General Carlos Prats and his wife in Buenos Aires. The Chilean military did not oppose Contreras's sentences in 2002 or later and did not try to prevent Contreras from being jailed. On the contrary, it dissociated itself from the former head of DINA and CNI. This change in attitude makes apparent the evolution and progress of civil-military relations between the two periods.

A second major source of tension was the debate on the possible impeachment of Augusto Pinochet in 1998. The former dictator was due to retire from the army in March to become a senator for life, according to the 1980 constitution. This placed the government in a difficult situation that was illustrative of the dilemma that all Chilean governments had to face during the period: how to make a significant political gesture, attacking the least democratic aspects of the constitution while respecting the rule of law and avoiding any unconstitutional action. The government, supported by former president Aylwin, opposed impeachment on the grounds that it was detrimental to the transition itself.

The debate took place largely within the ruling coalition, but other moves to change the constitution were opposed by the right, which was closely allied with the military. The National Congress opposed President Frei's proposals to change the composition of the NSC by adding the president of the Chamber of Deputies to upset the balance of power within the NSC in favor of civilians, abolish appointed senators, and reform the constitutional tribunal. The Frei administration managed, however, to consolidate civilian power through a mix of accommodation and bargaining. If Manuel Contreras ultimately went to jail, the president suspended all action in a famous corruption case known as the "cheque case." He also raised the salaries of the armed forces and reached out to the liberal sectors of the right-wing party on human rights issues, trading the army's demand for closure on the human rights issues for a reduction of the army's prerogatives.

Another factor also deserves particular mention: the progressive reduction of the military budget relative to the overall national gross domestic product during both the Aylwin and Frei presidential terms. Although Aylwin had wanted to reduce the military budget in absolute terms, he had been prevented from doing so by his lack of a two-thirds majority in both houses of Congress. He then had to follow the law, which stipulated that the military budget had to be the same as the budget had been in 1989 except for adjustments for annual inflation. As a result of the growth of the Chilean economy, the military budget significantly declined in relative terms—a trend that continued under Frei—from 2.96 percent in 1989 (17.20 percent of the national budget) to 1.56 percent in 1997 (8.94 percent of the national budget). As a consequence, the legitimacy of successive civilian governments increased as the military budget declined.

At the end of Frei's term, civil-military relations had reached a modus vivendi. The military could no longer block all government policies, even when they affected major military interests. The military respected court decisions, although together with its civilian allies it sought ad hoc measures to mitigate the rulings' effects. As observed by Gregory Weeks: "The key to civil-military stability was refraining from criticizing the armed forces, attempting gradual reforms, and fostering a better technical and more apolitical relationship with the Defense Ministry."

The presidential victory of Ricardo Lagos in January 2000 did not change the trend. Although he was the first socialist since

Salvador Allende to be elected president, he immediately demonstrated his willingness to establish a solid working relationship with the military by nominating a defense minister, Mario Fernandez, whom the military trusted. From the perspective of civil-military relations, Lagos's presidency was the continuation of those of his Christian Democratic predecessors.

The defining event for the evolution of civil-military relations took place in Chile across two presidencies—the arrest of Augusto Pinochet in London in 1998. The arrest further stimulated military subordination to the civilian democratic authorities. Both the Frei and Lagos administrations mobilized their diplomatic resources to prevent the extradition of the former dictator to Spain, where he was charged by Judge Baltasar Garzon for torture and conspiracy to commit torture. The arrest inevitably provoked political tensions but did not result in a renewed civil-military crisis; on the contrary, it displayed relative national unity. The military institution expressed its solidarity with its former commander in chief but maintained a subordinate attitude toward President Frei. It complied with requests to provide new information on the disappearances of political dissidents during the dictatorship as part of the "dialogue roundtable" initiated by President Frei, which included the participation of the military, victims, and civil society representatives.

But the Chilean judicial system continued its work in parallel. A number of Chilean judges increased their efforts to bring military officials guilty of atrocities to court to face charges of murder, kidnapping, and torture. Pinochet was soon stripped of his immunity and the Supreme Court reinterpreted the 1978 amnesty, stating that the amnesty could be applied only to persons, not institutions, but only after an investigation had been carried out and a judicial decision had been reached. The decision affected not only Pinochet but also many other officers. By January 2002, more than a hundred retired officers had been charged for known deaths and disappearances.

This slow but continuous work of the judicial process is one of the defining characteristics of the Chilean transition toward democracy. Although Eduardo Frei was, at times, tempted to address the problem of human rights violations as a political instrument to deal with the military, successive civilian governments have tried to avoid that trap and have shifted the problem where it belongs—to the judiciary. Although difficult and at times dangerous, using the judicial process did help establish solidly civilian supremacy over the long term. The military ultimately officially endorsed the democratic system and rejected human rights abuse as an instrument of power.

At the end of the Lagos presidency in 2006, the two radically opposite views of civil-military relations that had been contradicting each other in Chile since 1990 were gradually reconciled. The armed forces had long maintained that civil-military relations were still to be governed by the 1980 constitution and the legal and practical changes introduced in 1989 at the end of the military government.

All civilian governments, in contrast, had worked to restore civilian supremacy over the armed forces in accordance with the pre-1973 constitutional and customary principles. The polarization of society, on the one hand, and the polarization of civil-military relations, on the other, persisted. It took time before Pinochet finally resigned from his senate post.

The civil-military relationship emerged relatively unscathed at the end of the Lagos era, during which General Cheyre, commander in chief of the army, acknowledged in a 2003 speech the institutional responsibility for past wrongdoing and announced that the army was "on the way to adjusting to the principles and values of democracy as a political system and respect for human dignity as the vital element for a sound national and international coexistence."

Ultimately, Lagos's presidency was marked by the adoption of a new set of constitutional reforms that drastically restricted military autonomy. The election of Michelle Bachelet in 2006—herself the daughter of an air force general and member of Allende's cabinet who had been arrested after the 1973 coup and who had died in prison after being tortured—marked the beginning of a new era. Chilean armed forces are still able to exert various pressures on civilian policy makers, but there is no longer the threat of a rebellion or a coup d'état. The Chilean military, to a large extent, has returned to its tradition of professionalism, legalism, and constitutionalism.

Process of reforming intelligence agencies. Debates over the reform of the intelligence agencies and the reforms themselves reflect the evolution of Chile's political system, illustrating the constant tension between civilians and the military and reflecting the gradual change in the balance of power between the two. More important, they also demonstrate the long and difficult process of confidence building.

Reforming intelligence had always been part of the centre-left coalition agenda. The objective has been to centralize intelligence in an institution controlled by the president and put an end to a situation in which each branch of the military has had its own intelligence service accountable only to the commander in chief. Yet nothing could really be done during the four years immediately following the reestablishment of democracy. The total mistrust between civilians and the army and the willingness of the army to demonstrate that democrats were not able to control society and deliver on security prevented all serious cooperation between the two.

The situation was understandable given recent history but paradoxical because the main threat the new regime was actually facing was not coming from the right-wing parties allied to the military but from the far left. The terrorism emanating from groups such as Movimiento de la Izquierda Revolucionaria, Lautaro, and the Frente Patriótica Manuel Rodríguez was a greater problem for Chile's young and fragile democracy than the military, which had agreed to the transition. The same groups that had fought the dictatorship were now a problem for the nascent democracy and had to be eliminated although through different means than those used by DINA and the CNI. Former employees of the CNI, disbanded after the resignation of Pinochet, were also seen as potentially dangerous, but the threat never really materialized. Some members later joined organized crime syndicates, but they never reconstituted a politico-military force able to challenge the government.

Department for Public Security and Intelligence. Reforming the agencies in a situation in which civilians received no information from a totally uncooperative military was very difficult but necessary. The dissolution of CNI after the resignation of Pinochet from his position as commander in chief of the military had created an organizational vacuum.

Political repression had stopped but coordination mechanisms had disappeared in the process, leaving each agency to return to its previous autonomy and, to some extent, the civilian-military standoff. Moreover, the new civilian governments had no previous experience in intelligence work. Before they could embark on intelligence reform, they faced significant obstacles in dismantling structures the military considered central to the nation's protection, and they were also deprived of any effective intelligence instrument by the uncooperative military.

Intelligence cooperation had to be built before it could be institutionalized. This was done gradually through the Ministry of Defense and the Ministry of Interior and involved meetings in which government officials and the heads of intelligence of the army, air force, navy, and police took part.

Bilateral meetings and personal contacts also happened more frequently. A division of labour naturally occurred, with the police producing intelligence on domestic affairs, including ordinary criminality and activism of the far left, while the army was concerned with external intelligence, although it kept an eye on the domestic political process and the agents of political mobilization within the country.

The institutionalization of the process was both symbolic—given the role of intelligence during the dictatorship—and operational as an integral part of the assertion of civilian preeminence. At the same time, the new institutions could be meaningful only if they reflected the actual balance of power between civilians and the military within the country. Therefore, if the law that created the Department for Public Security and Intelligence (Dirección de Seguridad Pública e Informaciones [DSPI]) in 1993 was the first real attempt to control intelligence in Chile, it was a limited one.

The DSPI depended on the Ministry of Interior to be in charge of coordinating the activities of domestic public security. Its function was to "provide the information, studies, analysis and assessment of intelligence required for the government to formulate policies and adopt specific measures and actions with respect to terrorist actions and conduct" as well as crime and threats to public order. In this context, the role of the new agency was essentially a coordinating one. Through the Ministry of Defense, its role was to obtain information from the intelligence organs of the armed forces and to provide the government with the analysis and planning necessary for the conduct of its policy. It was also tasked with coordinating the exchange of information between the public agencies in charge of gathering intelligence and providing the public agencies with the domestic information entering the scope of their own responsibilities. The Consultative Intelligence Committee was created for this purpose. It was composed of an under secretary of the Ministry of Defense, the deputy chief of staff of the Ministry of Defense, the under secretary for external relations, the director of public security and information, the heads of intelligence of each branch of the armed forces, and the heads of intelligence of the public security institutions. The committee was chaired by the under secretary of the interior.

The new institution had no independent means of collecting intelligence and was entirely dependent on the goodwill of the intelligence branches of the armed forces and police. Its efficiency and relevance were therefore entirely the result of the good or bad personal relations entertained by the various protagonists, and the military linked its cooperation to the position of the government on the question of past human rights violations. The suspicion toward civilian power remained high, and several cases of government officials' being spied on were reported during the 1990s. The police, however, played a more positive role than the military and proved to be more cooperative.

The civilian government was aware of the weaknesses of the new intelligence mechanism, but it was prevented from acting more decisively by the links between the military and the parliamentary right, as the electoral system gave the military parliamentary representation that was far above its actual electoral weight. The military could therefore continue acting indirectly through its political allies. In 1995, a proposal by President Frei to centralize intelligence and establish more civilian control was defeated in Parliament before it could even be debated.

Creation of the National Intelligence Agency (ANI). It was no surprise that during the presidency of Ricardo Lagos a new reform of the intelligence system took place. The relationship between civilians and the military had, by then, built sufficient confidence to allow a new step. The process that led to the creation of the new institution was, however, another example of the unease in civilian-military relations.

The Chilean Congress started debating the creation of ANI as early as 2001. It soon became clear that the autonomy of the existing military and other existing intelligence agencies would not be challenged. As the new agency did not affect any of the military's prerogatives, the military did not oppose its creation.

The debate between civilian and military elements focused essentially on the scope of the mandate of the agency. Concerned with antiterrorism, the military wanted the mandate to be as broad as possible. It initially supported the creation of ANI and lost interest when it perceived the new agency would be too weak to fulfill what was to be its main mission, counterterrorism. By contrast, the civilian branch, the left in particular, was concerned about internal surveillance, while the government wanted to limit the scope of the agency.

ANI's creation was finally approved by the Senate in May 2003 and final legislation was passed in October 2004. The law that created ANI stated in Article 20 that "the conduct of military intelligence services corresponds to the appropriate military institution to which they belong," their objectives being set by their respective commander in chief. Similarly, the internal controls remained under the supervision of the heads of the agencies, who in fact define the role of their organizations.

The differences between ANI and its predecessor organization were important. The law of 2004 stated that if the Intelligence Committee was composed of the heads of other intelligence agencies and had a coordinating function, the existing intelligence agencies were now required by law to provide ANI with the requested intelligence. Although such provisions are always difficult to implement in practice because the various agencies could always pretend that they did not possess the information they were requested to provide, the decision to cooperate was in theory no longer solely the prerogative of the military.

Even more significant was the fact that the new agency was no longer confined to a coordinating role but was also responsible for collecting intelligence. In practice it still relied on intelligence provided by the intelligence agencies of the armed forces, but it also had independent intelligence-gathering capabilities that, among other things, allowed it to verify information, although the law still left a considerable degree of autonomy to the agencies. ANI was, for example, provided with the power to enact measures against narcotics trafficking and terrorism. Activities involving "national security," such as tapping telephones and surveillance of the electronic media, were left to the intelligence services of the armed forces. Permission had to be requested but could be granted by a military judge.

Of particular importance also was the fact that ANI was responsible not only to the Ministry of Interior but also, through the ministry, to the president himself, who appointed the director of the agency.

An intelligence committee was created in the lower house of the legislature, but the actual control exercised over the intelligence agencies is difficult to assess, given the secrecy of their activities. Some observers consider that Chile's military intelligence agencies have been left to themselves. The creation of an ANI that did not bring individual military agencies under civilian control could also have raised some suspicion that it might again be used as an instrument of repression by the power of the day. Whatever the reality of this assertion, the existence of parliamentary oversight, even if symbolic, is an integral component of the assertion of civilian predominance over the military.

As a result, if the creation of a civilian agency is considered in isolation, it is not clear whether it in fact advanced civilian supremacy over the armed forces. The highly autonomous intelligence agencies created by the military regime continue to elude civilian oversight. This is considered a failure by some observers, given the successes of the Senate in increasing civilian power over commanders in chief and the elimination of designated senators. In the field of intelligence, however, the Senate seems to have been unable to totally overcome the resistance of the military, revealing a lack of consistency as well as the absence of a clearly defined policy vis-a-vis the military.

The creation of ANI should, however, be considered in a larger perspective. There is no doubt that the creation of ANI was an imperfect attempt at democratic control of intelligence agencies in Chile. It was, however, an essential and necessary step in the assertion of civilian power. ANI was the result of the evolution of military-civilian relations in favor of civilian authority and, to some extent, it helped to create the conditions for further evolution. Despite the imperfections of the system, a return to the abuses of DINA and CNI is now unthinkable, as are the prospects of a new coup d'état in Chile. The political polarization of the country may persist, yet the peaceful transition toward a more transparent system and the acceptance by the military of the rules of the democratic game are undoubtedly models to be sought in Pakistan and elsewhere. Chile's military was not a loser in the process: it gradually regained its popularity as it accepted its own depoliticization.

Lessons from the Chilean and Indonesian Cases

Because all democratic transitions are different, the process by which a new democratic government establishes control over its intelligence agencies is unique and depends on a number of specific variables. It would be futile to compare the experiences of different countries too narrowly, regardless of their successes or failures. Some lessons for Pakistan can nevertheless be drawn from the Chilean and Indonesian experiences.

Establishing democratic control over intelligence agencies is a long-term process. It took, for example, fourteen years before Chile could pass a law establishing a civilian agency, ANI, with real, although limited, power over its military counterparts.

The main characteristic of the Chilean case is that the institutionalization of democratic control over the intelligence agencies follows very closely the evolution of the political balance of power between civilian institutions and the military. Intelligence agency reform reflects the evolution of the polity as a whole. Indonesia, by contrast, has institutionalized the control of its intelligence agencies much faster than it established the predominance of civilians. As a result, control is formal but not always effective.

Time is therefore an important component of the sustainability of any reform process, not least because it takes time for mentalities to evolve. The change of generations in military leadership is an integral component of democratic evolution.

Reforms of the institutions must be consistent with the reality of the political system. A distinction also has to be made between the democratic process and the reality of the balance of power between the civilian and military realms. The degree of institutionalization of the control system of the intelligence agencies is not an absolute indicator of the extent of this control.

The democratic process—of which the control of the intelligence agencies is a part—should be a permanent effort. There should, however, always be a relative consistency between the level of institutionalization and the control of the intelligence agencies.

This may imply pauses in the reform process as well as temporarily incomplete or unsatisfactory control. A significant gap between the law and the reality can be counterproductive, as it can be used by the agencies as a pretext to oppose necessary changes.

The military must cooperate. No democratization process has taken place without the consent and participation of the military. Consequently, no control of the intelligence agencies has ever been established without the military's cooperation or at least assent. It is only when he understood that he no longer had the support of the military—some of his generals had urged him to resign—that Suharto stepped down. Similarly, in Chile, the transition toward democracy had been prepared by the military itself. The mechanism the officers established was biased in their own favor as they introduced constitutional amendments and distorted the electoral process to give the right wing power much greater than its actual electoral weight. Nevertheless, they respected the process set in place and established the framework in which reform of the intelligence agencies took place. Even if they did not initially cooperate, they did not sabotage the process. Their resistance was, moreover, linked to concern over accountability for involvement in political repression more than to principled opposition of a certain degree of political control. The process itself consisted of building a confident relationship with the military.

Civil society and public opinion must play roles in the reforms. The role of civil society is an essential, yet complex element of establishing democratic control over intelligence agencies. In both Indonesia and Chile, the population's intolerance of security establishment abuses has been a defining factor in the democratic transition and the dismantling of the most repressive state institutions. In Indonesia, civil society and public opinion constitute the best guarantee that there will be no return to the situation that prevailed during the dictatorship.

In both countries the success of the civilian governments in establishing their predominance over the militaries and their agencies can partly be explained by their capacity to temper the expectations of civil society and larger opinion. This careful management gave them the necessary room for maneuver with their militaries and allowed the compromises necessary for the creation of working relationships that later developed into confidence building.

This was particularly obvious in the case of Chile, where the civilian government always operated between two major constraints: the demands for justice from a substantial part of the population and the government's weakness vis-a-vis the military agencies that it did not control. The policy of not using as a political instrument the human rights violations committed by the agencies during the dictatorship and, instead, transferring them to the judiciary allowed the government to maintain public pressure and constrain the military, but this policy also gave the government and the military the capacity to compromise by individualizing the process. The army had long rejected its own officers guilty of atrocities in DINA and later the CNI. By the time the army chief of staff, General Juan Emilio Cheyre, publicly acknowledged the responsibility of the army for some of the abuses, the institution had gradually lost much of its power through the process. The military institution could then cooperate fully again with a civilian government whose predominance it had accepted.

A cautious use of symbolism in this context was useful for managing public expectations. The Aylwin government, for example, always put forward symbols of civilian supremacy without humiliating the military, and at the same time it never gave up its willingness to bring to trial the major human rights violators during the repression.

Civilian indifference after major violations are in the past can also be a problem. In Indonesia, for example, the lack of motivation on the part of civilians for intelligence reforms has prevented successive civilian governments from establishing as much control over the agencies as the political balance of power would have allowed. Other fields of the democratization process proceeded more quickly and more successfully.

The international context is of vital importance. The international context is also a central factor in any democratic transition and, therefore, in the democratic control of the intelligence agencies. It can, however, influence the process positively and negatively. Even though the national situations were decisive in the coups d'état of both Suharto and Pinochet, there is no doubt that the Cold War context greatly facilitated the projects of the aspiring dictators. Their respective endeavors were at the very least tolerated by the international community, and in the case of Chile were helped by the United States with little concern for the methods employed. Similarly, between 500,000 and 800,000 people were massacred in Indonesia in the name of anticommunism without much international protest. Although comparable in scope, the abuses of the Chilean regime have been well documented since the end of the Pinochet regime in 1990. It should be acknowledged that the progressive change of position of U.S. administrations was initiated by an operation conducted as early as September 1976 on U.S. soil by Chilean intelligence agencies—the murder in Washington, D.C., of Orlando Letelier, a former minister in the Allende government.

In turn, the end of the Cold War greatly facilitated the acceptance of regime change in both Indonesia and Chile. As the communist threat disappeared, right-wing dictators were no longer necessary. Human rights and democracy therefore became the order of the day and the use of intelligence agencies as instruments of political repression insufferable.

Policy Recommendations

Because of the importance of Pakistan to the issue of terrorism, the community of nations, including Pakistan itself, is vitally concerned about the role of the intelligence agencies in Pakistan. The main obstacle the international community is confronted with, however, is of a psychological nature, the belief that the supremacy of the intelligence agencies in Pakistan is a fact of life and that nothing can be done about it. The examples of Indonesia and Chile demonstrate the contrary, even though change comes at a cost.

ROLE OF THE INTERNATIONAL COMMUNITY

From the perspective of the international community, the issue of democratic control of Pakistan's intelligence agencies is primarily the consequence of its concern with international terrorism. Western countries can be either a facilitating or an inhibiting factor, but they will be affected by the outcome of the process through the persistence or disappearance of terrorism emanating from the tribal areas along the Afghan–Pakistan border.

Most Western governments are reluctant to aid such a process, even passively. They believe that ending cooperation with the ISI would simply increase the terrorist threat on their national territories. For several reasons, this perception should be questioned:

- The threat of terrorism will persist as long as the ISI continues nurturing a number of extremist groups operating within and beyond Pakistan's borders. Therefore, compromises with Pakistan's main intelligence agency buy additional security only marginally and create a rent for the ISI. Besides creating an additional problem for the elected government, deals with the ISI perpetuate the ISI's dominance. As the ISI's control over terrorist groups diminishes, the rationale for the rent (the need for cooperation and the subsequent compromises) diminishes, too, although it does not totally disappear.

- The end of ISI interference would not automatically mean the end of terrorism and the insurgency in the tribal belt, but it would allow for real cooperation with Pakistani intelligence to take place.
- Given the likelihood of retaliation should any of these groups conduct a major terrorist operation on U.S. soil, the constraint is as much a reality for the ISI and its military patrons as for the ISI's Western partners.
- The control of the intelligence agencies is a component of civil-military relations. The ISI is a military body, and the operational responsibility to control it belongs to the military and its leadership. International policies intended to restrain the role of the Pakistani intelligence agencies will have to ensure that they do not weaken the civilian government in the process, a situation that would ultimately be counterproductive.

Any arm-twisting measures or mechanisms will have to be looked for between this set of constraints and structural factors, considering the risk for the West but also the Pakistani security establishment's objectives. International actors with an interest in Pakistan's situation should aim for the long term, taking into account current Pakistani vulnerabilities.

Work through the Pakistan government. Most of the countries involved in the region are now aware of the double-dealing of the ISI and are asking the Pakistan government to better control its intelligence apparatus. The problem is that the same Western governments that today blame the Pakistani state for its inability to control its agencies are maintaining working relations with these very same agencies, thus undermining their own purpose and the credibility of the Pakistan government as well as its legitimacy. This situation diminishes the Pakistan government's leverage to take control of the intelligence agencies. The ISI is, in turn, vindicated.

Mobilize all of the countries with some degree of influence on the Pakistan military. Because China is itself a victim of Islamist terrorism, it is a potential partner whose influence on the Pakistan military is far greater than any Western country. Beijing may still be reluctant to cooperate with Western countries, but China is likely to become a target of extremism owing, for example, to its role in the Red Mosque incident, during which Beijing convinced former president Musharraf to intervene militarily.

Condition all assistance to the Pakistan military on actual results, not only in the fight against terrorism but in controlling its intelligence agencies. Experience has shown that Pakistan can hand over international terrorists as a way of achieving restraint from the West in demands regarding the Taliban. Concentrating exclusively on this kind of result is at best insufficiently effective, hence the need to concentrate on the structures and institutions that actually support terrorism.

One may argue that the resistance may be strong and the risk of retaliation real if the Pakistan government cooperates in the fight against terrorism. The argument has validity but is gradually weakening as the Pakistani intelligence agencies seem to have lost control of some of the groups they initially supported. More important, however, is that Pakistan's security forces are themselves victims of terrorism. This convergence of interests should be emphasized through technical assistance whenever cooperation is sincere and unbiased but should leave no room for compromise with regard to the terrorist organizations targeted by Pakistan's security apparatus and to the need to place intelligence agencies under authoritative civilian control.

Diminish the importance of Pakistan for the international community's engagement in Afghanistan. Pakistan is currently in the unique position of supporting both sides in the Afghan conflict, whereas the international community is inhibited in its relations with Islamabad because Pakistan was until recently the only country of transit for support and supplies for the international troops in Afghanistan. The opening of a Russian route has not solved this problem as the International Security Assistance Force (ISAF) remains dependent on its relations with Moscow, which are at the mercy of issues external to Afghanistan but extremely important for almost all the actors in Afghanistan.

There is, in fact, no ideal situation as almost all the regional actors have some problems with the NATO component of the coalition. The solution can therefore come only from more countries' accepting transit of ISAF supplies through their territory. These could include China and Iran, because both countries have at least partially convergent interests with ISAF in the area. Islamabad's leverage would thus be greatly diminished and the room for maneuver of the international community increased.

These actions would help to gradually reverse the link of dependency between the international community and Pakistan without violating Islamabad's sovereignty. They could also help reinforce civilian predominance.

RECOMMENDATIONS TO THE GOVERNMENT OF PAKISTAN

Pakistan's intelligence agencies cannot be reformed in isolation. Because the Pakistani intelligence agencies, the MI and ISI, are part of the military, a policy aiming at establishing civilian control over these agencies is only part of the larger design of asserting civilian predominance. Several of the recommendations listed below would apply equally to this more general objective. They are also relevant to the specific issues at stake. Some are more concerned with the intelligence agencies. None of the recommendations is decisive if taken individually. All concentrate on a more transparent system and, therefore, more accountability.

Strengthen and develop the police. In the short and medium term, the Pakistan government will have no choice but to cooperate with the existing intelligence agencies. This should not prevent the government from maximizing the separation between the agencies and giving each of them its due role and corresponding means.

The two processes are closely linked. Problems facing the armed forces, the police, and the intelligence agencies are interconnected. The weakness of one of these institutions tends to reinforce the extension of the others beyond their expected roles. As observed by Felipe Agüero: "A weak or ineffective police will put pressure on officials to use the military in policing roles for which it is ill prepared, or to militarize the police. The existence of several poorly controlled intelligence agencies may harm the professionalism of military and police."

In both Chile and Indonesia, strengthening the police was integral to the reassertion of civilian control over the intelligence agencies, although with different degrees of success. The police in Indonesia are seen as a corrupt, inefficient institution, whereas the perception in Chile is the opposite.

In Pakistan, the domestic extension of the ISI presence (down to the district level) has been the reverse of the weakening of the police. Diminishing the ISI's domestic role will therefore require the strengthening of the police in parallel with the redefinition of the ISI's role, which should no longer interfere in domestic affairs.

The police force is known for its corruption, politicization, and basic inability to perform its duty of protecting citizens against crime and violence. Its reform will therefore be a prerequisite for a more balanced relationship among the intelligence agencies. According to the International Crisis Group, the police are also not immune from penetration by sectarian and jihadist elements as a result of deliberate state policies, but the police resent the Musharraf government for its neglect of the police force. Reforming the police would therefore be a difficult endeavor but a promising one, as this resentment would most certainly benefit any government willing to help the institution fulfill the role—implementing law and order— that should normally belong to it.

The question of police capabilities remains a major issue that could be greatly eased by international assistance. The international community has ultimately everything to gain in the strengthening of the police, as it would be a much more effective counterterrorism mechanism if trained and equipped properly. As the International Crisis Group recently recommended: helping the police "with training and technical assistance would pay counter-terrorism dividends." Such aid would be of great help in establishing the credibility of Pakistan's new government both domestically and internationally, creating the basis for a more confident relationship with the military as well.

Reinforce the separation between military and civilian intelligence agencies. To be effective, the reform should not stop at the police. The incestuous relationship between the ISI and the IB should be stopped, and the possibility of ISI agents' moving into civilian bodies should be controlled and limited. The ISI's ability to gain influence in the NAB by providing funding in exchange for the recruitment of former ISI agents is a good example of how one agency can gradually develop influence over another. Such cross-recruitment should be stopped if the organizations are to become independent.

Civilianize the debate on foreign and security policies. No democratic control of the intelligence agencies will be possible without a prior reappropriation by the Pakistani polity of the public debate on Pakistan's foreign and security policies. Only such a debate can help establish a consensus on the objectives and thus provide a framework for the agencies' own task. The agencies' actions would no longer be left only to their own initiative nor to the sole decision of the military. Moreover, public debate and civilian policy formulation would provide a reference point against which the actions or nonactions of the agencies could be assessed.

What is essential in the process is the delegitimation of the political role of the intelligence agencies and the redefinition of their role in conformity with the national interests of the country, as decided by the newly elected government and approved by Parliament as the expression of the nation's common political will. The absence of consensus on foreign and security policies would make the problem intractable. When confronted with international accusations of ISI responsibility in the recent terrorist attack against the Indian embassy in Kabul, President Musharraf and the COAS, General Kayani, playing once again on the nationalist feelings of the population, promptly denounced the accusations as a conspiracy against the ISI and the Pakistan military that supposedly endangered Pakistani security. It is therefore essential to adopt a common definition of the national interest. This redefinition will allow a clearer separation of what, in the Pakistani context, is patriotic or unpatriotic.

The reappropriation of the debate on foreign and security policies is the primary responsibility of Pakistan's Parliament. It would undoubtedly be difficult to prevent the political parties from playing emotional cards in a context where the traditional—in particular, religious—identity issue is likely to confuse the debate, but such a debate is essential. Civil society and public opinion more generally should also be involved through the press.

Stand up to the military whenever necessary. A fine line will inevitably have to be drawn between unnecessarily confronting the military and the need to stand up to it whenever constitutional order requires.

Although the director general of ISI is theoretically nominated by and accountable to the prime minister, the director general is in fact accountable primarily to the COAS. Every attempt by civilian prime ministers thus far to nominate an ISI director general of their own liking, without the consent of the military, has ended in failure; this illustrates the fact that legality is often at odds with reality in Pakistan.

There can be no soft substitute for the fact that the director general of the ISI is legally accountable primarily to the prime minister and not to the COAS. This does not and should not prevent discussions and the reaching of a consensus before the nomination itself takes place. Once decided, however, the director general is constitutionally accountable to the prime minister and no one else. One may argue that examples presented in these pages show that this is wishful thinking; however, two points about this need to be made.

First, it is unclear whether, after eight years of Musharraf's rule, the military is ready for yet another coup. The decision of the COAS, Parvez Kayani, to maintain relative neutrality during the February 2008 elections was understood by many in the military as necessary for restoring the prestige and professionalism of the army. It was preferable to let the civilians bear the burden of day-to-day government and reap the unpopularity inevitably associated with it.

Second, since the 2008 elections, the ISI seems to have launched a series of offensives both on the Afghan border and in Kashmir, which, besides their specific geostrategic objectives, also create a credibility problem for the civilian government.

This raises a number of questions regarding the real position of the Pakistan military. If it seems unlikely that it again wants to assume direct control, it also seems clear that the military intends to signal that it is still a force to reckon with. If compelled to clarify its position, the military could find itself faced with a dilemma between its willingness to adopt a low profile and protecting the ISI as the executor of the military's dirty work, a position it may find uncomfortable. The current situation favors the military only as long as the civilians refuse to confront it, but this could turn in favor of civilians if a confrontation arises.

Restore the Supreme Court and bring ISI's violations of legality to the court. Nowhere, except in a dictatorship, do intelligence agencies operate outside a legal framework. Such a framework exists in Pakistan but is ignored by the institutions concerned. It is therefore a necessary part of the democratization process to bring the intelligence agencies' violations before the courts to reestablish the preeminence of the judiciary, not out of revenge, but to assert civilian power. It is also essential to avoid using forgiveness for past abuses as an asset for a political bargain with regard to the control of the intelligence agencies. The natural judicial instance for such a matter would be Pakistan's Supreme Court, which is at the origin of the current political crisis and whose fate is not yet sealed. In the short term, this situation is in obvious contradiction with the necessity to depoliticize the process as much as possible. But the establishment of the rule of law is a prerequisite not only for the demilitarization of Pakistan's political life but also for obtaining control of the agencies.

It could be argued that the weakness of the current judiciary will inevitably be another obstacle to establishing such control. The Chilean example demonstrates that similar difficulties can be overcome and that it is essential not to bargain the political control of the agencies against any form of amnesty that would leave the agencies' legal violations unpunished.

Judicial control does not contradict the nature of intelligence agencies and the secrecy of their activities. Control should be over the purpose, reach, and objects of the agencies' work, not about how they do their job under the law.

Manage public expectations. The careful management of public expectations is ultimately an important factor of failure or success. The difficulty stems partly from the fact that, coming after years of military rule during which the practices of the intelligence agencies were at once an open secret and a taboo, nobody really dares to confront the agencies.

Opening a debate about the control of the intelligence agencies could raise popular expectations beyond reasonable objectives. Yet no reform of the system will be possible without mobilizing the population. Whatever the country, the primary driver of intelligence reform in relation to domestic political affairs has always been the intolerance of the population. This intolerance is often the best guarantee against a return to previous practices after reform has taken place. The press undoubtedly must play a central role in keeping intelligence agencies in the public eye.

At the same time, however, no reform of the intelligence agencies in general or simply of the ISI will be possible without the cooperation of the military. To achieve both the objective of reform and the cooperation of the military, the reform itself will have to be discussed with the military and the military's role recognized within the limits of the consensus produced by an eventual public debate on foreign policy.

4

Indian Mujahideen

Indian Mujahideen (IM) is a terrorist group based in India. The group has carried out several attacks against civilian targets in India.

Police investigations have revealed the group to be a front for the Pakistan based Lashkar-e-Taiba. The Indian Mujahideen on 4 June 2010 was declared a terrorist organisation and banned by the Government of India. On 22 October 2010, New Zealand declared it aterrorist organisation. In September 2011, the United States officially placed the Indian Mujahideen on its list of foreign terrorist organisations, with the State Department acknowledging that the group had engaged in several terrorist attacks in India and had regional aspirations with the ultimate aim of creating an "Islamic caliphate" across South Asia. The group was banned by UK as it aimed at creating an Islamic State and implementing Sharia law in India, by use of indiscriminate violence.

A number of botched arrests and custodial deaths have continued to raise questions in the mainstream media and even conspiracy theories particularly among India's besieged Muslim community that the so-called Indian Mujahideen is a fake organisation set up by vested interests with the intent to tarnish the Indian Muslim community with the Al Qaeda tag that was until then never used in reference to Indian Muslims, as confirmed by then US President George W. Bush during his official visit to India.

- Investigators believe that Indian Mujahideen is one of many groups composed of lower-tierSIMI members.

According to the Indian Intelligence Bureau, SIMI took new titles because the top leadership of SIMI have been detained and would be available for interrogation. The change in names is believed to signal a change in tactics as SIMI affiliated militants attempt to garner more support from India's Muslim community rather than be seen as a group consisting of foreigners. Two days after the 13 May 2008 Jaipur bombings, the extremistgroup sent an e-mail to Indian media in which they claimed responsibility for the attacks and said they would *"demolish the faiths (all religions apart from Islam) of the infidels of India"*. The biggest and boldest attack to date by the group was the 2008 Ahmedabad serial blasts, where it gained national notoriety with a casualty count towards 50.

BACKGROUND

Factionalism

Even though IM came to light in 2008, in the same year it was already seen to have a faction. The 30 October 2008 Assam bombingswere claimed by alleged offspring of the IM, Islamic Security Force-Indian Mujahideen, though police were still investigating this link.

Members

It is suspected that these are the major leaders of the Indian group.

- Abdul Subhan Qureshi alias Tauqeer, 36, sought: A software engineer from Mumbai. An expert In bomb-making and is an expert bomber.
- Safdar Nagori, 38, under arrest: Architect the transformation from SIMI to Indian Mujahideen.
- Mufti Abu Bashir, 28, under arrest: A preacher from Azamgarh In Uttar Pradesh.
- Qayamuddin Kapadia, 28, under arrest: A trader of Vadodara, He started the first-ever mosque of the Ahle Hadis Tanzeem In Vadodara a few years ago.

- Sajid Mansuri, 35, under arrest: A graduate In psychology and formerly a marketing executive.
- Usman Agarbattiwala, sought, 25: A PG diploma holder from Vadodara In human rights
- Alamzeb Afridi, 24, sought: A jobless youth from Ahmedabad. He purchased bicycles and then planted them In Ahmedabad after tying bombs.
- Abdul Razik Mansuri, 27, sought: An embroidery unit owner.
- Mujib Shaikh, 25, sought: A stone polishing artisan.
- Zahid Shaikh, 27, sought: A mobile phone repair shop owner from Ahmedabad.
- Amil Parwaz, sought: A native of Ujjain. Believed to Be involved In the court bomb blasts In Uttar Pradesh In November 2007.
- Yasin Bhatkal, 30, under arrest: Native of Bhatkal in North Karnataka.

Delhi group

The local group at Delhi is thought to include the following, most of them from Azamgarh:

- Mohammad Atif (24) aka Bashir: alleged planner and recruiter, killed In Batla House, Jamia Nagar encounter on 19September. Alleged to have planted a bomb at M-block market in Greater Kailash-I, and Varanasi bombs.
- Mohammad Saif arrested from Batla House in Jamia Nagar after 19September encounter. Alleged to have planted a bomb at Regal Cinema in Connaught Place.
- Zeeshan: arrested after the Jamia Nagar encounter. Alleged to have planted a bomb At Barakhamba Road In Connaught Place.
- Mohammed Sajid (16) aka Pankaj, killed during the Batla House encounter. Alleged to have planted a bomb at Barakhamba Road in Connaught Place.
- Junaid: Escaped during the Batla House encounter. Alleged to have planted a bomb at M-block market in Greater Kailash-I, and Varanasi bombs.

- Mohammad Shakeel (24): arrested him on 21September from Jamia Nagar. Alleged to have planted a bomb at Nehru Place in south Delhi
- Zia-ur-Rehman (22): arrested on 21September from Jamia Nagar. Alleged to have planted a bomb at Connaught Place and on a cycle in Ahmedabad.
- Saqib Nisar (23): arrested him on 21September from Jamia Nagar.
- Shahzad alias Pappu: Arrested from Azamgarh by UP STF, He was escaped during the Jamia Nagar encounter. Alleged to have planted a bomb At in Central Park, Connaught Place.
- Alihas Malik: sought. Alleged to have planted a bomb At Central Park, Connaught Place.
- Mohammad Khalif: sought.
- Arif: sought.
- Salman: Arrested by Special Cell.

ATTACKS CLAIMED BY INDIAN MUJAHIDEEN

The emails sent by Indian Mujahideen claimed that they were responsible for the following terror incidents. One warning email was received 5 minutes before the first blast in Ahmedabad. Another was received soon after the first blast of Delhi bombings. The timing makes it impossible for any other groups to have sent the two emails.

- 2007 Uttar Pradesh bombings
- 13 May 2008 Jaipur bombings
- 2008 Bangalore serial blasts
- 2008 Ahmedabad serial blasts
- 13 September 2008 Delhi bombings
- 2010 Pune bombing
- 2010 Jama Masjid attack
- 2010 Varanasi bombing
- 2011 Mumbai serial blasts
- 2013 Bodh Gaya blasts

Suspects and arrests

On 28 August 2013, in a major breakthrough Yasin Bhatkal, co-founder of IM and another IM terrorist have been arrested by Indian Police and NIA near Indo-Nepal border. According to Gujarat police, the breakthrough in 2008 Ahmedabad serial blasts case came from five 'switched-off' mobile phone numbers. Joint Commissioner of Police (crime) Ashish Bhatia said that the terrorists had procured five SIM cards of phones that were switched off on the day of the blasts — 26 July. The analysis of the phone calls made to those SIM cards from PCOs provided them the key leads.

The arrest of ten suspects included the leader, Mufti Abu Bashir Ishlahi alias Abdul Wasir, who was arrested the help of Uttar Pradesh police At his father's home At Sarai Mir In Azamgarh UP on 14August 2008. Bashir studied in the local Madarsatul Islah and later in Deoband in Saharanpur. According to the reports Bashir claimed that the bombings cost Rs 75,000 a SIMI activist sold his house in Kutch to get the amount.

Bashir, who had stayed in Ahmedabad along with Abdul Subhan Qureshi alias Tauqeer, a Co-conspirator, had bought five SIM cards using local names and addresses. He had used these cellphone numbers to remain in touch with the other members of the module at the planning stage of the conspiracy. Bashir had given the SIM cards to the bomb planters on 26 July, who had used them carefully. Each member had contacted the others through STD-PCO booths after successfully planting the bombs. These numbers were used only for receiving calls. Many of the calls were from Juhapura, where Zahid Shaikh, one of the key members of the group, lived at Sandhi Avenue near the Sarkhej highway. These numbers had become inactive immediately after the blasts.

Also, the Government suspects Indian mujahideen for the two blasts in Hyderabad, on 21 February 2013 at 7:01 pm.

Key members of the Indian Mujahideen in Mumbai police custody want to turn approver. In March 2014, a special cell of police in India arrested four members of IM, out of which one was Waqas alias Javed a bomb making expert in this group. They were arrested in Jaipur and Jodhpur in Rajasthan.

Jamia Nagar encounter

On 19 September 2008, the police raided an apartment in Jamia Nagar, near Jamia Millia Islamia In Delhi. There is speculation that the prime suspect in the Ahmedabad blasts, Mufti Abu Bashir, a madrasa teacher from Azamgarh, may have pointed out the apartment.

The raid resulted in the death of terrorists Bashir alias Mohammed Atif Amin (son of Mohammed Amin, cloth merchant in Bhiwandi, Mumbai), Mohammad Sajid and a decorated police officer Mohan Chand Sharma In the gunfight. Mohammad Saif (the son of Samajwadi Party leader Shadab Ahmed) was arrested while two hostiles managed to flee by possibly jumping the rooftops. All of the suspects were from Azamgarh district'S Sarai Mir town. They claimed to be students, but that was denied by Jamia Millia

The five were responsible for manufacturing bombs used in Ahmedabad, Jaipur and Delhi blasts.

Atif claimed to have been studying for a diploma in Human Resources Development from Jamia Milia Islamia University. However Jamia Milia denied having him As a student. Some residents of Sarai Mir thought He was pursuing his bachelors In technology from Jamia Hamdard.

Atif was said to have been the leader of a group of 14 young men belong to Azamgarh in Uttar Pradesh, all claiming to have been studying in Delhi: Atif (24), Sajid alias Pankaj (19), (both now dead), Shehzad alias Pappu (22), Junaid (27), Shahdab Bhai alias Mallick (27), Sajid (24), Mohammad Khalid (25), Arif (22), Shakil (26), Zia Khan (24) and Salman (25), Zeeshan (24) and Mohammad Saif (23).

Zeeshan Jawed was arrested from the offices of a private TV station, He worked for a private company, Monarch International on Vikas Marg, and is also said to be studying management. Both him and Saif claim to have been recruited by Atif.

It is reported that Mohammad Saif has said that the plans to carry out several blasts across the country were mooted about three years ago when the Indian Mujahideen (IM) was formed.

Although the blasts spanned over a period of 10 months (the first blasts took place in August 2007 in Hyderabad), the planning was made far back in 2005. After that series of explosions occurred Uttar Pradesh, Jaipur, Ahmedabad and Delhi.

There is considerable resentment In Sarai Mir over the death of the local boys. Villagers have blamed the media for giving a bad name to Azamgarh by calling it a "nursery of terror". Mafia don Abu Salem hails from here. Azamgarh used to export its famous country-made pistols, known as kattas, whose factories dot the region. The district was also known for young sharpshooters who joined Mumbai gangs. Individuals from the area have been accused of the murders of Bollywood producer Gulshan Kumar in Mumbai and Left leaderShankar Guha Niyogi in Chhattisgarh.

THE INDIAN MUJAHIDEEN: A RESURGENCE OF TERROR

The blood that flowed through Varanasi on the evening of December 7, 2010, marked yet another appalling episode in the history of India's prolonged combat with the various subversive elements spread throughout the length and breadth of the country. Soon after the devastating attack that rocked the portals of the temple town, an e-mail was sent to various prominent media houses by the Indian Mujahideen claiming responsibility for the attack. The e-mail claimed that the blast was in retaliation to the verdict in the Babri Masjid-Ram Janambhoomi title suit case. Security agencies traced the Internet Protocol address of the five-page e-mail signed by 'Al-Arbi' to the suburbs of Mumbai.i Police teams were immediately despatched to the area for further investigation, the results of which are awaited.

At this juncture, it would be prudent to look into the inception as well the activities of the Indian Mujahideen (IM) in order to understand their composition, terror tactics, modus operandi, as well as the issues that inflame their operations. Thus, this chapter focuses on the inception of the IM, their links with the Students Islamic Movement of India (SIMI), the ideology that they profess, and the various attacks that have been attributed to the same. Since the subject requires an in-depth research into the intricacies of the terror group as well as its links with other groups, this chapter deals with certain aspects of the same. It is the initial part of a series of papers based on a study of the Indian Mujahideen.

THE INCEPTION OF THE INDIAN MUJAHIDEEN (IM)

A study of the modus operandi of the IM has shown that the role of educated and technologically advanced youth in masterminding and executing terror attacks is of utmost importance. Such subversive elements have been indoctrinated with assorted ideologies like the Wahhabi and Deobandi schools of thought, to give legitimacy to their version of terror in the name of Islam. Drawing their own interpretations of the Quran, there has been a rapid spread of 'radical' teaching in the mushrooming *madrasas*. During the recent times there has been a sudden surge in the formation of such destructive organisations throughout India. One such organisation is the Students Islamic Movement of India (SIMI), which gave birth to the IM.

SIMI was founded with 250 members on April 15, 1977, by Mohammed Ahmedullah Siddiqui, as the students' wing of the Jamaat-e-Islami Hind (JIH).v JIH was the first organised Islamic reformist movement in India formed in Lahore on August 26, 1941, under the leadership of Sayyid Abul Ala Mawdudi.vi However, the alliance between the JIH and SIMI lasted only till 1981, when radical student members of SIMI protested against Yasser Arafat's visit to India, while the senior JIH leaders saw him as a champion. The rift in ideologies led JIH to abandon SIMI and float a new students' wing, the Students Islamic Organisation, while SIMI continued as a separate hard-line Islamic organisation.

After breaking away from JIH, SIMI underwent radicalisation, and its fanatical position was dictated entirely by geo-political events taking place in the world, which were interpreted as direct attacks on Islam and Muslims. Events, both domestic and international, which led to a shift in SIMI's philosophy, were:

- The Soviet invasion of Afghanistan and toppling of the Shah of Iran by Ayatollah Khomeini.
- The imposition of harsh Shariah laws in Pakistan by General Zia-ul-Haq in 1980.

- The demolition of the Babri Masjid in Ayodhya in December 1992.
- The militancy in the Kashmir Valley since 1989.

Provoked by the Godhra carnage of 2002, the divide, assisted by the ISI, LeT and HuJI, eventually led to the creation of a new militant organisation of SIMI called the Indian Mujahideen. It was co-founded by Riyaz Shahbandri and Abdul Subhan Qureshi. The IM, at this point in time, consisted of students, most of them Kashmiris, studying in Deobandi madrasas in South Gujarat, Andhra Pradesh, Karnataka and Maharashtra. The Indian Mujahideen was, thus, born, taught by its masters to spread jihadist doctrines in India, through homegrown militants, aided, abetted and calibrated from across the borders.

The Ideology

The name Indian Mujahideen is apparently drawn from a book on a *Jihad* waged by two Islamic warriors in north-west India around 1831 in Balakot, now in Pakistan-occupied Kashmir (POK), and which suited the terror mission devised by the Students Islamic Movement of India.x The IM ideology primarily draws inspiration from the Wahhabi philosophy of the Deobandi School, which practises a rigid, puritanical version of Islam. All the arrested members of the IM and SIMI, so far, have been students of Deobandi *madrasas* from Bharuch, Ujjain, Azamgarh and Saharanpur.

The Deobandi Wahhabis advocate that a Muslim's first loyalty is to his religion and only then to his country. Secondly, Muslims should recognise only the religious frontiers of their *ummah* (community) and not national frontiers. Thirdly, they have a sacred right and obligation to go to any country to wage *Jihad* to protect the Muslims of that country.xi The Deobandi and Ahle-e-Hadith schools were revived in India through funding by Saudi charities, when oil prices skyrocketed in the 1970s. Significantly, a majority of terror groups like the JeM, HuJI, LeT, HuA and now the IM owe 'allegiance' to the Deobandi *madrasas* and the Mawdudi school of thought. Thus, the Deobandi school of thought and Wahhabism combined to form an extremist version of radical Islam, which advocates the prominence of *Jihad* for Islamisation.

The Leadership

The leadership of the IM can primarily be traced to a man from Mumbai named Abdul Subhan Usman Qureshi, code name "Kasim" or "al-arbi" who has signed the e-mail manifestos sent by the IM before and after the multiple blasts of 2008. It has been reported that he may have escaped into Bangladesh recently. Interestingly, Qureshi's background refutes the theory that most IM cadres come from deprived backgrounds or are schooled in radical *madrasas*. Qureshi studied at the Antonio DeSouza High School ran by a Christian missionary in Byculla, Mumbai, and came from an economically priviledged background. In 1995, he obtained a diploma in industrial electronics and in 1996, a specialised software maintenance qualification from the CMS Institute in Marol. After obtaining these degrees, he joined various software and computer firms. However, somewhere during this period, Qureshi was also harbouring radical ideologies and in 2001, he left his job at the firm stating in his resignation letter that "I have decided to devote one complete year to pursue religious and spiritual matters."

According to Mumbai police intelligence, by 1998, Qureshi was one of the most committed SIMI activists to edit one of SIMI's house-magazines, *Islamic Voice,* from New Delhi. By then, SIMI's growing links with global Islamic movements like the Egyptian Brotherhood and Hamas were clear. Links with Bangladesh based HuJI and Pakistan based LeT were also coming to the fore. Since 2007, Qureshi succeeded in training hundreds of SIMI-IM cadres and was the mastermind of the Delhi blasts undertaken by Mohammad Bashir, Mohammad Fakruddin and Saif Ahmad in September 2008.

According to a UP based IM cadre, Sadiq Shaikh, hailing from Azamgarh district and who was arrested on September 23, 2008, IM modules exist in Uttar Pradesh, Karnataka, Pune and Mumbai. Most arrested IM cadres are computer professionals and bomb makers. Among those arrested are Pune based Mohammed Mansoor Asgar Peerbhoy and Mubin Kadar Shaikh, who jointly designed the IM logo and hacked into unsecured Wi-fi connections. Another significant intelligence input from the UP police indicates that UP based IM cadre Fahim Arshad Ansari who was arrested in UP in February 2008 was in direct contact with the LeT in masterminding the Mumbai attacks of November 2008. Ansari studied at the Malad Municipal Secondary School in Mumbai, from where he graduated in 1989 but later on went onto Dubai. In 2005, another Hyderabadi, Sami Ahmad who was arrested by the police in 2006 revealed that he had had agreed to put Ansari in touch with the LeT.

Conclusion

At present the Gujarat Police suspect that the same absconding Indian Mujahideen (IM) terrorists wanted for the 2008 serial bombings in Ahmedabad could be behind the December 7, 2010, blast in Varanasi. The IM, which claimed responsibility for the Ahmedabad blasts by sending emails to media houses, reportedly owned up the Varanasi blasts in a similar fashion. The two mails bore striking similarities in both language and content, a senior ATS officer said.xvi Fifty-nine people were killed and over 200 injured in the Ahmedabad blasts. "The two mails have great similarities. Both mention the Godhra riots, both mention the name of (Chief Minister) Narendra Modi and state in a similar way how he had presided over the massacre of Muslims in his state but is still free. Both mails also say the motive was to avenge the Godhra riots," the officer said.xvii ATS sources said there were strong indications that two top IM men, Riyaz and Iqbal Bhatkal — believed to be holed up in Pakistan and wanted for the Ahmedabad blasts — were involved in the Varanasi bombing. According to them, there were inputs suggesting that Riyaz had supported Dr Shahnawaz, a top IM operative suspected to have overseen the planning and execution of the blast in Varanasi.

A senior ATS officer added: "Riyaz and Iqbal are remote-running the banned SIMI outfit in the name of IM. They adopted the method of low-intensity blasts in Varanasi, just like the Ahmedabad bombings. Even the mail in which their outfit claims responsibility for the blast is strikingly similar to the one they sent out after the Ahmedabad blasts."xviii It is thus beyond doubt that terror groups have established a pan-Islamic network, with a large number of sleeper sells in the hinterland, with extreme linkages with J&K, the global terrorists, and the ISI. In the recent past, a number of terrorist modules have been broken up in all metropolitan cities, and hitherto unaffected areas in the country. It remains to be seen as to whether such horrific carnage as meted out in Varanasi will follow in the near future or effective counter terrorism measures would be successful in annihilating the menace of domestic terrorism from within the heartland of India.

DEVELOPING STRATEGIC LEADERS FOR THE 21ST CENTURY

It is remarkable how the scope and focus of American national security policy have changed since September 11, 2001 (9/11). The United States has fought two major wars in Afghanistan and Iraq and is engaged in the daunting challenges of post-conflict stability operations in both countries.

The "war on terrorism" continues both here in America as well as throughout the globe. Policymakers remain engaged with the challenges of globalization, international trade, the spread of AIDS, etc., that predate the 2001 terrorist attacks. Now, however, they must view these problems through a new lens and confront emerging challenges with Iran and North Korea. Finally, these conditions are not transitory—the nation must expect that the threat of multiple crises having an immediate effect on American security will continue indefinitely. The old adage that Washington is "a one crisis town" can no longer apply.

These events have changed how we think about "national security." They have dramatically expanded not only the number and scope of issues, but also the overall complexity of the process. Americans who felt safe at home and viewed security threats as distant from our shores no longer feel this way.

The government that is supposed to protect us has also felt the winds of change. The requirement for interagency decisionmaking has accelerated, demands for greater policy flexibility have increased, and a process that was largely confined to a few agencies of the Federal government now involves a multitude of new players and allied states. Clearly, the sad and apparently unexpected aftermath of the Iraq War underscores the critical need for significant changes in the planning of military operations, preparation for post-conflict requirements, *and* oversight of their execution.

As the nation embarked on this new era at the turn of the century, the *2002 National Security Strategy* noted that we must "transform America's national security institutions to meet the challenges and opportunities of the 21st century." The Bush administration responded initially with the creation of the Department of Homeland Security, the largest change in the structure of the Federal government since the National Security Act of 1947. But we must also transform existing institutions, the policy process, and how we "think" about the defense of the nation. Furthermore, as General Richard Myers, former Chairman of the Joint Chiefs of Staff, observed, this transformation cannot wait—"It must take place as we wage the war on terrorism."

Crucial to this effort is developing a system that places the right people in the right places in government at the right moment. The nation critically needs civilian policymakers who can manage change and deal with the here and now.

This monograph will examine the development of career civilian leaders for strategic decisionmaking in the national security policy process. Such development must include the recruitment of high-quality personnel, experiential learning through a series of positions of increasing responsibility, training for specific tasks or missions, and continuous education that considers both policy and process. Consequently, it requires people who are not only substantively qualified and knowledgeable of policy issues, but also possessed of the leadership abilities to direct large complex organizations.

This monograph will first consider existing efforts in the Office of the Secretary of Defense (OSD), State Department, and Central Intelligence Agency (CIA) and then make appropriate recommendations for each. It will further consider what changes must be made to existing personnel management systems and development programs to encourage the creation of an effective cadre of civilian "national security" professionals for the policy process. Such recommendations may be applicable to other executive agencies as well. These three departments were selected since they are in many ways those with a clear traditional role in the development of foreign and defense policy. Clearly, there are additional considerations with respect to current and growing requirements for those with technical expertise, human resource management, finance/comptroller skills, etc. The development of personnel with such talents for these three agencies will not be the subject of this monograph.

Some critics might observe from the outset that the nation is at war and can ill-afford reorganizations or changes at this critical moment. The sad tragedy that has been the Iraq War would suggest otherwise. It became clear almost immediately following the invasion in 2003 that fundamental errors had been made in intelligence and policy analysis. From the very beginning the United States not only required additional troops for the occupation of Iraq but also enhanced civilian leadership and capacity to reconstruct Iraqi society. Without both these components, efforts to forestall the ensuing chaos as well as the resultant insurgency were doomed to failure.

Poor civilian leadership and mismanagement have been clearly documented in numerous studies, books, reports, and articles. Official reports provided by Stuart W. Bowen, Jr., Special Inspector General for Iraq Reconstruction (SIGIR), are particularly critical of American efforts in Iraq. In early 2007, SIGIR reported that despite nearly $108 billion budgeted for the reconstruction of Iraq since 2003, the country's electricity output and oil production were still below prewar levels. Stocks of gasoline and kerosene had actually plummeted to their lowest levels in at least 2 years. Consequently, Mr. Bowen testified before the Senate Judiciary Committee in March 2007 that his office planned to "aggressively pursue" the suspension and prosecution of contractors who are determined to have engaged in fraudulent contracting activities in Iraq. He further observed that the failure of the American-financed reconstruction program in Iraq threatened to be repeated elsewhere unless structural changes were made in the U.S. Government. Mr. Bowen compared his recommendations to the

Congress as not dissimilar to proposals made in the 1980s that resulted in legislation strengthening the Joint Chiefs of Staff.

Prior to this, the Iraq Study Group (ISG) noted in its comprehensive report in late 2006 that "civilian agencies also have little experience with complex overseas interventions to restore and maintain order—stability operations—outside of the normal embassy setting." The ISG described the mission in Iraq as "unfamiliar and dangerous." As a result, the report observed that the United States had great difficulty filling civilian assignments in Iraq with sufficient qualified personnel. The ISG recommended that the constituent agencies (State, Defense, the U.S. Agency for International Development [USAID], Treasury, Justice, Intelligence community, etc.) train for and conduct joint operations across agency boundaries. It further suggested that the State Department expand its efforts to train personnel to carry out civilian tasks associated with such complex stability operations, concluding that a Foreign Service Reserve Corps with personnel and expertise to provide surge capacity for such operations be established. This effort should provide a model for other civilian agencies to include Treasury, Justice, and Agriculture. Such ideas, however, were hardly new. They had been recommended a year or more prior to the release of the ISG report by leading government experts and officials.

As American patience wears thin over the failure to achieve progress in Iraq the argument might be presented that this venture has been a tragic aberration. Once the United States withdraws from Iraq, it can simply avoid future efforts to rebuild societies torn apart by conflict. Unfortunately, this global conflict will not allow us that luxury. We are confronted by an enemy who would replace secular governments with theocratic regimes hostile to our national interests and values. Their strategy amounts to "a global series of insurgencies, competing for the right to govern" in many predominantly Muslim nations around the globe. State collapse will continue to challenge the national interests of the United States and its allies for decades to come. If we are to prevail, we must mobilize and synchronize all elements of our national power—diplomatic, military, economic, social, and informational—

to confront these new and extremely dangerous adversaries. The key actions required in a counterinsurgency involve "work we associate with civilian skill sets and even agencies—but the uniformed military is often placed in the position of having to undertake such activities." Consequently, a rebalancing of roles between military and civilian leaders is required. Regardless of what the final outcome is in Iraq, that outcome may not be our past so much as our future. This new security environment requires better qualified civilian leaders to think in different patterns in order to accomplish these daunting tasks.

Terms

Understanding certain assumptions is crucial to this analysis. First, some observers may take exception to the distinction between the words "training" and "education." They may argue that they are synonymous, as we frequently use them interchangeably. They are *not* the same, there being a significant denotative difference. While training is more concerned with teaching *what* to think and what the *answers* ought to be, education is all about teaching *how* to think and what the *questions* ought to be: "Training is focused on the development and performance of specific tasks or skills, and education is oriented toward more generalized and abstract knowledge that may or may not be tied to specific tasks or action." Training is most frequently used when the goal is to prepare an individual or an organization to execute specified tasks. It often includes repetition of tasks, not unlike an athletic team learning to execute plays. Finally, it is normally the preferred method of learning when the goal is to perform operations in which success, failure, and completion can be clearly measured. Education has more to do with how to think about problems and how to deal with those things that may not lend themselves to categorical solutions. It becomes a matter of intellect, thought, indirect leadership, advice, and consensus building.

Second, we must also differentiate between "leadership" and "management." *Management is about coping with complexity*. It is a response to a significant development of the 20th century, namely, the emer-gence of large, complex organizations. Good management brings order to what would otherwise be chaos. *Leadership, by contrast, is about coping with change.* An expert in human development once wisely observed, "If you don't like change, you will like irrelevancy even less." American business recognized this phenomenon as competition in the market and volatility in business cycles became more intensive and jarring. Doing the same thing only slightly better was no longer good enough. *Management* remains important for the day-to-day success of any organization, focusing as it does on such issues as planning/budgeting, organizing/staffing, and controlling/problem solving. By contrast, *leadership* begins with setting directions, aligning people, and motivating them to achieve success. The successful development of government policy for the war on terrorism is wholly dependent upon developing leaders of substance at all levels of executive agencies. They must be able balance the pressing requirements of management with the critical need to provide leadership for their organizations and the collective effort.

These expanding requirements for improved leadership and management preceded 9/11, and remain an integral part of dealing with the rapid pace of change. In his widely acclaimed book, *The Lexus and the Olive Tree,* Thomas Friedman described the importance of change in the international system along with the corresponding demands placed on both organizations and individuals. He argued that "Globalization" had replaced the Cold War as the new defining international system. But "the globalization system, unlike the Cold War system, is not frozen, but a dynamic ongoing process." Friedman observed that "if the Cold War were a sport, it would be sumo wrestling." Quoting Professor Michael Mandelbaum, he continued: "It would be two big fat guys in a ring, with all sorts of posturing and rituals and stomping of feet, but actually very little contact, until the end of the match, when there is a brief moment of shoving and the loser gets pushed out of the ring, but nobody gets killed." Globalization, by contrast, "would be the 100meter dash, over and over and over. And no matter how many times you win, you have to race again the next day. And if you lose by just one-hundredth of a second, it can be as if you lost by an hour."

In this new environment, any program that places "the right people, in the right place, at the right time" must acknowledge that it seeks to develop policy substance as well as management and leadership in its workforce to confront the changes engendered by globalization and the new security environment. If the policy process is to be improved, it must have well-qualified policymakers who understand the issues. Many must also develop into leaders as they move through their careers. These future leaders must be able to set goals, inspire performance, and monitor progress for the success of their organizations and the overall process.

HISTORICAL BACKGROUND

Problems with the recruitment, retention, and development of individuals for the national security process are not new. The last 20 years are replete with studies conducted by leading American policymakers, think tanks, U.S. Government Accounting Office (USGAO) Reports, Congressionally-directed studies (such as *The 9/11 Commission Report*), and even presidential directives that focused either on a single government agency (the most studied appears to be the Department of Defense [DoD]), the interagency process, and government service in general. For example, the National Commission on the Public Service was formed in 1987 following a symposium entitled, "A National Public Service for the Year 2000." The symposium concluded that a "quiet crisis" existed in government. Too many of the nation's best senior executives were prepared to leave government, and not enough of its most talented young people were prepared to join.

The commission, headed by former Federal Reserve Board Chairman Paul Volcker, included 36 distinguished Americans including former presidents, senators, congressmen, cabinet-level officials, corporate executives, university presidents, and leaders of major nonprofit organizations. Former Secretary of Defense Donald Rumsfeld served as a member of this commission. The commission uncovered wide dissatisfaction among those in senior and mid-level positions of government. For example, only 13 percent of the senior executives interviewed by USGAO as part of the effort said they would recommend that young people start their careers in government. The report embraced three themes that shaped its findings— leadership, talent, and performance. It recommended making more room at senior levels of departments for career executives, enhancing efforts to recruit quality young people, and more effective executive development. In this last area the report observed, ... the education of public servants must not end upon appointment to the civil service. Government must invest more in its executive development programs and develop stronger partnerships with America's colleges and universities.

It further recommended increases in compensation and a reduction in presidential political appointees by 1,000 in order to create room for more career civilians to advance.

In May 1997, the Clinton administration issued Presidential Decision Directive (PDD) 56. The directive acknowledged that the federal government requires the capacity to prepare agency officials for the responsibilities they will be expected to assume in planning and managing agency efforts for complex contingency operations. It further noted the need to create a "cadre of professionals" familiar with this integrated planning process to improve the government's ability to manage future such operations. It was issued at a time when the Dayton peace enforcement mission in Bosnia that had been predicted to last 1 year had become an open-ended operation with no end in sight, and when many in the Clinton administration were still feeling the effects of the bitter lessons from the Somalia.

PDD 56 directed the State Department, Defense Department, and the National Security Council to work with the "appropriate U.S. government educational institutions—including the National Defense University, the National Foreign Affairs Training Centre, and the U.S. Army War College—to develop and conduct an interagency training program." It further directed that this training effort be held at least annually and focus on the development of mid-level managers (Deputy Assistant Secretary level) in the preparation and implementation of political/military plans for complex contingency operations.

A. B. Technologies reported in a study prepared for the Joint Chiefs of Staff that "the spirit and intent of PDD 56 directed training is not being followed" and that as a whole the directive was not implemented.

The need for a cadre of professionals to deal with the emerging security environment was reiterated in December 1997 with the issuance of the National Defense Panel Report. This report recommended the creation of "an interagency cadre of professionals, including civilian and military officers, whose purpose would be to staff key positions in the national security structures." The panel argued that this cadre should be similar in spirit to the "joint" products envisioned by the 1986 Goldwater–Nichols Act. Their report made the following specific recommendations:

- create personnel management systems to provide greater attention to the education, development, and career development of these personnel,
- identify "interagency" slots within the national security community including domestic agencies that have foreign affairs responsibilities (e.g., Justice, Commerce, and Energy) which are staffed by this interagency cadre, and
- establish a national security curriculum, combining course work at the National Defense University and National Foreign Affairs Training Centre.

In 1999 the Clinton administration convened the Panel on Civic Trust and Responsibility. This group prepared a report entitled "A Government to Trust and Respect" that, sad to say, identified many of the same problems that had been highlighted 10 years before.

The panel reported that in 1960 20 percent of law school graduates nationwide worked for the Federal Government at some point during their first 10 years of employment, with 35-40 percent of those having received a Masters in Public Administration (MPA). At roughly the same time, between 1,200 and 1,500 young Americans applied for the 39 positions available as part of the White House Fellows Program. By 1999, however, there were only 300 applicants for White House fellowships. Schools of Public Administration were sending percentages of their graduates in the low teens to Washington, and the law schools were sending only about 13 percent.

The report found that Americans remained proud of their country, but they were deeply concerned and distrustful of their government. Furthermore, the public was not willing to invest significantly higher levels of trust and confidence in the government until they perceived improvements in the way decisions were made. The study urged improvements in the quality of public officials to be achieved through greater leadership appeals in behalf of public service with the hope of attracting the "best and the brightest." It further recommended higher standards for government performance, improvements in the technological tools provided government civilians, and formation of public-private partnerships for enhancing government performance.

At nearly the same moment, Paul Light, Director of the Brookings Governmental Studies program, presented his report entitled, "The New Public Service" (1999). The Light Study argued that a flexible range of government, private, and non-profit opportunities had begun to replace traditional government-centered public service. In 1974, for example, 76 percent of the graduates of major public administration or public policy graduates schools took their first jobs in the government sector; 11 percent took private sector jobs; and 12 percent went to nonprofit organizations.

In 1993, 49 percent went to government positions; 23 percent went to the private sector; and 24 percent to non-profits. These numbers continued to drop between 1993 and 1999. While there is a multitude of reasons for this phenomenon, Light concluded that three were paramount: (1) recent graduates believed they had a better chance to help people in the private sector or working in non-profit organizations; (2) they also believed the private and non-profit sectors managed money more wisely than government; and (3) these graduates believed their opportunities for professional advancement and personal growth and skill development were far better in the non-public sector work place.

Light observed that the public servant of the 21st century wants and expects to change jobs and sectors frequently. Young people are not solely focused on job security and salary but rather on getting a job with a tangible impact. Overall, he concluded that the government system falls short in recruiting, training, and management. The study recommended that the government:

- *Declare a human capital crisis,* recognizing it is in a talent war with the other sectors;
- *Be more aggressive in recruiting* mid-and upper-level positions from the outside;
- *Recognize that recruitment must be followed* with challenging work and the opportunity for growth.

This effort also uncovered two interesting demographic phenomena in the civilian government workforce. First, Light concluded that the career civil service faced the potential for a steady stream of retirements at a rapid rate through 2014. A managing partner of the Andersen Consulting firm quoted by Light described this situation as a "human-capital time-bomb ticking." For example, approximately 40 percent of the career Senior Executive Service (SES) force became eligible for early or regular retirement by 2003, and almost 70 percent qualified by 2006. In DoD the figures were 64 percent already eligible, and 74 percent eligible in 2005. Second, the federal hierarchy was shifting from a traditional bureaucratic pyramid into an ellipse or diamond. The year 1998 marked the first time in history that the number of middle-level federal employees outnumbered the lower-level employees. A decade ago there were 1.2 lower-level employees (General Schedule 1-10) for each middle-level employee (General Schedule 11-15). Only a year later, the lower-level number had dropped to 0.93 for every middle-level position. If this trend continues, the federal government's last front-line employee will retire sometime in 2030, with his or her job having been contracted out or downsized forever. Obviously, these changes will have serious impacts on the education and development of both senior policymakers and civilian agencies in the future.

In 2000 two reports focused solely on this issue in DoD. The first was the Defense Science Board report on the Task Force on Human Resources Strategy of that year. It noted a "growing shortage of managers in place to fill career positions that... become available as more than half of the civilian workforce becomes eligible to retire in the next 5 years." The report concluded with the following critical issues for the civilian workforce in the DoD:

Insufficient number of properly trained candidates in the pipeline, an aging workforce with little turnover, limited professional development opportunities, and weak compensation and incentive systems for SES and career civil service.

- *Lack of a continuing professional development program* for most career civilian employees.
- *Need for an integrated personnel management plan* that includes planning for an increased use of personnel from the private sector.
- *Continuing problems with the confirmation cycle, inadequate compensation, financial disclosure rules, and post-employment restrictions,* all tending to create a limited, less qualified applicant pool.

The second report in 2000 was that of the USGAO titled "Human Capital: Strategic Approach Should Guide DoD Civilian Workforce Management." This report noted that strategic human capital planning has been a weak link in the management of federal departments and agencies. It further concluded that:

High performance organizations in the public and private sector have come to recognize that people are an organization's key assets. It is through the talents and dedicated work of staff that missions get accomplished.

The USGAO report further observed that DoD was like other federal departments and agencies that are required to deal with the myriad social, economic, and technological changes that have become *de rigueur* in 21st century America. This report was particularly relevant in that it encompassed over 700,000 civilians or 37 percent of all nonpostal civilian federal workers.

Furthermore, DoD had also largely been the "bill payer" for government-wide civilian reductions since 1989. Between 1989 and 1999, DoD reduced its civilian workforce by about 400,000 positions, from approximately 1,117,000 to 714,000, a 36 percent reduction. Reductions continued until early 2005, totaling 41 percent. As a result, the DoD civilian workforce aged from 41.6 to 45.8 years, leaving fewer employees today in their 20s and 30s. This raises serious questions about the department's ability to replace retirees in the future of whom (as previously mentioned) 74 percent had reached retirement eligibility by 2005. For example, employment in the youngest age groups, under-31 and 31-to-40, declined 76 percent and 51 percent, respectively, during the period 1989 to 1999. Still, the largest reductions occurred in clerical positions and blue-collar wage grades while the smallest reductions (8 percent) were in the professional grades GS-9 through SES. As a result, the professional force encompasses a higher percentage of the workforce and in general is better educated. In many ways, the civilian workforce in executive departments of the federal government has evolved over the past several decades from one qualified by early "training" to one needing "educational development" today.

Finally, this report pointed out serious issues with the actual conduct of personnel reductions. First, it discovered that civilian force reductions (unlike those on the military side) were less oriented toward shaping the makeup of the workforce in the future. Little attention was paid to maintaining a balance of skills needed to maintain in-house capabilities as part of the defense industrial base. Second, little concern was paid to the fact that the resulting workforce would be significantly older and thus more retirement eligible.

Third, many senior officials voiced concerns that the reductions had adverse effects upon the morale of the residual workforce. They observed that in many cases these changes resulted in limited career development opportunities, reduced chances for promotion, job insecurity, and longer working hours.

The USGAO report concluded that a five-part framework is essential if DoD is to create an effective human capital management process. The five parts are as follows:

- *Strategic planning*—Establish the agency's mission, vision for the future, core values, goals, and strategies.
- *Organizational alignment*—Integrate human capital strategies with the agency's core business practices.

- *Leadership*—Foster a committed leadership team and provide reasonable continuity through succession planning.
- *Talent*—Recruit, hire, develop, and retain employees with the skills needed for mission accomplishment.
- *Performance culture*—Enable and motivate performance while ensuring accountability and fairness for all employees.

The USGAO report further concluded that a strategy for human management must include "an effective approach to 'growing leaders'—identifying employees with leadership promise and providing them with a variety of professional development and learning opportunities designed to pass along the values and competencies that the agency has identified as important to its leaders."

Since 1990 the USGAO has also periodically reported to Congress on operations across the entire federal government that it identified as being at "high risk." This effort is supported by the Senate Committee on Governmental Affairs and the House Committee on Government Reform. It has brought a much needed focus to problems that were perceived as impeding effective government and wasting money. In responses to recommendations from these reports, Congress has enacted a series of government-wide reforms to strengthen financial management, improve information technology practices, and instill a more results-oriented government.

The "high risk" report that was issued in January 2001 at the start of the new Bush administration included a section entitled "Strategic Human Capital Management: A Government-wide High Risk Area." This report noted that "the federal government has often acted as if people were costs to be cut rather than assets to be valued," arguing that the federal government's human capital strategies were not adequate to meet the emerging needs of the nation. As a result, the USGAO warned that the inattention to human management strategies had created a government-wide risk that was fundamental to the federal government's ability to function effectively. This risk had arisen for a number of reasons. First, the dramatic downsizing of the federal government that had occurred during the 1990s was set in motion without sufficient planning for the overall effect on individual agencies' performance capacity. Second, during this time agencies attempted to save on workforce-related costs by reducing investments in other human capital investments such as training and professional development. This occurred despite the fact that these programs were critical if their smaller workforces were to compensate for institutional losses in skills and experience.

The 2001 "high risk" update further argued that the inadequate human capital strategies would have serious future implications in a number of ways. Personnel turnover at top management positions would complicate efforts to transition to modern performance management techniques. The report observed that 45 percent of career SES members across all agencies and departments of the federal government were projected to retire by fiscal year 2005. An additional 26 percent would become retirement-eligible by that time but were expected to remain in their existing positions. This would obstruct attempts to invest in training and development of younger rising personnel to meet the specific needs of individual agencies.

This report highlighted as a particularly critical need that of focusing better on training personnel in contract management. It argued that agencies must have more personnel properly trained in contract management particularly "where agencies must... oversee the quality, cost, and timeliness of products and services delivered by third parties." This point was all too prescient in view of the revelations concerning problems that have bedeviled the American use of contractors during recovery/reconstruction operations in Iraq.

The Commission on National Security for the 21st Century—more commonly known as the Hart-Rudman Commission after its two chairs, former Senators Gary Hart and Warren Rudman—was created in 1998 to conduct a comprehensive review of national security for the newly emerging era. Enjoying the support of the Congress and White House, it was originally chartered by the Secretary of Defense to conduct what was called "the most comprehensive review of American security since the National

Security Act of 1947." This endeavor resulted in three reports by the spring of 2001.

The first, *New World Coming: American Security in the 21st Century,* focused on the emerging global security environment for the first 25 years of the new century.

The second, *Seeking a National Strategy: A Concert for Preserving Security and Promoting Freedom,* outlined a new national security strategy that reflected emerging challenges. The final report, *Roadmap for National Security: Imperatives for Change,* offered a prescription for a significant overhaul of the structure and processes of the American national security establishment.

This final report by the Hart-Rudman Commission noted a critical need for reform within the government personnel system, echoing many of the findings of the studies previously mentioned. For example, the Hart-Rudman commission observed that the United States was "on the brink of an unprecedented crisis of competence in government." This was due in large measure to problems that had been identified by the National Commission on the Public Service in 1987, i.e., recruiting, developing, and retaining America's most promising talent. While specific recommendations with respect to the State Department, OSD, and the CIA will be discussed in more detail in subsequent sections, it is important to note here the commission's emphatic conclusion:

If we allow the human resources of government to continue to decay, none of the reforms proposed by this or any other national security commission will produce their intended results.

The Hart-Rudman Commission report was significant for several reasons. First, it remains the most recent comprehensive review of the federal government, long-term threats, and strategy. Second, the report was amazingly prescient in many important respects. The findings of this report and its recommendations thus remain salient despite the fact that the report was completed before the terrorist attacks of 9/11.

Also at the time of the arrival of the Bush administration in January 2001, Dr. Robert Moffit of the Heritage Foundation produced a study entitled "Taking Charge of Federal Personnel," which examined the balance between federal employees, political appointees, and contractors. Many regard this study as the blueprint for the approach to personnel management adopted by the newly arrived administration of President Bush. Moffit argued that those who seek to reform government "have little appreciation for the immense power and political sophistication of the federal employee network and its allies and the intensity of its resistance to serious change." Moffit argued that his analysis of past efforts to improve the federal bureaucracy demonstrated that a President must (1) make liberal use of his power of appointments and do so in a timely fashion; (2) use only political appointees for implementing the President's policies and for making all key management decisions; (3) provide a clear rationale for any reductions in the size of the federal work force and work to reform the benefits program provided to federal employees; (4) use the Civil Service Reform Act to improve accountability; and (5) make every effort to use good management and contract out government services to save money.

Critics have argued that the report viewed the government bureaucracy as an obstacle to the administration's new agenda. The report makes no recommendations with respect to improving the career civilian workforce for executive positions. It clearly argues for "smaller government" and use of the private sector to provide many of the services and expertise that had traditionally been part of the career civil service in the federal government. Moffit further recommended that party loyalty should take precedence over expertise when selecting officials.

Clearly many of the ideas argued in the report were adopted by the Bush administration such as reform of the civilian personnel system in DoD. There is no doubt this study served to encourage the new administration to adopt a dramatic increase in outsourcing and contracting to reduce costs while providing the government with outside expertise. These measures were accomplished in many cases while reducing the overall number of civil servants. As a result, government contracts have soared during the Bush administration to about $400 billion in 2006 from $207 billion in 2000. An analysis prepared by the *New York Times* suggests that fewer than half of all contract actions are now subject to full and open competition. In 2005, 48 percent were competitive, down from 79 percent in 2001. Executive agencies, according to the *Times*, are unable to seek low prices, supervise contractors, and intervene when work goes off course because the number of government workers overseeing contracts has remained constant or been reduced, while contract spending has skyrocketed.

These problems were illustrated in October 2007 by a special audit of State Department contracts with DynCorps for private security guards conducted by the Special Inspector General for Iraq (SIGIR). The audit reported that until early 2007 the State Department had only two government contracting officers to oversee contracted work by as many as 700 DynCorps employees. The SIGIR report stated that this shortage resulted in "an environment vulnerable to waste and fraud." Stuart Bowen, Chief of SIGIR, observed during an interview that "when you put two people on the ground to manage a billion dollars, that's pretty weak."

Some observers believe that the trend towards increased use of contractors has resulted in their having too great a voice in the actual determination of policy. The Acquisition Advisory Panel appointed by the Congress and White House in late 2006 reported that this trend "poses a threat to the government's long-term ability to perform its mission" and could over time "undermine the integrity of the government's decisionmaking." This conclusion was echoed by David Walker, Comptroller General of the United States. He observed that the problem ultimately was a matter of loyalty—"the duty of loyalty to the greater good—the duty of loyalty to the collective best interest of all rather than the interests of a few. [Contracting] companies have duties of loyalty to their shareholders, not the country."

Interest in government human capital adjustments became more apparent in the aftermath of 9/11. The National Commission on Terrorist Attacks Upon the United States (often referred to as *The 9/11 Commission Report*) observed that the federal government's interagency process was unable to adapt how it manages problems to the new challenges of the 21st century, explaining that:

The agencies are like a set of specialists in a hospital, each ordering tests, looking for symptoms, and prescribing medications. What is missing is the attending physician who makes sure they work as a team.

The report charged that a missing element contributing to the 9/11 disaster was effective management of transnational operations.

Even prior to the final release of *The 9/11 Commission Report,* the Centre for Public Service at the Brookings Institution established its National Commission on the Public Service. The Commission was composed of Chairman Paul A. Volcker and 10 distinguished Commissioners. They included former Comptroller General of the United States Charles Bowsher; former U.S. Senator Bill Bradley; former Secretary of Defense Frank Carlucci; former White House Chief of Staff Kenneth Duberstein; former Office of Personnel Management Director Connie Horner; former Office of Management and Budget Director Franklin Raines; former head of the New York Metropolitan Transit Authority Richard Ravitch; former Treasury Secretary Robert Rubin; former Secretary of Health and Human Services Donna Shalala; and former Congressman Vin Weber. Their report, *Urgent Business for America: Revitalizing the Federal Government for the 21st Century,* was issued in January 2003. The Commission underscored the urgent warnings contained in the Hart-Rudman Commission Report, calling for immediate action in a number of areas. These included improvements in federal personnel management practices and a concerted effort to recruit and retain employees for the federal government. It further called for (1) reform of the presidential appointment process to include a reduction in the overall number of Executive Branch political appointees; and (2) careful examination of competitive outsourcing practices to ensure they did not undermine core competencies of the government.

That same year USGAO conducted a study of how and whether agencies in four countries—Canada, Australia, New Zealand, and the United Kingdom— are adopting a strategic approach to managing the succession of career civilian senior executives and other public servants who have critical skills. This study, entitled *Human Capital: Insights from Other Countries Succession Planning and Management Initiatives*, was delivered to Congress in September 2003. The study observed that: leading public organizations here and abroad recognize that a more strategic approach to managing human capital should be the centerpiece of any serious change management initiative to transform the cultures of government agencies.

It concluded that several key practices were used by agencies in these nations to deal with succession issues and overall human capital management. They included (1) ensuring that the top leadership of the agency or department actively participates in planning for succession and other management initiatives; (2) linking this effort to the organization's overall strategic planning; (3) identifying talent (particularly with critical skills) at multiple levels in the organization and early in employees' careers; and (4) emphasizing developmental assignments in addition to formal training. Obviously, these efforts in democratic nations outside the United States are consistent with many of the recommendations contained in the various studies and analyses commented upon above, all of which are focused on the goal of protecting and enhancing organizational capacity.

In the summer of 2004, the RAND Corporation published a broad examination of the career development strategies of three U.S. employment sectors—government, private corporations, and not-for-profit organizations. It concluded that "America's ability to shape the world this century will depend on the quality of its leaders," but that the nation was producing too few future leaders with sufficient depth and broad international experience. The two authors, Gregory Treverton and Tora Bikson, conducted over 135 interviews of leaders in all three sectors. They observed that while all three sectors had major problems, the federal government was the most striking in its failure to address practices that were contrary to attracting and developing future leaders. The report did find, however, that a new sense of urgency had emerged in the aftermath of 9/11, and that young people were attracted by the opportunity to serve.

Treverton and Bikson concluded their study with several recommendations, many of which echo those made by previous such studies and reports. They include (1) making the hiring process quicker and more transparent; (2) requiring individuals to serve rotational assignments in other government agencies as a requirement for promotion; (3) facilitating temporary movement of officials from one department to another as required; (4) developing mechanisms for the lateral entry from other sectors (business or nonprofits) to fill mid-career positions; (5) expand targeted fellowship programs particularly at the graduate level to nurture talent; and (6) reserve some number of senior positions (particularly at the deputy assistant secretary level) for career civil servants to encourage retention.

In late 2005 the federal government launched "Project Horizon," designed to bring together U.S. Government senior executives from agencies with global responsibility and the National Security Council (NSC) staff to explore ways to enhance interagency coordination. This effort, which embraced nearly every department and agency of the federal government, was funded/managed by the participants with active involvement from the NSC. The Executive Summary of its initial progress report, released in the summer of 2006, states that the department participants identified the building of "a more flexible and deployable corps of U.S. Government professionals with deep interagency experience and global affairs expertise" as critical to the government's ability to deal effectively with the current operational environment. The report concludes with 10 discrete interagency capabilities needed to deal with anticipated challenges and opportunities. Two are particularly relevant to this monograph. First, a revised set of human resource policies, procedures, and incentive structures was needed to facilitate the rapid assembly of capable, experienced, and integrated personnel. These changes were essential to create a "global affairs career path" that would include required interagency rotations/training, formal education, and provisions for flexible assignments and deployments.

Second, a network of global affairs training institutions was needed, one that mutually leveraged member curricular offerings to create an enhanced curriculum for the development of global affairs professionals. Project Horizon is now exploring possibilities for institutionalizing appropriate curricular offerings as found through quarterly meetings of an interagency strategic planning group (ISPG).

Obviously, this brief review of studies, reports, directives, etc. with respect to recruiting, retention, and development of career civil servants for the national security process over the past 20 years is not comprehensive.

There are many other studies that focus on an individual agency or department, or on an aspect of the problem. Still the 15 documents treated here have many points in common. First, they show that problems associated with the recruiting, retention, and development of the "best and the brightest" for a career as a civilian in the national security process are not new.

Second, they demonstrate that this problem has taken on an increasing urgency in the last decade and in particular in the aftermath of the attacks of 9/11. Third, many of the recommendations converge, e.g., greater opportunities for development, lateral entry, required rotational assignments, etc. Finally, this litany of negative reports is sad testimony to the federal government's refusal or inability to adequately confront these issues despite their growing importance.

A TALE OF THREE AGENCIES

The following three subsections examine how three agencies—State, OSD, and CIA—currently develop career civilian leaders for participation in the national security decisionmaking process and then makes specific recommendations that apply to each, respectively. As previously suggested, such development must include the recruitment of quality personnel, experiential learning through a series of positions of increasing responsibility, training for specific tasks or missions, and continuous education that considers both policy and process. But if change characterizes the environment that descended upon America after 9/11, do the cultures of these three organizations facilitate or retard change and growth? To answer this question, in the sections that follow we shall undertake a compact review of each of their cultures with respect to the professional development of its members.

"Organizational culture" is a powerful force within any organization or group. It is concerned with group norms or traditional ways of behaving that any set of people develops over time. Organizations, like people, have a past as well as a future.

Such group norms are not solely recurring behavior patterns that can be observed by outsiders, but are those actions, attitudes, and assumptions that are unconsciously reinforced by everybody in the organization.

Frequently these accepted actions might even be counter to what is printed as organizational policy. Something is "cultural" when, if a member does not behave in the normal manner, the others (or the organization itself) automatically nudge him or her back towards the accepted ways of doing things. As a result, "culture" will triumph over "planning" every time. Any effort focused on organizational growth that fails to consider culture is doomed from the outset. Clearly, the CIA, OSD, and State reflect this phenomenon; consequently, any improvement must include appropriate alteration of their respective culture, or what we might think of as group norms.

Indicative of these group norms was a survey of members of the SES conducted in August 1999 at roughly the same time as the Hart-Rudman Commission deliberations. This survey was sent to all Senior Executive Servants throughout the federal government, numbering over 6,500. Approximately 2,500 (40 percent) responded. Among the significant findings:

- Over 75 percent oversaw a budget in excess of $1 million.
- Two out of three reported rewarding teamwork, creativity, and innovation.
- Most believed creativity and innovation were rewarded though subordinates did not share this belief.
- The most important core qualifications for them were leadership, communications, focus on results, leading change, and technical competence.
- Many believed that recruiting more leaders outside the Federal Government for career SES positions would improve the SES.

- Over half believed a rotation assignment to another agency would be a positive developmental experience, but only 9 percent had been afforded the opportunity.
- Most had to do any personal development on their own time as it was not offered as part of their formal development.

The wars in Afghanistan and Iraq have placed new requirements on executive agencies to play a role in post-conflict resolution that many were ill-prepared for. In many ways, these conflicts have forced the leaders in these agencies to confront fundamental aspects of their organizational culture. In the aftermath of the attacks of 9/11, many senior officials have pointed to the difficulty of getting executive agencies to adopt a war mentality, an indication of both the problem and power of organizational culture. Former Defense Secretary Rumsfeld was repeatedly quoted as believing that the majority of the federal government was not at war. He also took the view that the demands placed upon these agencies were frequently beyond what they had been trained, organized, and equipped to accomplish.

Department of State

It is a badge of honor among Foreign Service Officers to avoid any education once they join the department.

A Senior Foreign Service Officer

The Department of State has perhaps the most unique culture of the three agencies in several ways. First, Foreign Service Officers (FSOs) normally enter the organization with a graduate degree and frequently with some familiarity in foreign language. Most are nearly 30 years of age and frequently have already had a previous career. Consequently, they are normally somewhat older than their colleagues entering OSD and CIA. Second, the values of the institution reveal much about its culture. The State Department's core values include loyalty to the United States, character that exhibits the highest ethical standards, and excellence in service. All of these underscore the State Department's representational function abroad and requirement to provide assistance to Americans and businesses abroad. This representative function leaves little time for development of a core competency for the organization.

FSOs view themselves as focused on performing the various functions required at an embassy or developing policy. The majority of FSOs serve a significant portion of their career in a core area such as political officer, economics, consular services, information management, etc. Unlike the military that "trains" and "prepares for operations," FSOs view themselves as continually conducting generic diplomatic functions week after week. Consequently, long-term planning is rarely put forth as a core competency of the organization.

Finally, the remaining organizational values emphasize accountability/individual responsibility and a sense of community that includes teamwork and the customer-service perspective, both of which are essential to the functioning of an embassy. As a result, the State Department has largely eschewed the tendency to focus the development of its officers on a particular regional background but rather sought "generalists" who are fungible and thus deployable worldwide. Most FSOs measure the ultimate success of their respective career by whether they are ultimately selected for an ambassadorial position. This perspective has traditionally discouraged specialization in a particular region or culture since the pool of prospective ambassadorial positions remains worldwide in scope.

A strong difference exists, however, between the denizens of "Foggy Bottom" in Washington and those serving in overseas assignments. The fact that the latter venue is the clear preference of the majority of FSOs reflects in many ways the historical ethos of the organization. Moreover, promotions in the organization seem to favor those who achieve their success overseas. Consequently, most FSOs seek to stay in regional bureaus or abroad and avoid functional agencies (Bureau of Intelligence and Research, arms control, legislative affairs, etc.) despite the fact that these organizations are not only critical to the success of the institution but also provide valuable experiential learning opportunities. This status difference may also result in bifurcation within the organization. For example, the economics section of State may be more closely aligned with Treasury or the Office of the Trade Representative on a particular issue than with the regional bureaus. This organizational tendency often results in poor integration of goals between regional and functional policies, and a lack of sound management, accountability, and leadership.

Another essential value of the culture is that individual performance trumps group effort by a division or directorate. Recognition is often the derivative of having your "name on the byline" of an important cable to Washington. Consequently, rotation assignments outside State are acceptable but *not* truly encouraged, particularly as an individual becomes more senior in rank. Most believe such assignments are ill-advised as it rarely affords them sufficient recognition within State to undergird subsequent promotions. This belief is also due in part to the long narrative format for State Department evaluations and a corresponding fear that few outside the culture will fully understand it. The department has begun an effort to coordinate many of its personnel policies with USAID, a major component of State, and encourage rotations between the two, but it remains to be seen whether this move will be truly embraced by the organization.

Finally, the FSO community has been the most successful of the three organizations in ensuring that a number of its career diplomats are placed in Assistant Secretary or even Undersecretary positions as new administrations arrive. There was even a grievance leveled by the FSO association against an administration when a particular position that had been traditionally held by an FSO was given to a political appointee. Ultimately, the decision was reversed. State has also occasionally been successful in placing career FSOs in senior positions in OSD that had normally been held by political appointees, but there have been few, if any, examples of a career OSD person being offered a senior position at State.

From the overall standpoint of recruiting, retention, and culture, the Hart-Rudman Commission observed in 2001 that the State Department, "in particular, is a crippled institution, starved for resources by Congress because of inadequacies, and thereby weakened further." The commission went on to state that only if these internal weaknesses were cured, would State become an effective leader in the formulation and conduct of policy. Such cures were critical to securing necessary funding from Congress. This was highlighted in the summer of 2000 when 1,400 Foreign Service personnel (roughly a quarter of the entire FSO corps) attached their names to an Internet protest of their working conditions.

The challenges to the State Department brought about by the conflicts in Iraq and Afghanistan were perhaps greater than to any other organization in the federal government. The Hart-Rudman Commission had suggested even prior to 9/11 that the capacity of the department to support post-conflict resolution efforts had deteriorated and was insufficient to meet an explosion of requirements. One need only consider that in 1950 the budget of the Department of State was roughly half that of DoD. By 2001 it was only 1/20th. During the Vietnam War, USAID had nearly 15,000 employees. By 2001, this number had been reduced to roughly 3,000. As a result, Secretary of Defense Gates has described USAID as essentially an "outsourcing and contracting agency." The total number of FSOs was only 5,000 in 2000. Even prior to 9/11, the number had not increased significantly despite the fact that the number of countries and international institutions requiring diplomatic representation had grown significantly in the years following the end of the Cold War.

This record is particularly stunning if one compares State to DoD. In 2007 the U.S. defense budget accounted for approximately half of total global defense spending, and American armed forces had over 1.5 million uniformed personnel. By comparison, the State Department employed 6,000 FSOs (a 1,000 increase from 2000), while USAID employed 3,000. In other words, by 2007 DoD was about 167 times the size of the State Department (including USAID). As one observer noted, "There are substantially more people employed as musicians in Defense bands than in the entire U.S. Foreign Service." President Bush himself seemed to underscore the pressing need for a greater civilian effort in post-conflict recovery efforts during his State of the Union Address in January 2007. The President expressed his desire to "design and establish a volunteer Civilian Reserve Corps." This corps would function much like military reserves and ease the burden on the military by allowing the government to hire civilians with critical skills to serve on missions abroad. So far, at least, this effort is at best in the embryonic stage, and a full-scale effort is unlikely prior to the end of the Bush administration.

The challenge posed by Iraq for the State Department was underscored in President Bush's "Surge Speech" on January 10, 2007. In his remarks to the nation, the President outlined a new strategy for Iraq that included a 30,000-soldier increase in military forces deployed to Iraq as well as a doubling of Provincial Reconstruction Teams (PRTs) and the better integration of their efforts with brigade combat teams. This PRT increase was proposed despite the fact that maintaining staffing even in existing PRTs in Iraq had been a significant challenge, with frequent turnovers and lengthy vacancies. The results of PRTs have been neither surprising nor impressive. The Initial Benchmark Assessment Report released on July 12, 2007, noted that while the military had been able to achieve the targeted increase in troop deployments by early June, the expansion of the PRT program was still not complete with only about half of the approximately 300 additional PRT personnel having been deployed by that date. The report noted that "the full complement of *civilian surge* personnel will be completed by December 2007" (emphasis added). Some might plausibly argue that taking nearly 1 full year to increase civilian deployments by 300 is hardly a *surge.* In fact, a very senior Pentagon official remarked that he had greater confidence that the Iraqi government would deliver on its promise to provide additional military forces for security in Baghdad than that the State Department would be able to deliver on its planned PRT increase to meet the expanded requirements as outlined in the President's surge strategy.

For a number of years the State Department had been unable to recruit sufficient new FSOs to replace those departing owing to normal attrition. This was due in part to budgetary restrictions. Consequently, by 2002 there were 25 percent fewer people taking the entrance examination than in the mid-1980s. The opportunity to live abroad, learn a foreign language, and develop negotiating skills which had traditionally attracted young people to the Foreign Service were now available in the private sector and many nongovernment organizations (NGOs). These competitor organizations offered higher salaries, lacked the level of austerity or danger often faced by State Department employees, and imposed fewer constraints on two-career families. There was also some indication that attrition itself might be a growing problem. While most Foreign Service entering classes have suffered an attrition rate of 12 to 17 percent by the eighth year of service, two classes in 2000 and 2001 had sustained 23 and 32 percent, respectively, by the same point in their careers. While these results were not conclusive, they were supported by two major studies on departmental talent by McKinsey and Company as well as the Overseas Presence Advisory Panel.

The department's own policies had also been a detriment to attracting and retaining the best personnel. The recruiting process was slow, and candidates frequently waited 2 years from the date of their first written exam until the first day of work. The required oral exam also discouraged many qualified people from applying, particularly if they had a broad range of knowledge as opposed to specific skills. This distinction was compounded by the exam's antiquated "blindfolding" policy whereby the examiners (who determined which applicants were offered positions in the Foreign Service) often knew nothing about the individual's background. While this procedure had the admirable goal of ensuring a level playing field for all applicants, it ran completely counter to the need to recruit the most qualified individuals. As of March 2003, this process had been eliminated for the individual assessment portion of the exam.

Upon assuming his responsibilities as Secretary of State, Colin Powell quickly enunciated his desire to enhance recruitment and the development of FSOs. Secretary Powell observed:

For America... leadership begins and ends with having the best men and women in the Department of State. It is absolutely imperative that on the front lines of freedom, democracy, and open markets we have men and women who are excited about the possibilities and superbly talented in orchestrating and managing the kaleidoscope of changes that colors our todays and brightens our tomorrows.

Consequently, the Department began the "Diplomatic Readiness Initiative" in FY2002. The initiative was a 3-year plan to hire 1,158 staff over and above attrition. It was hoped that this would ensure that the department could respond to crises and emerging priorities, cover gaps, and provide employees appropriate training/development. The program focused on entry-level positions, disallowing lateral entry at higher levels (for example, GS 12-14). An Alternative Examination Program was initiated, allowing applicants (limited to government employees) to advance to the oral examination on the basis of their professional experience.

By 2004 the department had redressed almost the entire personnel deficit of the 1990s and increased diversity and quality of FSOs and specialists. The Department dramatically increased its investment in marketing, expanded outreach efforts, and student programs. As a result, applicants for the Foreign Service examination doubled from about 8,000 in FY 2000 to nearly 20,000 in FY2004. Candidate refusals of job offers from State plummeted from 25 percent in FY2000 to 2 percent in FY2004, while the quality of those hired in terms of academic background and critical skills improved significantly. By 2007 State Department officials proudly announced that, for the second consecutive year, the department had been placed in the top five ideal employers in an annual poll of undergraduates reported by *Business Week*. Still, despite these laudable successes the department was only able to stabilize its overall strength at a total of roughly 5,500 FSOs. It was unable to create a significant surge capability.

Efforts were also made to redress what had been a difficult relationship between the State Department and USAID, while at the same time expanding USAID's capacity to deal with complex international emergencies and post-conflict resolution issues. The administration established the President's Management Agenda to ensure that both organizations maintained well-qualified and well-trained workforces. This included a USAID Development Readiness Initiative to increase surge capability, joint training, and the establishment of formal Department-USAID cross assignments, etc. Still, these remained largely voluntary programs and were never adequately resourced.

In February 2004, Senators Richard Lugar, Joseph Biden, and Chuck Hagel introduced the Stabilization and Reconstruction Civilian Management Act (commonly referred to as the Lugar-Biden Initiative). This legislation sought to establish a more robust civilian capacity to respond quickly and effectively to post-conflict situations as well as complex international emergencies. An Office of the Coordinator for Reconstruction and Stabilization (S/CRS) was created in the Department of State, but its work to improve planning and coordination was largely undermined by a lack of resources that drew criticism from a number of sources.

In response, President Bush signed National Security Presidential Directive 44, titled Management of Interagency Efforts Concerning Stabilization and Reconstruction, in December 2005, but the NSC Deputies Committee did not approve the interagency management system to commence serious planning across the government until March 2007.

Currently, the S/CRS consists of only 70 experts. After 3 years of effort, it has trained 11 active members for deployment and an additional 300 Standby Corps volunteers. The recurrent concern about the shortage of funds for S/CRS was reiterated by the Secretary of State in testimony before the Senate Foreign Relations Committee in February 2007.

In January 2005, Dr. Condoleezza Rice assumed her new role as Secretary of State. She took control of the department as it was continuing to undergo rejuvenation based on the Diplomatic Readiness Initiative created by her predecessor, and she subsequently endorsed this effort. One year later, she outlined her vision for the department, which was described as "transformational diplomacy." Dr. Rice argued that American diplomacy must now seek to "create a more secure, democratic, and prosperous world." To accomplish this grand task, she outlined three management objectives:

- Reposition personnel, particularly from the European epicenter of the Cold War, to dispersed and linguistically/

culturally difficult posts that are home to emerging powers as well as problems.

- Shift the professional focus from a reporting role to managing programs and building institutions with a special emphasis on public diplomacy.
- Expand training, especially in difficult languages, and require senior FSOs to maintain functional expertise in two languages and regions.

The Secretary also announced her commitment to expanding the capabilities of State's S/CRS that had been created by former Secretary Powell and endorsed by the Biden-Lugar Initiative. Following the announcement of the new plan, legislation was enacted transferring $100 million DoD funds for post-conflict operations to S/CRS to empower it for critical situations. Still, as previously noted, many experts argued that at least $400 million or more annually was required if S/CRS was to be adequately resourced. Finally, Secretary Rice used the word "transformational" to describe her belief that "like any great changes of the past, the new efforts we undertake today will not be completed tomorrow." She described this effort as a "work of generations." Consequently, this endeavor was aimed at altering the organizational culture of the department as it had developed throughout the Cold War, obviously not an overnight task.

During the initial year of this effort, Secretary Rice also sought to overhaul the department's hiring process. State Department Director General George Staples stated that under the plan announced in December 2006 the department would use a new "Total Candidate" approach. The goal would be to improve the department's ability to find and compete for the best candidates and improve the overall hiring process. The effort would weigh resumes and references in making hiring selections but would also consider intangibles such as "team-building skills." The written examination for candidates would be retained but shortened and automated.

This effort occurred against the backdrop of expected personnel losses due to retirement and increased competition with the private sector and other government employers for top-quality personnel.

The Partnership for Public Service, a nonprofit organization based in Washington, estimated in 2007 that 60 percent of federal workers would reach retirement age in the next decade. In the State Department it is estimated that 90 percent of senior officers will be eligible for retirement in the next 5 years. Overall, State's civil service cohort has aged from an average of 41 in the 1990s to 47 in FY 2006. Streamlining of the department's recruiting and hiring process was thus timely.

Criticisms of changes in the hiring process were largely based on two arguments. First, many career FSOs openly expressed their concern that the changes would lead to a politicization of the selection process. Some pointed at the earlier expanded use of contractors as a clear attempt to introduce political correctness into the policy process, and they interpreted the latest changes as a complementary effort. Second, even proponents had to agree that the written examination had been a proven predictor of candidate success. Consequently, many viewed the change to automated format as a lowering of standards for entry.

Secretary Rice requested additional resources in her initial year in office for her transformation effort but remarkably did not request a significant increase in subsequent fiscal years. The 1,000-plus positions that were added as part of the Diplomatic Readiness Initiative have now been absorbed by assignments to Iraq, Afghanistan, and other difficult positions in Washington and around the globe. An independent assessment of the Secretary's "transformational diplomacy" effort suggested the department needs a minimum of 1,000 additional trained officers just to meet existing requirements. This was further corroborated in the report, *The Embassy of the Future,* prepared by the Centre for Strategic and International Studies in October 2007. This study describes how the State Department by its own analysis has a shortage of 1,079 positions for transit, training, and temporary needs (these include language training, professional education, rotational assignments, etc.). The report further outlines the need for joint agency training, rotational assignments to other departments, educational opportunities at universities, and further leadership training as essential to accomplishment of the State Department mission in the future.

The issue for the Department of State is not solely one of shortages in personnel and resources, as difficult as those challenges might be. Many experts have also argued that in addition to expanding overall strength, the Department of State must better protect its developmental resources, including leadership/management programs, from personnel "raids" to cover operational emergencies. One report suggested that "sending people abroad without the requisite training is like deploying soldiers without weapons."

The department's Foreign Service Institute (FSI) describes itself as the federal government's primary training institution for officers and support personnel of the American foreign affairs community. It annually provides more than 450 courses, including instruction in 70 languages, to more than 50,000 employees from the State Department, over 40 other government agencies, and the U.S. military.

As part of the Diplomatic Readiness Initiative, some efforts were made to enhance developmental opportunities for FSOs offered at FSI and elsewhere. Mandatory courses in basic, intermediate, and advanced leadership for employees at the level of GS 13, 14, and 15 (Foreign Service grades 03, 02, and 01, respectively) were established, as well as the Senior Executive Threshold Seminar for those recently selected for senior Civil and Foreign Service. Career candidates for Ambassador or Deputy Chief of Mission (DCM) appointments have an advantage if they have demonstrated leadership qualities. Unfortunately, the four required courses total only 17 days, of which 2 are equal opportunity and diversity awareness. The Senior Executive Seminar, 3 weeks in length, is somewhat more robust. Overall, training offered at FSI expanded by 25 percent from 1.9 million student classroom hours to 2.4 million from 2002 to 2004.

Still, many of these courses are primarily "training" as opposed to "education." Furthermore, the FSI reports to the Undersecretary of State for Management, whose duties include security, human resources, building operations, and administration, rather than to those departmental leaders responsible for the future direction of the institution as well as overall policy. Consequently, many of the courses offered are focused primarily on preparing a diplomat or his/her family to be successful in a particular assignment abroad. They do not provide broad-based education on policy or problems that do not lend themselves to textbook solutions.

Consequently, the State Department offers little in the way of formal education and development for its officers during their career. Most current FSOs are forced to learn either experientially or by their own outside efforts. There are individual developmental opportunities to attend the military's senior service colleges or participate in such programs as congressional fellowships. Unfortunately, these are not formalized development programs for the organization, not numerous, and not perceived as career enhancing due to the long period of separation. These impediments are compounded by manning shortages, which mean that there is frequently no officer available to fill a position for an educational or development experience for an extended period.

With these points in mind, several recommendations specific to the State Department seem appropriate. First, a successful Foreign Service requires officers who are consistently building new knowledge and skills. The State Department requires a 1015 percent increase in personnel to allow for that proportion of the overall service to be in training or education at any given moment. This number must be rigorously fenced off solely for these purposes to allow for adequate training and development. Failure to do so will result in personnel being simply absorbed into ongoing operational efforts. Second, expanding requirements and the pressing need to maintain a surge capacity require more flexibility for admission to the Foreign Service. Horizontal entry and exit should be considered whereby those with a particular background or linguistic skill could enter laterally at grades far above entry level. Furthermore, greater allowances should be made for career FSOs to take a leave of absence for personal reasons and subsequently return to duty. Third, any use of "blindfolding" for selection to the Foreign Service should be ended, and overall recruiting practices reviewed.

Fourth, the Alternative Examination Program should be broadened to include those in the military (both active and reserve) or who complete graduate degrees in areas of particular need. Fifth, control of the FSI should be passed from the Undersecretary of Management and placed directly under the Deputy Secretary. This shift would give FSI greater prominence, underscore the importance of FSO development, and allow the department leadership to better control course offerings and selection policies. Sixth, opportunities for development assignments at think tanks, congressional staffs, military war colleges, etc., should be actively sought as part the department's overall development programs.

Seventh, critical problems exist with respect to pay, allowances, and retirements. FSOs serving in Iraq and Afghanistan pay taxes while serving abroad, unlike uniformed military, and effectively take a pay cut during these assignments.

Foreign Service retirement is capped, and, unlike the military or other government agencies, State Department retirees cannot accept another government position without forfeiting a significant portion of their retirement pay. These compensation issues must be addressed.

Finally, the Hart-Rudman Commission made one final internal recommendation for the State Department in 2001 that still deserves consideration. The report recommended changing the Foreign Service's name to the United States Diplomatic Corps. Some might argue that this is superficial rhetoric mongering, but it could have a significantly beneficial impact. It would serve as a reminder that this group of people do not serve foreign interests but are rather central to U.S. national security. Such a change would further rationalize the value of diverse assignments in regional bureaus, abroad in an embassy, and in the functional components of the organization. This change might help to better depict a career pattern for young people considering diplomatic service as a possible profession. Finally, it would also serve to emphasize that the traditional mission of the State Department to provide national representation abroad has dramatically changed, as revealed in the recent report *The Embassy of the Future*. This report observes that diplomats of the future will need traits and skills that are different from those of diplomats a decade ago and even those hired today.

A change in organizational culture is required, as the "new diplomat must be an active force in advancing U.S. interests, not just a gatherer and transmitter of information."

Office of the Secretary of Defense

I have had 2 days of formal development in my 30 years as an OSD employee... 1 day of AIDS awareness and 1 day of sexual harassment training....

As an organization, that portion of the Office of the Secretary of Defense (OSD) that deals with policy differs significantly from State and CIA. First, it is a smaller group of professionals, numbering only about 400. In fact, they are outnumbered by others within OSD (human resource management, finance, comptroller, acquisition, research/development, etc.). Second, the State Department has a focused competency in diplomacy, and the CIA deals with intelligence gathering and analysis. OSD Policy shares its competency in defense planning with the military to a degree but is primarily focused on the security relationships between the United States and foreign powers. Obviously, this focus changed dramatically when, in the aftermath of the invasion of Iraq, DoD assumed responsibility for the initial efforts at post-conflict resolution instead of the Department of State. Third, development of an official within OSD primarily deals with his/her substantive background on a particular policy question as opposed to broad understanding of national security policy, the interagency process, or any effort to develop the skills necessary to manage a large and complex organization.

The Defense Science Board Report of the Task Force on Human Resources and the USGAO report ("Human Capital: Strategic Approach Should Guide DoD Civilian Workforce Management") both pointed out many of the existing problems in DoD. They include insufficient numbers of properly trained candidates in the pipeline, limited professional development opportunities, weak incentives/compensation plans, an aging workforce, etc. The department overall suffered the largest force reductions in its history at the end of the Cold War, resulting in a professional staff that views itself as largely over-tasked. Fewer personnel have not resulted in fewer requirements, particularly in the aftermath of the attacks of 9/11. Despite this fact, reductions in personnel strength that were planned prior to these tragic events remained "on the books" to be implemented.

For the middle to upper grades, some believe that DoD recruiting has benefited markedly in the last few years by the change in the dual compensation laws that affected military officers upon retirement. These now allow military professionals upon retirement from active duty to accept government positions without any reduction in their retirement compensation. While this step has offered the department a source for recruiting mid-level management with significant policy experience, it may have masked or even contributed to the longer-term problem of an aging workforce. This problem could be exacerbated if coupled with the absence of a robust recruiting program. Over time, this might cause the OSD policy community additional problems due to the impending retirement of a significant portion of the staff. It may also, if not managed effectively, lead to a perception among younger employees that their opportunities for progression are inhibited by the lateral entry of a significant number of military retirees.

Still, the overall job satisfaction in OSD and Defense agencies is relatively high, similar to what is found in the private sector. Civilian job satisfaction is somewhat lower for those assigned to the service staffs (Army, Navy, and Air Force), but these still exceed 50 percent approvals. While this is encouraging, these professionals give lower ratings to their supervisors and the quality of work produced than one finds in similar private sector analysis. This may indicate that a larger percentage will seek retirement at the earliest age possible under the existing personnel system.

Overall, DoD does not have an aggressive recruiting program. For many years, the department largely depended upon the Presidential Management Fellows Intern Program for entry-level positions in policy, but in the aftermath of the Cold War, these numbers shrank significantly. Proposals were made prior to 2001 to increase the number of selectees per year for the coming decade, but they were not acted upon. In November 2003 President Bush announced the Presidential Management Fellows Program (PMF) to modernize this effort. The new program sought to increase standards, rigor, and prestige of the program, and it lifted the annual hiring cap for all Federal agencies.

The PMF program is a paid government fellowship sponsored by the Office of Personnel Management (OPM) for recent graduate students who seek a 2-year fellowship in a U.S. government agency. Selection begins with the nomination of the student by the Dean, Chairperson, or academic program director of their graduate program. This is followed by a rigorous assessment process. Agencies that hire PMFs include the Departments of Agriculture, Commerce, Defense, Education, Energy, Health and Human Services, Homeland Security, Housing and Urban Development (HUD), Interior, Justice, Labor, State, Transportation, Treasury, Federal Bureau of Investigation (FBI), Library of Congress, National Aeronautics and Space Administration (NASA), and USAID. Following the conclusion of the 2-year fellowship, PMFs usually have the opportunity to convert their fellowship into a full-time permanent position. In 2007, over 3,900 applicants were screened, 790 were determined to be finalists, and 383 received appointments. Consequently, OSD has seen some increases in both the numbers and quality of applicants from the PMF program.

These facts, coupled with OSD's unwillingness to actively recruit new employees, could suggest a problem of organizational culture—a tendency to view career civilians as replaceable parts versus valuable professionals who need to be aggressively recruited, managed wisely, and retained. It appears, however, that the current generation of young Americans does see government service in agencies such as OSD as attractive. For example, since 1997 OSD has received between 100 and 140 applications each year for the six to eight open PMI positions.

Consequently, the federal government should attempt to eliminate recruitment hurdles and seek to expand the National Security Education Program (NSEP, also referred to as the David L. Boren National Security Education Act) that links educational benefits to government service requirements. This act directed the Secretary of Defense to create the program, provide oversight, and award scholarships. The NSEP was established in December 1991 with the following objectives:

- Provide resources, accountability, and flexibility to meet U.S. national security education needs, especially as such needs change over time.
- Increase the quantity, diversity, and quality of the teaching and learning of subjects in the fields of foreign languages, area studies, and other international fields critical to the Nation's interests.
- Produce an increased pool of applicants for work in the departments and agencies of the U.S. Government with national security responsibilities.
- Expand, in conjunction with other Federal programs, the international experience, knowledge base, and perspectives on which the U.S. citizenry, government employees, and leaders rely.
- Permit the federal government to promote the cause of international education.

Since 1994 the NSEP has awarded over 3,000 undergraduate and graduate scholarships for study abroad. Each recipient is required to spend 1 year working in the federal government in a position of national security responsibility. This is normally associated with DoD, Department of State, Homeland Security, or an element of the intelligence community. This opportunity seems to be particularly attractive to those who have recently completed degrees at schools of public policy and seek entry-level positions/ experience. Efforts might also be considered to create an ROTC-like program for particularly promising young undergraduates who are in relevant disciplines and seek a career in government service.

Experiential learning through rotation assignments to other government agencies, the National Security Council, or other outside developmental experiences are largely discouraged by the OSD culture and leadership. Many quality OSD personnel have sought such assignments in the past and performed brilliantly, but this was largely due to their own initiative. They were rarely, if ever, rewarded upon their return with promotions or positions of increased responsibility. In the late 1990s, OSD policy created a number of other professional developmental opportunities at the various war colleges, State Department, Council on Foreign Relations, as well as sabbaticals at major universities for GS 15 or SES-level employees. These were all largely discontinued with the arrival of Secretary of Defense Rumsfeld, and any future assignments outside of OSD policy could occur only if an assistant secretary was willing to give up the necessary body. Clearly these decisions were driven in part by the operational reality that every OSD employee who was sent to a developmental assignment outside of the organization meant that in theory his/her position would remain vacant until the incumbent returned.

Reluctance may be due to the fact that, in general, OSD senior positions have a higher percentage of political appointees than commensurate subcomponents of CIA and State. As a result, the organizational focus is on the immediate needs of policy as opposed to the professional health and development of career employees. The presence of Schedule C or political appointees in many (if not most) senior OSD policy positions further discourages career advancement.

Many civilian professionals increasingly see their progress reaching a "glass ceiling" prior to any consideration for a deputy assistant secretary position. Furthermore, many see that they must not only compete with political appointees for senior positions but also with senior military officers and even FSOs who periodically have been offered senior DoD positions.

This tendency may contribute to earlier retirement or the loss of valuable employees to the private sector. Unfortunately, DoD does not conduct exit interviews for those departing the department as part of its overall recruitment/retention efforts. Consequently, it is difficult to assess the relative importance individuals ascribe to particular factors in deciding to depart service in the Department.

In the early 1990s, DoD attempted to establish a more formalized development program. Senior officials realized that the implementation of the Goldwater-Nichols Act had begun to yield an officer corps that was more highly educated and equipped with a stronger joint perspective than in the past. There had not, however, been a similar investment on the civilian side. Civilian career professionals in OSD had very few opportunities for developmental assignments and little exposure to national security decisionmaking. Since 1997, OSD has initiated at least two new programs focused on enhancing leadership and management development among its civil servants and expanding their overall understanding of the policy process— the Defense Leadership and Management Program (DLAMP) and Policy Career Development Program (PCDP).

DLAMP was established partially in response to the Commission on Roles and Missions of the Armed Force. It was designed as a systematic effort to prepare civilians for key leadership positions at GS 14-15 and SES levels for DoD. It had three components:

- A 1-year rotational assignment outside one's occupation or component.
- A minimum 3-month course in professional military education at the senior level that was established at the National Defense University.
- At least 10 advanced graduate courses in subjects important for Defense leaders (in essence a DoD-focused MBA program).

At one time DLAMP had 1,100 participants with 83 enrolled at 10-month professional military education courses (such as the war colleges).

While this program was endorsed by the Defense

Science Board, it suffered from several difficulties over time. First, DLAMP was designed for all DoD civilian employees regardless of background. There was no distinction between those in technical fields versus those in policy positions. Those assigned to policy positions rarely were afforded the opportunity to attend, while many with a technical background found experiences such as the senior service college interesting but somewhat irrelevant to their career patterns. Second, DoD was unable to generate a personnel delta from which to fill positions left vacant when individuals were attending schooling. Consequently, managers were reluctant to send their best to schooling. As a result, GS 12s and 13s began being assigned to meet requirements. Third, selection for attendance was based on performance and not potential. Administrators claimed that existing personnel regulations precluded them for making development assignments based on future potential, arguing they were forced to focus solely on improving a person's background for their existing position. As a result, no clear link was established between DLAMP attendance, subsequent assignments to positions of greater responsibility, or promotions. Fourth, OSD Policy found DLAMP of less and less interest as it was more and more successful at attracting entry level applicants who already possessed a master's degree. Finally, graduation criteria seemed unclear to many based on the three tasks involved, and this made management of the program more difficult. This, coupled with rising costs for temporary assignments and overall mismanagement, resulted in the program being downsized solely to attendance at the senior service colleges. In 2007, roughly 50 DLAMP students are in attendance at the various war colleges.

Significantly, none have been sent from DoD policy positions. The PCDP was created specifically to deal with the development of OSD personnel in policy positions in the latter part of the Clinton administration. This effort's goal was "to develop career national security professionals of the Office of the Secretary of Defense Policy (OSD Policy) who are motivated, professionally developed and trained, and during the course of their careers, increasingly able to shape and affect the changing security environment." In formulating PCDP, its authors observed that historically civilian employees in OSD Policy had very limited career development opportunities. Consequently, career advancement as reflected in more responsible, more senior, and varied assignments was at best episodic and difficult to predict or plan for. They also noted that this was not a new phenomenon. Senior Defense officials had noted an ever increasing need for enhanced career opportunities and options for professional OSD Policy personnel in studies completed in 1961, 1978, and 1994. This last study stimulated the PCDP effort, and it was formally inaugurated in 1995.

PCDP had four interlocking elements. These included: (1) a training/development program; (2) a rotation process that sought challenging assignments both inside and outside of OSD Policy; (3) an improved recruitment and hiring process; and (4) a career advancement program. The program included detailed guidance on when and how personnel could apply for development or rotation assignments as well as the creation of panels to review applications, monitor evaluations, and consider subsequent assignments. In many ways, this program seemed ideally designed not only to confront existing problems in OSD Policy, but also as a model that other agencies of the federal government might consider. Unfortunately, this group has not met in several years, and the program is largely moribund.

Secretary Rumsfeld made "transformation" a centerpiece of his efforts as the new secretary upon the arrival of the Bush administration in 2001. He observed in a *Washington Post* editorial that "transformation of our military capabilities depends on our ability to transform not just the armed forces and the way we fight. We must also transform DoD." Consistent with this effort, Secretary Rumsfeld chartered a study to examine joint defense capabilities in March 2003. This report, *The Joint Defense Capabilities Study*, was completed in January 2004. While this was an exhaustive study of planning, resourcing, and execution, it largely ignored any changes to DoD personnel practices. The report provided only a single page on "workforce planning" and no detailed analysis of its recommendations. It did note that "workforce development is often reactive to decisions concerning joint capabilities, rather than being fully considered when those decisions are made." The report concluded that to support a revision in the planning process effectively, a more systematic effort had to be made to address human capital requirements. It recommended two additional efforts: (1) conduct a careful analysis of personnel requirements and training; and (2) increase the number of overall experts available to the department.

Perhaps in partial response to these recommendations the Bush administration also proposed the Defense Transformation Act in 2003 that was designed to assist the department in better managing its civilian personnel. Secretary Rumsfeld underscored the importance of this effort to the nation's security: "The DoD cannot meet the challenge of the future with an organization anchored in the past. We must be permitted to be as agile, flexible, and adaptable as the forces we field in battle around the world." This effort sought to restructure how DoD hires, pays, promotes, and disciplines its more than 650,000 civilian employees. It proposed a new National Security Personnel System (NSPS) that would: (1) accelerate the hiring process that at the time took nearly 5 months, (2) introduce pay-for-performance bonuses; (3) streamline the promotion process; (4) provide greater flexibility for DoD senior managers to move personnel rapidly as required; and (5) facilitate the transfer of as many as 300,000 jobs then performed by military personnel to civilians. It also proposed new legislation that sought to reduce the number of labor unions that DoD had to negotiate with from as many as 1,300 to half a dozen. Finally, it proposed expediting the firing of

DoD personnel when necessary. Congress approved NSPS in November 2003. It required OSD to establish a program office to oversee the design and implementation of this new system in partnership with the Office of Personnel Management (OPM). This effort began in early 2004 and included six design working groups encompassing over 100 participants from DoD and OPM. Implementation of the new system began in the summer of 2005 and was scheduled to be completed over the next 2 years.

Obviously this new system was controversial

Supporters emphasized improved hiring and firing, a $500 million "performance fund" to provide federal executive incentive bonuses, enhanced collective bargaining arrangements, moving uniformed personnel out of positions that could be performed by civilians, and incentives for risk taking. They also argued that the NSPS would reduce the department's need to turn to contractors for missions abroad. For example, during Operation IRAQI FREEDOM, over 80 percent of civilians deployed to the theater were contractors. This was due in part to the fact that DoD regulations at that time precluded the department from moving its employees quickly. The associated performance management system was described as the cornerstone for the program's overall success. It required supervisors to establish performance goals and expectations in concert with their employees and provided personnel management training for supervisors and managers. Obviously, this requirement could over time enhance the managerial skills of at least the existing DoD leadership.

Critics noted that a pay-for-performance system had proven a failure in the 1970s and 1980s. They also complained that previous systems to improve the ability of DoD managers to assess their employees accurately had failed. Furthermore, assessments of this type are particularly difficult to conduct for policy-related positions in comparison to administrative, clerical, or technical jobs. Consequently, some believed that while the NSPS might be appropriate for many portions of DoD, it would be less useful to OSD Policy.

Detractors further argued that overall the new law provided the Secretary of Defense "sole and unreviewable discretion" to implement change over the objections of OPM, labor unions, and Congress. Consequently, the Secretary could bypass federal personnel regulations to hire and promote any persons who are declared "essential to national security." An official with the American Federation of Government Employees (a union representing 200,000 employees) said reducing OPM's role would "open the door for every subsequent defense secretary to tailor the department's personnel system to his or her political tastes." As a result, a coalition of several federal labour unions has initiated a number of court cases that seek to halt or modify NSPS.

This new discretionary authority, coupled with the expanding number of political appointees in DoD Policy, could actually result in a significant increase in the use of contractors for policy analysis. If this were to occur, it is likely that Secretaries would utilize those "think tanks" that support administration policies and deprive the policy process of alternative views. Finally, NSPS does little to nothing to improve the development of career employees in OSD Policy. While the enhanced pay system is important particularly with respect to recruiting and retention, it ignores other incentives such as educational opportunities, variety of assignments, etc., that may be more appealing, particularly to those in policy positions. In response to these concerns, members of Congress approved an amendment to the defense appropriations bill for fiscal year 2008 that would deny funding for key parts of NSPS. The White House responded that this effort was "in essence a total revocation" of the new system.

Not unlike their colleagues in the Department of State, new policy professionals in DoD are engaged in interesting work on a vast variety of issues that in many ways are more challenging than during the Cold War. It would be unfair not to note that efforts have been made to encourage the "best and the brightest" to seek a career with DoD, and the recent applicant pools have had outstanding credentials. Programs have been initiated to allow positions to be shared that include currently at least one SES billet. There has also been an attempt to create a few positions for DoD policy professionals with Regional Combatant Commands. The question remains whether or not these efforts will result in a dramatic improvement in overall development and serve as an incentive for the retention of the very best in a policy career.

Still, any DoD civilian joining the policy staff is confronted by a system that largely leaves career planning and individual development as a matter of personal responsibility and choice. They are joining a staff that has at best an ill-defined career pattern, particularly for those in policy positions. It places little value on educational development, training, outside experiential learning, or rotation assignments to broaden the knowledge of its personnel. This is despite the fact that most experts would agree that interagency experience is critical to the development of effective policy professionals in today's and tomorrow's defense climate.

In addition to the suggestions previously made, the following internal departmental improvements would seem appropriate. First, OSD, in concert with the Department of State, should expand the number of overseas postings for its personnel at American embassies and international organizations. Second, establish a clear rotational program for those working in regional bureaus at the GS 15 and SES level at the various regional centers established by OSD (e.g., the Marshall Centre in Europe, the Asia-Pacific

Centre in Honolulu, the Africa Centre at the National Defense University, etc.) This would not only broaden the understanding of regional issues for these personnel but also improve the exchange of ideas on policy questions between the departments and the centers it oversees. Third, revise the DLAMP and place a career OSD civilian in charge.

A new revitalized program must link the selection of an individual for training or educational development to his/her demonstrated performance and potential. It must further seek to align better attendance and completion with subsequent assignments to positions of increasing responsibility. Fourth, establish avenues for horizontal entry of highly qualified individuals with particular specialties into senior career positions.

5

Attacks Claimed by Indian Mujahideen

2007 UTTAR PRADESH BOMBINGS

Six consecutive serial blasts rocked Lucknow, Varanasi and Faizabad courts in Uttar Pradesh on 23 November 2007 afternoon in a span of 25 minutes, in which reportedly many people were killed and several others injured.

Bombs were explicitly targeted to the lawyers who were working in courts premises at these cities. The first blast occurred in Varanasi civil court and collectorate premises between 13:05 and 13:07 pm. Two successive blasts occurred in Faizabad district court around 13:12 and 13:15, closely followed by one at Lucknow at 13:32.

The blasts came a week after the Uttar Pradesh police along with central security agencies busted a Jaish-e-Mohammed terrorists which planned to abduct Rahul Gandhi. The blasts may be in retaliation to the arrested terrorists being beaten up by lawyers and not being assigned even a counsel to defend them in the court.

Lucknow blasts

In Lucknow two bomb were found one triggered panic after explosion and other unexploded powerful live bomb was deactivated by bomb disposal squads. Both the bombs were planted in bicycles in civil court premises. Lucknow blast was mildest among all other blasts in Faizabad and Varanasi.

Varanasi blasts

Three consecutive blasts claimed most lives in Varanasi at least 11 people were killed including four lawyers and 42 injured. Bomb were tied to bicycles which exploded around 13:05-13:15.

Faizabad blasts

Two successive blasts occurred in Faizabad which were strongest among all. In these blasts at least four people were killed on spot and about 15 were injured.

Terror Mail just before blasts

A little known group Indian Mujahidin has claimed responsibility of these blasts. This group apparently sent an email to some private TV channels just five minutes before the blasts. This email says the Jihad in India is in retaliation against the injustice to Muslims in India, the demolition of the Babri Masjid and the Gujarat riots.

Indian Mujahideen also claimed responsibility for the blasts in Delhi and Hyderabad but refused any association with the attacks on theMecca Masjid, the Samjhauta Express and the 2006 Malegaon blasts.

HuJI's hand suspected

Investigating agencies suspect the hand of Bangladesh based terrorist outfit Harkat-ul-Jihad-al-Islami(HuJI) pointsman who goes by the name Guru has emerged as a prime suspect. Intelligence agencies suspect that Guru may have planned the attacks executed by sleeper cells of Lashkar-e-Taiba and Jaish-e-Mohammed possibly under the banner of al-Qaida-fil-al-Hindi (meaning al-Qaida in India).

Lawyers' strike to protest blasts

Bar Council of Uttar Pradesh decided to go on strike to protest against these terrorist activities. In the state capital, lawyers moved about in groups in the court compounds and raised slogans against terrorism. The government has tightened security arrangements in the courts throughout the state after the Friday blasts. Lawyers from other states also join state bar council and observing the day as shok diwas.

Reactions

- The Union Home Ministry of India said it's a terrorist strike meant to disturb communal harmony.
- Uttar Pradesh's Chief Minister condemned serial blasts and announced a compensation of Rs.200,000 to the next of kin to each of those killed and Rs.50,000 for those injured in the incidents. She also said that it is a complete failure of central intelligence agencies.
- The Prime Minister of India, Dr. Manmohan Singh condemned serial blasts and announced a compensation of Rs.100,000 from thePrime Minister's National Relief Fund to kin of each of those killed in blasts.
- British High Commissioner to India Richard Stagg said in a statement *"We condemn all forms of terrorism. It is a particularly worrying development that the judiciary and the legal system have been attacked. Our thoughts are with the affected families"*.

JAIPUR BOMBINGS

The 13 May 2008 Jaipur bombings were a series of nine synchronized bomb blasts that took place within a span of fifteen minutes at locations in Jaipur, the capital city of the Indian state of Rajasthan, and a tourist destination. A tenth bomb was found and defused. Official reports confirm 63 dead with 216 or more people injured. The bombings shocked most of India and resulted in widespread condemnation from leaders across the world with many countries showing solidarity with India in its fight against terrorism.

This was the first time terrorists had targeted Jaipur, India's tenth largest city and one of its most popular tourist destinations. The bombs went off near historic monuments at one of the busiest times of the day. One of the bombs exploded close to Jaipur's most famous landmark, the historic Hawa Mahal (palace of winds).

Two days after the blasts, a previously unknown Islamic militant group known as *Indian Mujahideen,* sent an e-mail to Indian media in which they claimed responsibility for the attacks and said they would "demolish the faith (Hinduism)" of the "infidels of India". Though the Indian authorities said that the e-mail was genuine, they also added that there were some contradictions and the primary motive of the e-mail might be to mislead investigating agencies. Indian Home Ministry sources said that a Bangladesh-based organization, Harkat-ul-Jihad-al-Islami (HuJI) or "Islamic Holy War Movement", was suspected to be behind the attack. The police were also able to find credible evidence linking the suspected bombers to Bangladeshi militants which resulted in backlash against illegal Bangladeshi immigrants in Rajasthan. India plans to expel more than 50,000 Bangladeshi migrants in Rajasthan.

Bombings

The following areas were bombed using RDX placed in bicycles:

- Bari Choupar
- Manak Chowk Police Station area
- Johari Bazar
- Tripolia Bazar
- Choti Choupar
- Kotwali area

Nine bombs at seven locations exploded within fifteen minutes, starting at 7:10 PM. The blasts were synchronized to inflict maximum casualties. The first two blasts occurred at Manak Chowk and as the crowd ran towards Johri Bazar another two blasts near the National Handloom Centre blocked the exit point, pushing back the panicked crowd towards Tripolia Bazar and Chandpol area, where subsequent blasts caused maximum fatalities.

Aftermath

The serial blasts created panic among Jaipur residents following which several units of police and Indian Paramilitary Forces were deployed throughout the city. Most of the victims were taken to Sawai Man Singh Hospital. The doctors used the mobile phones of the dead to inform the victims' relatives. A curfew was imposed in parts of Jaipur and the state government of Rajasthan had ordered all units of police to maintain extra vigilance across the state. The Government of India deployed several units of the elite National Security Guards in Jaipur to aid the law and order forces in the city. 400 men from Rapid Action Force were also sent. A few hours after the blasts, India declared high alert across several major Indian cities including Delhi, Mumbai (Bombay) and Chennai (Madras). Security in other major Indian tourist destinations like Panaji and Agra was also increased. Delhi Police also sent a team to Jaipur to check whether the terrorist attacks there had any links with previous terrorists attacks in Delhi.

Investigations

India ordered an inquiry into the blasts while the Indian Home Ministry raised concerns that certain 'foreign elements' might be behind the bombings. The police has found credible evidence linking the bombing suspects to Bangladesh-based militants. Consequently, Rajasthan state government took severe measures against illegal Bangladeshi immigrants in the state.

Four people were detained for questioning by Rajasthan police regarding the blasts. A lead has already been traced by the police. Initial police investigations suggested the involvement of several Islamic militant organizations like Bangladesh-based Harkat-ul-Jihad-al-Islami, Student's Islamic Movement of India or Pakistan-based Lashkar-e-Toiba. Concerns are also being raised about the possible involvement of al-Qaeda.

Police officials say that the bomb blasts in Jaipur follow patterns similar to those observed during the bomb blasts in Hyderabad andVaranasi. The Indian Police revealed that the bombs planted were of low intensity but by placing them in highly crowded areas, the terrorists had ensured that the death toll would be high. The *Times of India* quoted Additional Director General of Rajasthan Policeofficer as saying that the terrorists had planted "highly explosive RDX" with timers on bicycles, a technique which was also used during the terror attacks in Uttar Pradesh in November, 2007 (in which the involvement of Bangladesh's Harkat-ul-Jihad-al-Islami is also suspected). The police have also found striking similarity between the Jaipur bombings and Hyderabad bombings. On May 15, a police officer said,

About 1.5 kg of Neogel with metal ball-bearings was put in boat-shaped wooden cases in Jaipur and Hyderabad. In both cases, timers were used. The similarities in the signatures of the bombs are shocking.

The police said that they had identified the people who had sold bicycles to the attackers. The bicycle sellers said that the bombers spoke Bengali language, adding credibility to police claims that the terrorists might be Bangladeshis. A police official said,

The employees [of the bicycle shop] have told us that they did not look like Rajasthanis and spoke in broken Hindi. In fact they were speaking Bengali, which has again given rise to speculation that the militants were from a Bangladeshi outfit.

On May 14, the Indian police released a sketch of a suspect. A day later, the police released sketches of three additional suspects. A shop owner in Udaipur claimed he saw one of the suspects a few days back.

Claim of responsibility

A little-known group *Indian Mujahideen* claimed responsibility for the attacks and sent a video to *Aaj Tak* via e-mail supposedly featuring the bicycles wrapped with explosives used during the terror attacks. The address from which the e-mail was sent was reported to be "guru_alhindi_jaipur@yahoo.co.uk". News agencies reported that the video showed a serial number on one of the bicycles as '129489'. Police officials confirmed that the bicycle used in Choti Choupad blast had the same serial number. However, Rajasthan Chief Minister Vasundhara Raje also suggested that a secondary objective of the e-mail could also be to mislead the investigating authorities.

In the e-mail, the group threatened an "open war against India" unless it stops supporting the United States and United

Kingdom on "international issues". It also said that it would "demolish the faith (Hinduism)" of the "infidels of India".

Domestic reactions

"This is not a crime, we are in the middle of a war."—Vasundhara Raje, Rajasthan Chief Minister

The President of India, Pratibha Patil expressed her grief at the loss of lives in the blasts and appealed for calm while the Prime Minister of India, Manmohan Singh, pledged the Government of India's support to the state Government of Rajasthan and the victims' families. The Prime Minister also said:

The terrorists have the advantage of attacking by stealth but there is no lack of firmness in dealing with this menace. All possible precautions are being taken. It would be premature on my part to comment anything as it will interfere with the investigations.

Singh also defended the Government's intelligence mechanisms saying the number of cases that the intelligence agencies had anticipated and prevented was "significant". He observed:

There are many cases where security agencies have foiled attempts. Many cases were anticipated. I don't want to talk about what they were able to prevent.

Indian Home Minister, Shivraj Patil, conveyed his condolences to the victims' families. The Government of India announced 100,000INR compensation to the next kin of those dead in the terrorist attacks and 50,000 INR *ex gratia* to those seriously injured. An emergency meeting of Indian cabinet ministers was also held later during the day. Foreign Minister of India, Pranab Mukherjee, said he was going to raise the issue of 'cross-border terrorism' with Pakistan's government during his visit to Islamabad next week. Indian Finance Minister, P. Chidambaram, said that the blasts won't affect India's business climate. India's National Security Advisor, M.K. Narayanan, said that the intelligence agencies were looking into all possible aspects of the blasts and no major breakthrough in ongoing investigations were made.

The Chief Minister of Rajasthan, Vasundhara Raje, said "I condemn this blast. They have tried to ruin the communal harmony of the state but they will not succeed. Never in the history of Rajasthan such a heinous incident has happened and this is not an attack on the state but on the nation". She also added, "there are some slender leads on which the state agencies are working and its difficult to name any terror outfit at present". The Chief Minister also laid emphasis on a new anti-terror legislation either similar to POTA or to the one in the neighbouring state of Gujarat. She also criticised the President of India for not signing an anti-terror bill passed by the Rajasthan Legislative Assembly in 2006. Raje also expressed her concern that the terrorist attacks in Jaipur will negatively affect the tourism industry there. The Chief Minister also said that Rajasthan will have its own anti-terror force and also proposed a joint task force between Indian states.

India's main opposition party, the Bharatiya Janata Party (BJP), blamed the United Progressive Alliance (UPA)-government for not taking adequate measures against terrorism in India and re-newed calls for POTA were made. The BJP also demanded that Pakistan's Inter-Services Intelligence should be on international terror watch-list. India's Leader of Opposition, L. K. Advani, said "The blasts are reflective of the states' inability to preempt these strikes." Gujarat Chief Minister Narendra Modi accused the UPA government of adopting double standards on terrorism and said, "The UPA-led government at the Centre should make the people realise that it is committed to curb terrorism spreading in our country."

2008 BANGALORE SERIAL BLASTS

2008 Bangalore serial blasts occurred on 25 July 2008 in Bangalore, India. A series of nine bombs exploded in which two people were killed and 20 injured. According to theBangalore City Police, the blasts were caused by low-intensity crude bombs triggered by timers.

India already suffered from a similar series of blasts in Jaipur, in May 2008.

The Times of India has reported that either the banned organisation Students Islamic Movement of India or the militant organisation Lashkar-e-Toiba could be behind these blasts. The

Intelligence Bureau is not ruling out the involvement of these organisations, however the police maintain that it is too early to attribute blame to anyone.

This was followed by the 2008 Ahmedabad serial blasts occurring on 26 July 2008

The bombings

It was initially reported that three blasts took place at around 1:30 pm IST. Later reports indicated that four low-intensity blasts occurred: One at Nayandahalli (1:30 PM IST), two in Madiwala (at 1:50 pm IST), and the last in Adugodi (2:10 pm). Other blasts were reported from areas including the Mallya hospital, Langford Road and Richmond Circle. The Madiwala blast took place at a check post, behind The Forum, a popular shopping mall in Bangalore.

It has been reported that gelatin sticks were used in the bombs. Police indicated that all bombs had timer devices attached to them and that mobile phones were used to trigger the bombs.

The blasts were low-intensity but occurred in crowded areas.

- 1st blast: 1.20 pm, Madiwala bus depot
- 2nd blast: 1.25 pm, Mysore road
- 3rd blast: 1.40 pm, Adugodi
- 4th blast: 2.10 pm, Koramangala
- 5th blast: 2.25 pm, Vittal Mallya road
- 6th blast: 2.35 pm, Langford Town
- 7th blast: Richmond Town

There was another bomb found on 26 July 2008 in Bangalore near Forum Mall,Koramangala which was defused successfully by the Bomb Detection Squad.

Casualties

Current reports indicate that two people have been killed and 20 injured.

One of the confirmed dead was a woman waiting at a bus shelter in Madiwala on the Hosur road; her husband and another person were seriously injured. The injured were admitted to the St. Johns Hospital.

In response to the attack Prime Minister Singh sanctioned an ex gratia payment of Rs one lakh to the relatives of those dead and Rs 50,000 to those injured in the blasts.

Reactions

President Pratibha Patil, the Prime Minister, Manmohan Singh, Leader of the opposition L. K. Advani, Vice-President Hamid Ansari, Chief Minister of Karnataka, B. S. Yeddyurappa all condemned the violence and appealed for calm and communal harmony.

All India Anna Dravida Munnetra Kazhagam (AIADMK) general secretary J. Jayalalithaa called for the revival of special act like POTA to effectively counter terrorists and extremist outfits. The All India Muslim Forum also "strongly condemned" the attack.

Impacts

Calls by concerned and panicked citizens resulted in the telephone networks being jammed. Malls, schools and cinema halls across the city were shut down, and the police cordoned off the blast sites.

The effect of the blast on the Sensex was immediately visible with losses exceeding 3.5% reported on Friday after the Bangalore blasts. The 30-share BSE index was down 3.7%, or 529.28 points at 14,228.81, with 23 components in the red. The 50-issue NSE index was down 2.9 percent at 4,305.30.

The government has issued a statement that IT companies in Bangalore were not the target of the blast. This was reaffirmed when major IT companies based in the city-like Wipro and Infosys-reported that the blasts had no impact on their operations and that all employees were safe.

Employees were, however, urged to leave for home early. A new security plan for IT and other industries was announced byMinister for Home Affairs Shivraj Patil immediately after the Bangalore serial blasts. Under the new amendment of law Central

Industrial Security Force personnel could be used to safeguard private sector industries which till now was limited to public sector undertakings(PSUs).

Investigation

No one has claimed responsibility for the bombings. The Bangalore Police Commissioner, Shankar Bidari, termed the blasts "an act of miscreants" trying to disturb peace in the city. The Union Home Ministry of India named the Pakistan-based Lashkar-e-Toiba andStudents Islamic Movement of India, as the suspects.

The Bangalore Police said that attack "bore some hallmarks" of the Bangladesh-based militant group Harkat-ul-Jihad-al-Islami (HuJI).

The Central Government of India had warned the Karnataka state government one day earlier that state was high on the terror hitlist along with six other Indian states – Andhra Pradesh, Rajasthan, Uttar Pradesh, Maharashtra, Punjab, and Assam – and Union TerritoryDelhi.

There is a possible connection with the Andhra and Varanasi attacks. An official was quoted as saying "The aim of these groups, whether HuJI or LeT or Simi, is clear. Bangalore and Hyderabad are being chosen as targets to create panic in the US as the cities house [the] biggest IT companies from the US." The Andhra – Karnataka link involves Raziuddin Nasir, a Hyderabad resident, and his aide Hafiz Khan Adnan from Bangalore, were arrested near Hubli in Karnataka this year. Furthermore, another clear link between the terror elements in both blasts is the explosive material used. In the Bangalore blasts an explosive with an ammonium nitrate base was used, while in the Gokul Chat and Lumbini Park explosions in Hyderabad a similar ammonium nitrate base was used. These were also of low intensity with the aim of creating panic. Like the Malegaon and Mecca Masjid blasts, it took place on a Friday during or just after the prayers. In response to these blasts security was also beefed up in Andhra Pradesh.

It was also reported that sleeper cells have gained a firm foothold in Karnataka with the discovery of terror camps in the Karnataka forest early in the year. In this vein, near-simultaneous blasts – all having the footprint of the jehadi network that had carried out blasts in Varanasi, Jaipur, Mumbai and elsewhere – point to the strong foothold terrorists have made in the city.

On 29 July, the Bangalore police Anti Terrorism Squad (ATS) arrested a SIMI activist named Sameer Sadiq in connection with the blasts. According to the police, Sadiq had played a key role in the Surat riots. He was staying at Gurapanapalya in Bangalore, the area which incidentally housed the SIMI office before it had been banned.

On 30 July 2008, the Intelligence Bureau (IB) indicated that two men – Rasool Khan Parti and Mohammad Sufiya Ahmed Patangiya – currently living at Farahan Arcade Gulistan in Karachi were the masterminds behind the Ahmedabad and the Bangalore serial blasts. They used to reside in Hyderabad, Andhra Pradesh. Both are possibly members of Harkat-ul-Jihad-al-Islami. The Gujarat Police has been looking for them in connection to the murder of former Gujarat state minister Haren Pandya.

On December 2009, two Lashkar-e-Taiba terrorists including Lashkar's South India commander Thadiyantevide Nasir were arrested by the Indian Forces from the Bangladesh border. Interrogation of them lead to significant evidences to the serial blasts in several Indian cities in 2008 especially the Bangalore blasts. Nasir's arrest paved way for the arrest of several Muslim youth from Kerala involved in terrorism, as well as evidences for terror links of Kerala politician Abdul Nasser Madani. His wife Soofiya Madani was arrested by Kerala Police on 19 December 2009 on the ground that she had taken an active role in Kalamassery Tamil Nadu state transportation corporation bus burning case. She has also confessed to Kerala Police, her involvement in organising the bus burning and planting bomb near coimbatore press club in retaliation to poor treatment of her husband in coimbatore jail. The main accused in the case,T Nasir, an Islamik sevak sangh activist (wing of PDP) turned Lashkar-e-Taiba terrorist is said to had actively coordinated and obtained endorsement from Soofiya Madani. T Nazir is involved in the cases ranging from the attempted murder of former kerala chief minister [E K Nayanar] to the recentBangalore bomb blast for which he is under custody of

Karnataka police. Bangalore police has already obtained ample proof that T Nazir and his associates like Abdul Sattar has good link with Madani family. These sequence of events has brought serious question toKerala's position holding the image of a good secular fabric in its society.

2008 AHMEDABAD BLASTS

The 2008 Ahmedabad bombings were a series of 21 bomb blasts that hit Ahmedabad, India, on 26 July 2008, within a span of 70 minutes. 56 people were killed and over 200 people were injured. Ahmedabad is the cultural and commercial heart of Gujarat state, and a large part of western India. The blasts were considered to be of low intensity, and were similar to the Bangalore blasts, Karnataka which occurred the day before.

Several TV channels said they had received an e-mail from a terror outfit called Indian Mujahideen claiming responsibility for the terror attacks; Islamic militant group Harkat-ul-Jihad-al-Islami, however, has claimed responsibility for the attacks. The Gujarat police arrested the suspected mastermind, Mufti Abu Bashir, along with nine others, in connection to the bombings.

These bombings occurred a day after the Bangalore blasts and a day before a bomb blast in the Indian state of Jharkhand.

The bombings

The bombs were planted in Tiffin carriers on bicycles, a pattern similar to the 13 May 2008 Jaipur bombings. Many of the blasts targeted the city bus service of AMTS (Ahmedabad Municipal Transport Service), ripping apart portions of the vehicles. Two blasts took place inside the premises of two hospitals, about 40 minutes after the initial series of blasts. One of the blasts in the hospitals occurred when injured victims of the initial series of blasts were being admitted there. Another bomb was found and defused on the following day in the Hatkeshwar area. Two live bombs were also retrieved from Maninagar, Gujarat Chief Minister Narendra Modi's constituency.

Gujarat police recovered and defused two more bombs in Surat, another major city in Gujarat, a day after the Ahmedabad blasts. Two cars filled with materials required to make explosives, including detonators, were also found, one of them parked on a roadside near a hospital, and the other in the outskirts of Surat.

Warning of attacks through e-mail

Several news agencies reported receiving a 14-page e-mail five minutes before the explosions with the subject line: "Await 5 minutes for the revenge of Gujarat", apparently referring to the 2002 Gujarat violence which took place after the Godhra train burning incident. The e-mail was sent by the group known as Indian Mujahideen on 26 July at around 6:41pm IST.

The contents of the e-mail warned of attacks in 5 minutes: "In the name of Allah the Indian Mujahideen strike again! Do whatever you can, within 5 minutes from now, feel the terror of Death!"

The e-mail also contained threats against the current Chief Minister of Maharashtra, Vilasrao Deshmukh, and his deputy, R.R. Patil, with the claim, "We wonder at your memory. Have you forgotten the evening of 11 July 2006 so quickly and so easily?"

Furthermore, the threats went on to warn Indian businessman Mukesh Ambani of Reliance Industries to "think-twice" before "usurping and building a citadel on a land in Mumbai that belongs to the Waqf board...lest it turns into horrifying memories for you which you will never ever forget."

The e-mail also reportedly threatened several Bollywood actors, asking them to stop acting.

Police reported that they questioned U.S national Ken Haywood from whose IP address the threatening email was sent. Haywood's residence in the Sanpada area of Navi Mumbai was raided by ATS officials on 27 July after the IP address from which a threatening email was sent minutes before the Ahmedabad serial blasts was found to be his.

Casualties

56 people were killed by the bombing and over 200 people were injured.

Initially, Prime Minister Manmohan Singh sanctioned an ex gratia payment of Rs 100,000 (US$ 2,300) to the next of kin of the dead. However upon visiting Ahmedabad, he raised the ex gratia figure to Rs 350,000 (US$ 8,050). In addition, he also announced a compensation of Rs 50,000 (US$ 1,200) for those injured in the blasts.

Gujarat Chief Minister Narendra Modi announced a compensation of Rs 500,000 (US$ 11,500) to each victim of the bomb blasts.

Investigations

Harkat-ul-Jihad-al-Islami has claimed the responsibility of the blasts. The email mentioned that "the innocent Muslims arrested in the (Mumbai) bomb blast case are being tried for years and years."

Union Home Secretary Madhukar Gupta said the Centre dispatched one team of bomb experts and decided to convene a meeting of top officials of state governments to discuss the situation arising out of the recent explosions.

According to the *Times of India* the intelligence community believes that both blasts of Bangalore and Ahmedabad were executed by a network of Wahabi fundamentalists masquerading as Indian Mujahideen.

Leads in the case

- Several TV channels stated that they had received an e-mail from a terror outfit called Indian Mujahideen claiming responsibility for the terror attacks. This e-mail has been traced to a locality in Navi Mumbai. This outfit in the past claimed responsibility for the Jaipur bombings on 13 May 2008.
- The police investigation has centered around the claims made in two phone calls.
- A doctor who was visiting one of the hospitals where one of the blasts occurred has claimed to have overheard a person talking on his cellphone saying, "Bangalore was a failure, however Ahmedabad will be successful and we will celebrate if God wishes.". A sketch of this person, shown alongside, was released. The doctor described the

suspected culprit as being around "30–34 years old; wearing a pink shirt; clean shaven; and seemingly an educated person."

- A person has claimed to have received two suspicious phone calls at around 8:00pm IST. In one of the phone calls, it is reported that the caller said, "Ejaz, kaam ho gaya hai?", which translates to "Ejaz, has the job been done?"
- Two cars, both stolen Maruti Wagon R models with vehicle license plates reading "GJ-6-CD 3569" and "GJ-5-CD 2908" were also found in Surat. One of the cars had four live bombs which were defused. In addition, a wooden box with white powder, wires, a battery and shrapnel was also found near Nupur hospital. The cars used for bombings in Ahmedabad and those that were defused in Surat were eventually traced to Navi Mumbai, from where they had been stolen on 7 July and 15 July 2008. Investigations revealed that they were subsequently laden with explosives inVadodara, before being brought to Ahmedabad and Surat.
- On 30 July 2008, it was reported that the police had found CCTV footage of the driver of one of the cars used for the bombings. The photo was obtained from a toll booth near Pune. It had been earlier established that the bombers had stolen the cars from Navi Mumbai before driving it to Gujarat. The car used in the blast at the Ahmedabad Civil Hospital was driven 6 times between Ahmedabad and Surat between 7 July and 24 July.
- On 4 August 2008, the Gujarat police claimed to have their first breakthrough in the case with the identification of the shop from where the LPG cylinders used for the blasts were bought. The police also claimed that the crates in which the bombs were planted were made from locally purchased wood.

Suspects

- The Hindustan Times reported on 28 July 2008 that police and intelligence officials had zeroed in on three masterminds behind the blasts. The suspects, Rasool Khan Yakoob Khan Pathan *alias* Rasool 'Party', Sohail Khan and Mufti Sufiyan, are suspected to be key operatives of either the Lashkar-e-Toiba (LeT) or the Harkat-ul-Jihad-al-Islami (HuJI). They are also believed to have got to Pakistan after the 2002 Guajrat riots.

- On 29 July 2008, the police detained three suspects, Abdul Qadir, Hasil Mohammad and Hussain Ibrahim, near Limdi on Rajkot-Ahmedabad highway in Surendranagar district, while they were leaving Ahmedabad soon after the blasts
- On 30 July 2008, it was reported on Rediff that the Intelligence Bureau (IB) believed two men, Rasool Khan Parti and Mohammad Sufiya Ahmed Patangiya, who are currently living at Farahan Arcade Gulistan in Karachi were the masterminds behind both the Ahmedabad and the 2008 Bangalore serial blasts. They were previously residents of Hyderabad in Andhra Pradesh, and are members of Harkat-ul-Jihad-al-Islami. The Gujarat Police has been looking for them in connection to the murder of former Gujarat state ministerHaren Pandya.
- On 16 August 2008, the Gujarat Police announced that they had solved the case, making it the fastest terrorism case to be solved in recent years. According to the Gujarat Director General of Police P.C.Pande, Mufti Abu Bashir was the mastermind behind the blasts, and up to 10 of his accomplices had been arrested.
- On 20 November 2008, the Gujarat Police claimed that Amir Raza Khan, a HuJI operative from Kolkatta now in Pakistan, was also the mastermind of the blasts. In a chargesheet filed by the Crime Branch, SIMI members Safdar Nagori, Hafez Hussain, Sibli Abdul Karim, Kamruddin Nagori, Amil Parvez and Mufti Abu Basher planned the attack and asked Abdus Subhan alias Tauqeer and Qayamuddin Kapadia for executing the blasts. SIMI members organised terror training camps in Waghamon in Kerala and Halol nearVadodara. Qayamuddin and Tauqeer then held a meeting with their local contacts in

the city for arrangements of logistics and support to carry out the conspiracy. The local contacts were those who were associated with SIMI before it was banned in 2001 by the Central Government.

Arrests

- Maulana Abdul Halim, a suspected Students Islamic Movement of India activist, was arrested from Dani Limda in the heart of Ahmedabad on 27 July 2008. He was alleged to be involved in instigating the Muslim youth after the 2002 Gujarat violence and sending them to Uttar Pradesh for terror training. Charges have also been laid on him for sending 33 youths for terror training to Pakistan in 2003. After his arrest, he was remanded to a 14-day police custody by the Metropolitan Magistrate in Ahmedabad.
- On 15 August, the Gujarat police arrested Mufti Abu Bashir, and nine others, in connection to the bombings. Bashir belongs to Binapara village in Azamgarh district of eastern Uttar Pradesh, and was believed to be a SIMI activist.
- On 24 October, a SIMI activist, Abdul Razik Mansuri, a resident of Gomtipur area Nagda district, Madhya Pradesh, had been arrested along with Harun Rashid, a Gujrat residence and send to Gujarat for questioning. The Joint Commissioner of Police for the crime branch, Ashish Bhatia, said: "He was arrested from the Nagda district in Madhya Pradesh by our team. He was there staying with some of his relative. We have brought him to Ahmedabad for interrogation." He added that Mansuri was likely to be produced before a court in Ahmedabad to be remanded to judicial custody.
- On 11 November, the Madhya Pradesh Anti-Terror Squad (ATS) arrested Qayamuddin Kapadia, a top-ranking member of SIMI and a key conspirator and executor of the attack, In Ujjain. Police claimed that Kapadia admitted his involvement in the Ahmedabad blasts, and that he, along with Abdul Subhan Qureshi *alias* Tauqeer of Mumbai and Riaz Bhatkal of Karnataka, collaborated with the SIMI cell

led by Atif to carry out the Delhi blasts. Atif was later killed in an encounter with Delhi Police.

- On 13 November, Rafiuddin Kapadia, the brother of the key accused, Qayamuddin Kapadia, was arrested by the city police of Ahmedabad. His arrest took the toll of the total held by the police to 43. The Joint Commissioner of Police, Ashish Bhatia, who is heading the probe in the serial blasts case, said: "We have arrested Rafiuddin Kapadia, brother of Qayamuddin. He was present at the SIMI training camp in Halol near Vadodara. He originally hails from Vadodara and was arrested today from Ahmedabad by the crime branch officials."
- On 26 March 2012, Maharashtra ATS arrested one blast suspect Mohammed Abrar Babu Khan alias Abrar Shaikh in an encounter inSambhajinagar. Khaleel Qureshi was killed and Mohammed Shakeer was wounded in the encounter. All are alleged to be members of terrorist group Indian Mujahideen. A police constable was also injured during the firing.

Legal case

Controversy arose in the court case of the 26 accused as the state was alleged to have suppressed the legal rights of the accused. On 23 October lawyers of the accused walked out in protest against the stand taken by the Metropolitan Magistrate. The lawyers wanted to meet the accused alone, however, they had moved an application stating that police did not allow them to meet their clients alone and that the Court should direct the police not to remain present while they were talking to the accused. The Metropolitan Magistrate countered that it was not possible as police had to be with the accused. He is said to have hinted at collusion between the lawyers and the accused, causing a walk out by the accused's lawyers. The next day, in two different cases, the designated Metropolitan Court remanded all the 26 accused to police custody till 31 October.

As per the legal rules police have to file a chargesheet in any case before 90 days of the first arrest of the case. However, on 11 November, about three and half months after blasts and the late

July arrest, the Gujarat police filed a chargesheet, pertaining to the city civil hospital blast and L G hospital blast case, in a court naming 26 people, all with alleged linkd to SIMI, as accuseds in the case. A 2,000-page chargesheet was filed in the court of the Metropolitan Magistrate, G M Patel. The accused included SIMI activists Mufti Abu Basher, Safdar Nagori and Sajid Mansuri. The chargesheet also listed the names of 50 absconders, and that police had so far examined 511 potential witnesses.

Similarities

Similarities between the Bangalore and Ahmedabad bombings were investigated, where the former suffered from eight blasts and the latter 21. Union Minister of State for Home Affairs Prakash Jaiswal told reporters in Kanpur that the similarities between this and the Bangalore blasts was that both "blasts were of low intensity" and were planted in crowded areas. Furthermore, both states – Karnataka and Gujarat – have BJP led governments.

Further threats

The threat of terror continued even after Ahmedabad blasts. The Gujarat police discovered an active bomb which was set to detonate at 12:00am IST in Hatkeshwar, Maninagar. A bomb squad was quick to respond and successfully managed to defuse the bomb in front of a large crowd, which rose to jubilation and applause upon bomb's defusion.

Kerala

A phone call from Pakistan to a Karnataka journalist claimed there would be more blasts in Kerala on Sunday. Kerala police chief Raman Srivastava said: "I have been informed by the DGP of Karnataka about the terror threat to Kerala. We spoke to the journalist concerned, who said he had received two calls today – one at 1 pm and another at 3:30 pm."

Surat

On the following Monday, just days after the Ahmedabad blasts, another bomb was found in Varacha area of Surat. The bomb was placed near an electricity transmitter and contained a packet 700–800 grams of ammonium nitrate, a packet of shrapnel, two detonators, one battery, and a circuit. This was found after the two car bombs that were discovered immediately after Ahmedabad attacks.

On Tuesday, 29 July, eighteen bombs were found in Surat, and were subsequently defused. They were found mainly in the diamond-processing and residential areas of Surat, within a span of just four hours. According to the Times of India, a top government official believed that the planting of so many "unexploded" bombs was probably a means to divert attention of the police from the ongoing blast probe. After Gujarat Chief Minister Narendra Modi visited the city another bomb was found and defused by a bomb disposal squad. All in all, 23 bombs were found in three days in Surat.

Forensic investigations revealed that the bombs had not exploded because the circuits had been wrongly assembled. The police were not sure whether that was on purpose or a way to estimate the reaction time of the bomb squad, for planning future attacks.

Rajasthan

Three bombs were detected on the road in Pali district, near Marwar in Rajasthan. The bombs, put in half-litre oil containers, were planted on the Marwar-Ranawas Road at gap of one km and were spotted by onlookers. The box carried a bundle of fuse wire, 30–40 marbles, 8 iron plates, and detonator. There was no timer nor any electronic devise attached to the explosives. The bombs were defused by the bomb squad.

Tamil Nadu

In Tamil Nadu, Sheikh Abdul Ghaffoor, 39, was arrested with an alleged plan of carrying out bombings on Independence Day, 15 August 2008. The plot included bombing the state capital Chennai along with three other cities in Tamil Nadu and at least six trains. Meenakshi Amman Temple in Madurai is believed to be on top of the list for such terror attack. The man was detained with a large cache of explosives and two timer devices. Apparently, it is believed that the plot was revealed by an arrested leader, P Ali Abdullah, of a banned organisation, who has been serving sentences in an Indian jail since 2003. Chennai city police later on 1 August 2008 announced that the arrests were not linked with either the Ahmedabad or Bangalore blasts.

Kolkata

An E-Mail was sent to Kolkata on 29 July 2008 to bomb 8 different locations in Kolkata. Subsequently, high alert was placed in Kolkata but the E-mail turned out to be a hoax.

New Delhi

Another E-mail was sent to the Japanese Embassy in New Delhi on 30 July 2008 to bomb several locations in Delhi. The mail was soon forwarded to the Delhi Police from the Japanese Embassy and the city was placed under a Red Alert. The E-Mail threatened to bombSarojini Nagar which was a target in the October 2005 bombings. Further to these threats Japan closed its embassy in New Delhi on 31 July 2008 and also issue warning to its citizens living in India to avoid crowded places like markets and train stations. Nevertheless the initial examination of a youth arrested for sending emails to the Japanese embassy indicated that he might suffer from some mental problems. Delhi police revealed that the youth who sent the email was frustrated of a failed visa application to the embassy and the email threat was a hoax.

Criticism

In criticizing the central government Ajai Sahni, executive director of the Institute for Conflict Management said "India's police to population ratio is one of the lowest in the world, barring the poorer African countries. There is a high deficit of personnel in intelligence gathering. The IB has barely 3,500 field officers. We need to address these shortcomings." Security expert Prakash Singh added "they (terrorists) have no fear of being detected, arrested or prosecuted." PR Chari, a research professor at the Institute for Peace and Conflict Studies, said "the blasts were a demonstration of their (terrorists) capabilities and a terse reminder of the state's helplessness." BJP president Rajnath Singh also blamed the UPA government for its "soft approach" to terrorism that has allowed terrorists to grow bolder. He also took the government to task for repealing POTA and for "sleeping over the anti-terror laws like GUJCOCA (an anti-terror law adopted by the Gujarat Assembly)". Gujarat Congress chief Siddharth Patel said: "'The Gujarat government has failed miserably on the law and order front." Adding that the terror attack pointed to the "total failure' of the state's intelligence machinery."

Conspiracy theories

Sushma Swaraj, a senior leader of the BJP, at a press conference in Delhi, claimed the ruling UPA government had a conspiratorial hand in the blasts to divert attention from the allegations of bribery as well as to gain Muslim votes. Times of India called her comments as "scandalous" and "outrageous remarks". The Congress party's spokesman, Shakeel Ahmed said that Sushma Swaraj should be "tried for treason" and her comments have "given a clean chit to terrorists and anti-national, disruptive forces both within and outside India". Later on 31 July 2008, BJP's spokesperson, Prakash Javdekar, clarified that the allegation of conspiracy made by Sushma Swaraj was her personal view and to the contrary the party viewed the attacks not as a conspiracy of the Congress party but as an "an attack on the nation". Although Sushma Swaraj's comments were critically commented by some media and her own party, T. K. Arun, a columnist of The Economic Times suggested that investigations should also look into her point that some of the blasts occurred in Muslim locals of Ahmedabad and "*that a large share of those getting slaughtered by the terrorists are Muslims*". The US national to whom the suspicious e-mail was traced escaped from India even after a lookout notice was issued.

Reaction

Hindu–Muslim Unity

It is widely believed that the attacks were carried out to bring about the levels of unrest Gujarat had seen after the Godhra train burning. It is believed that by targeting communally sensitive areas such as Sharkej, Hindus and Muslims, attackers wanted to provoke and reignite communal disharmony and riots. However, the people of Gujarat stood tall in unity against such violence. Peaceful demonstrations held across Gujarat by both Hindus and Muslims called attacks an act of cowardice. Such demonstrations of unity were also held in Delhi and Bhopal where Hindus and Muslims held candlelight vigils.

Upon his visit to the region, PM Singh praised Gujarat's unity saying "I commend the people of Gujarat for the resilience they have shown. These terrorist acts are aimed at destroying our social fabric, undermining communal harmony and demoralising our people".

President Pratibha Patil, Prime Minister Manmohan Singh, Vice-president Hamid Ansari, Chief Minister Narendra Modi, all condemned the blasts and appealed for calm. Minister of State for Home Affairs Shakeel Ahmedexpressed surprise and shock at the successive attacks. Home Minister Shivraj Patil said: "we should assess the situation correctly and try to help the people, who have suffered and plan to see that these things do not happen afterwards."

Opposition Bharatiya Janata Party leader L. K. Advani condemned the blasts, and demanded that both Gujarat and Rajasthan should be allowed to go for their own anti-terror legislation.

The Bahujan Samaj Party questioned intelligence agencies failure to be alert to the blast conspiracy, and urged the state Congress to ask the UPA to approve GUJCOCAas. The Vishva Hindu Parishad announced it planned a nationwide anti-jehadi movement from 28 July, and urged the government to act against terrorism "before it is late." AIADMK general secretary J. Jayalalithaa called for the revival of special act like POTA to "effectively counter terrorists and extremist outfits".

A host of others who condemned the blasts included Head of the congress party Sonia Gandhi, Union Minister of State for Home Affairs Prakash Jaiswal, CPI M, the All India Muslim Forum, Sri Sri Ravi Shankar, Sanchetna, Sahrwaru, Safar, AMWA, Muslim Majlise Mushavirat, Sarkhej Muslim Welfare Organisation, Ahmedabad Muslim Welfare Society, Sirat Committee, Aman

Samuday, Anhad, Swabhiman Andolan, Lok Kala Manch, Samarpan, Sarvoday Sanskrutik Manch, Bharatiya Muslim Mahila Andolan, Bharatiya Moolnivasi Janjagran Abhiyan, and Action Aid (Gujarat).

13 SEPTEMBER 2008 DELHI BOMBINGS

The 13 September 2008 Delhi bombings were a series of five synchronised bomb blaststhat took place within a span of few minutes on Saturday, 13 September 2008 at various locations in Delhi, India. The first bomb exploded at 18:07 IST, and four other blasts followed in succession, with at least 30 people killed and over 100 injured.

Background

Three bomb attacks had already occurred the same year in India. The first of these was on 13 May in Jaipur. The series of nine blasts over a span of 15 minutes claimed 63 lives, and injured 216. The second series of nine bomb blasts took place on 25 July in Bangalore, and claimed 2 lives, while injuring 20. The next day, on 26 July in Ahmedabad, a spurt of 21 blasts killed 56 people and injured over 200.

The Indian Mujahideen claimed responsibility for the Jaipur bombings through an email sent to Indian media and declared "open war" against India in retaliation for what it said were 60 years of Muslim persecution and the country's support of United States' policies, most notably the war in Afghanistan. *The Times of India* has reported that either the banned organisation Students Islamic Movement of Indiaor the militant organisation Lashkar-e-Taiba could be behind the blasts in Bangalore. Similar to the Jaipur case, after the Ahmedabad blasts, several TV channels reported that they received e-mails from the Indian Mujahideen claiming responsibility for the terror attacks.

Police say the Indian Mujahideen is an offshoot of the banned Students Islamic Movement of India, but allege that local Muslims are given training and backing from militant groups in neighbouring Pakistan and Bangladesh.

Details

Five blasts took place within a span of 31 minutes from 18:07 to 18:38 IST (12:37 to 13:08 UTC) in busy markets or commercial localities. Four bombs were defused.

The first blast took place at 18:07 at Ghaffar market (a municipal market along a stretch of Ajmal Khan Road, Karol Bagh) in which at least 20 people were injured. They were rushed to nearby RML hospital. The explosive was kept near a car, and resulted in a cylinder blast in an auto rickshaw, which was subsequently thrown up several feet into the air.

Immediately after, two explosions took place in Connaught Place in which at least 10 people were injured. Police and witnesses said that the bombs went off in dustbins in and around Connaught Place, a shopping and dining area popular with tourists and locals in the centre of the city. The first of these blasts occurred on Barakhamba Road, near Nirmal Tower and Gopal Das Bhavan at 18:34. A minute later, the second bomb exploded in the newly constructed Central Park in the centre of the Connaught Place roundabout, built above one of the main stations of the Delhi Metro. An eyewitness reportedly saw two men place the bomb in a dustbin at Central Park.

Subsequently, two explosions rocked M-Block market in Greater Kailash-I at 18:37 and 18:38 – the first near the popular Prince Paan Corner, and the other near a Levi's store. The latter damaged 10 shops.

Preliminary examination of the blast site said that low intensity ammonium nitrate tied to integrated circuits with timer devices had been used in almost all the serial blasts.

Four bombs were also defused – the first one at India Gate, the second outside Regal Cinema in Connaught Place, the third in Connaught Place, and the fourth on Parliament Street.

On the evening of 13 September 2008, IBN reported at least 30 deaths and over 100 injured. AFP reported that "Indian police (New Delhi police spokesman Rajan Bhagat) said Sunday that 20 people were killed and close to 100 injured."

Response

Police and security

Security was tightened across the national capital, with police personnel fanning out to railway and Metro stations, hospitals, bus terminals, the airport and other sensitive points like cinema halls, shopping malls and religious places. Barricades were put up on most city roads to check traffic. Several major markets, including the Sarojini Nagar market, which was targeted in the previous Diwali-eve blasts in 2005, were shut down and evacuated. Cyber-café owners were asked to keep a tab on customers.

A Central Industrial Security Force (CISF) spokesperson state that "security has already been strengthened and frisking and checking of the commuters have been stepped up. The Metro is under constant vigil". He added that extra personnel had been pressed into service to keep an eye on commuters.

Press confusion

The confusion in the aftermath of the blasts was evident in the press reports immediately following. The general consensus was that the blasts had claimed 18 lives. However, there was some disparity, with CNN claiming as low as 15, to NDTV claiming as high as 30.

There was also some controversy over blast sites and the sites where bombs were defused, most notably that where Zee News reported a bomb being defused at Central Park, while the *Outlook* Magazine stated that the park was a bomb site.

Responsibility

The Islamist "Indian Mujahideen" sent an e-mail to all major TV channels, informing them of the blasts just after the first one occurred. In the case of the bomb blasts in Jaipur, and Ahmedabad, e-mails were sent before the blasts.

Indian Mujahideen strikes back once more. Within 5 minutes from now... This time with the Message of Death, dreadfully terrorising you for your sins. And thus our promise will be fulfilled. Inshallah...Do whatever you want and stop us if you can.

The email was sent from Arbi Hindi. The email threatened nine blasts. A 13-page attached document depicts photographs of the previous blasts under the caption "our Jihad". The Delhi blasts are, according to the email, a direct reaction to the raids carried on and after the Ahmedabad blasts, and "harassments imposed by your (Indian) ATS and the police on the innocent Muslims". The document also mentions Amarnath dispute, violence against Christians in Orissa, Babri Masjid demolition and Gujarat riots.

The email was traced to Chembur, an eastern suburb of Mumbai. Mumbai's anti-Terrorism squad (ATS) confirmed that WiFi of the owner firm "Kamran Power" was hacked and used for sending the mail.

Reports claim that the Indian Mujahideen called this operation "*Operation B-A-D*", encompassing the Bangalore, Ahmedabad and Delhi Bombings. Intelligence officials had intercepted a call made "from the across the border" claiming "Operation BAD is successful", after the Ahmedabad blasts, which the Gujarat police that interpreted as Bangalore, Ahmedabad, Delhi, though the dates and specific places were not known.

Investigation

Two persons were detained from Connaught Place area soon after the blasts. Delhi Police said an 11-year-old boy had claimed to have seen the perpetrators; he informed police that the suspects, clad in black kurta-pyjamas, were seen placing bags in a dustbin. The Delhi Police soon, within three hours of the blast, arrested another person who the police suspect to be the mastermind of the blast.

Preliminary investigation by police reveal Indian Mujahideen-SIMI cell led by Abdul Subhan Qureshi alias Tauqir, having information technology background from Mumbai, to be involved. Another person named Qayamuddin is also under investigation. Four more people have also been detained and questioned.

In the morning of 19 September, the Batla House encounter took place, in which Delhi Police shot down two persons, thought to be suspects, hiding in L-18 block of Jamia Nagar, Delhi. Two others suspects were arrested while one managed to escape. Bashir alias Atif, believed to be the mastermind was one of the two killed. Inspector Mohan Chand Sharma, who was injured in the encounter, died in a hospital.

He was credited with helping to have killed 35 terror suspects, 85 arrests and also the winner of 75-odd encounters, 150 medals and seven gallantry awards.

Later, the intelligence team said that the arrested allegedly had links with Dubai and further questioned if they had any link with Dawood Ibrahim.

On 23 September, the police arrested five more people from Mumbai and Uttar Pradesh. All five are suspected to be part of the Indian Mujahadeen's think tank. The men were:

- Sadiq Sheikh, 31, software engineer from Mumbai
- Afzal Usmani, 32, hotelier in western suburbs of Mumbai
- Arif Sheikh, 38, electrician from Mumbra, Mumbai
- Mohammed Zakir Sheikh, 38, scrap dealer from Mumbra, Mumbai
- Mohammed Ansar Sheikh, 31, software Engineer from Mumbai

On 4 October they were sent by the judicial Chief Metropolitan Magistrate to 12 days' policy custody.

The crime branch has claimed that these are the operatives who had introduced themselves as Pakistanis to perpetrators of 11 July 2006 Mumbai train bombings. After the 2006 bombings, police had claimed that a group of SIMI activists along with five Pakistan nationals had planted bombs in seven trains.

On 11 November, the Madhya Pradesh Anti-Terror Squad (ATS) arrested Qayamuddin Kapadia, a top-ranking member of SIMI and a key conspirator and executor of the Ahmedabad attack. Police claimed that Kapadia admitted his involvement in the Ahmedabad blasts, and that he, along with Abdul Subhan Qureshi *alias* Tauqeer of Mumbai and Riaz Bhatkal of Karnataka, collaborated with the SIMI cell led by Atif to carry out the Delhi blasts. Atif was later killed in an encounter with Delhi Police.

2010 PUNE BOMBING

The 2010 Pune bombing occurred on 13 February 2010 at approximately 7:15 pm IST when a bomb exploded at the German Bakery in the city of Pune, Maharashtra, India. The blast killed 17 people, and injured at least 60 more, including an Italian woman, two Sudanese students, and an Iranian student.

The German Bakery is located near the Jewish Chabad House and the Osho *ashram* (an international meditation resort) in Koregaon Park, Pune. The ashram and the bakery are frequented by foreigners and the bakery, which is popular with tourists and locals alike, was busy at the time of the blast.

Two little known groups, the Laskhar-e-Taiba Al Alami and the Mujahideen Islami Muslim Front, claimed they were behind the bomb attack. But, according to government agencies, the attack could have been part of a project by Lashkar-e-Taiba to use the Indian Mujahideen, called the Karachi project. David Coleman Headley, a Pakistani-American terror suspect, has been accused of involvement in the project.

Location and time

The site of the bombing was the German Bakery, a two-decade-old popular establishment in Pune. The bakery, situated on the ground floor of a corner building in the Koregaon Park area of Pune, was reduced to rubble, though the rest of the building was left intact.

At the time of the explosion, the bakery's limited seating areas were full of students and foreign visitors from the nearby Osho Ashram.

A security alert had been issued in October 2009 for a Jewish Chabad house in the vicinity of the German Bakery, but the Bakery was not deemed to be at risk at the time.

Initial media reports indicated that a Liquefied petroleum gas (LPG) cylinder used for cooking had caused the blast, but the Pune City Fire Brigade issued a statement that the cylinders at German bakery were intact. Security agencies confirmed shortly thereafter that the explosion was a terrorist strike.

Victims

Nine people were killed instantly. The rest of the victims succumbed to their injuries a few days later, while undergoing treatment. TheChief Minister of Maharashtra, Ashok Chavan, announced, "Regarding the compensation payment to the dead, the families will be paid Rs. 500,000 (US$ 11,000) per person who has died in the unfortunate incident. And whatever the medical expenditure is for the people who have been admitted in the hospitals will be entirely borne by the government".

About sixty people were injured in the bombing. Forty-six were men and the rest were women. Twelve of the injured were foreigners: five were Iranian, two were Sudanese and two were Nepalese, and one each from Italy, Taiwan, and Yemen.

List of victims:

[hide]Name	*Age*	*Nationality*
Saied Abdulkhani	26	Iran
Rajeev Agarwal	23	India
Suleiman Alfatah	21	Sudan
Atul Ganpat Anap	26	India
Anindyee Dhar	19	India
Ankik Dhar	24	India
Binita Gadani	22	India
Shilpa Goenka	23	India
Aditi Jindal	23	India
Nadia Macerini	37	Italy
Aditya Jaiprakash Mehta	24	India
Gokul Nepali	30	Nepal
Shankar Pansare	27	India
Abhishek Saxena	24	India
P. Sindhuri	22	India
Anaj Sulaiman	21	Sudan
Vikas Tulsiani	24	India

Equipment

Commissioner of Police, Satyapal Singh, after receiving the preliminary report from the Forensic Science Laboratory (FSL), stated thatRDX explosive had been used. Ball bearings and nutbolts were part of the bomb. He added, "According to the FSL report received last night, the material used for the explosive was a combination of RDX, ammonium nitrate and petroleum hydrocarbon oil (ANFO). However, the quantity used has not been determined yet. Also the trigger mechanism is being investigated yet." It is not known whether a remote detonator or a timer was used to carry out the blast.

Initial hypotheses about the perpetrators and motives

On 14 February, the Indian Home Minister P. Chidambaram stated that responsibility for the blast had not yet been determined, but that Indian authorities were making attempts to interview David Headley, a Pakistani-American businessman, accused of involvement with terrorism who was then undergoing trial in the United States. In connection with the bomb blast, the Indian Home Secretary, G. K. Pillai also referred to Headley. News organisations have reported that Headley had visited Pune in July 2008 and March 2009 toscout the area near the blast and described him as a suspected member of Lashkar-e-Taiba, one of the largest and most active South Asian Islamist terrorist organisations. G. K. Pillai also said that the attack could be part of a project by Lashkar-e-Taiba to use theIndian Mujahideen in what Headley apparently called the 'Karachi project' during his interrogation by the U.S. Federal Bureau of Investigation (FBI).

The attack occurred just a few days after an agreement was reached between India and Pakistan to resume dialogue at a meeting on 25 February in New Delhi. The incident added to the government's vulnerability, with the opposition asking for suspension of the bilateral talks.

A little known group calling itself the *Laskhar-e-Taiba Al Alami* claimed it was behind the bomb attack in Pune in a phone call to the Islamabad office of the Indian daily *The Hindu*. The caller appeared to be educated, and said the group had split from the Lashkar-e-Taiba due to its affinity to Pakistan's Inter-Services Intelligence. The call appeared to originate from the Miramshah or Bannu district inNorth Waziristan.

Ilyas Kashmiri was believed to have masterminded the attack. He was killed in a drone strike in Pakistan on June 3, 2011.

Investigation

The Maharashtra police had announced a probe was under way to establish the cause of the explosion, while a Central Bureau of Investigation team was sent from New Delhi to Pune to assist in the investigations. Consequently the entire country was put on high alert, especially Mumbai and Hyderabad. After a detailed review of the internal security situation in the wake of the attack, Prime MinisterManmohan Singh directed the Union and Maharashtra governments to take coordinated and effective action to speedily investigate the terror attack.

Investigation in the blast is being done by Maharashtra government's Anti Terrorist Squad along with the National Investigation Agency in Delhi. Maharashtra ATS Chief K P Raghuvanshi is heading the blast probe. The agency has got crucial closed-circuit television camera(CCTV) footage of the alleged bombers.

Investigators first focused their attention on the prospect that the attacks were carried out by a Pune Jihad cell known to have existed since at least 2006. This came out from the questioning of Mohammad Peerbhoy, an Indian Mujahideen operative held in the course of a national counter-terrorism operation that targeted the Lashkar-linked group in 2008.

Just moments before the explosion, Paras Rimal, a waiter at the German Bakery had noticed the bag (containing explosives). When Paras moved in to investigate the bag, he was called outside the bakery by an unknown motorist who paid him ₹200 (US$3.30) to fetch a glass of water. Since Paras was away from the blast he sustained mild injuries and has become an important eyewitness for the police.

Investigators are also including other Indian metropolitan cities like Bangalore and Mumbai in the probe. Popular destinations where foreigners are often seen are being searched. Similarly people who checked in or out of hotels in the surrounding areas are also being tracked down. Over 40 people have been arrested during the investigation. Among them are four Kashmiris arrested in Hampi, Karnataka. Pune police arrested two suspects from Pune's suburbs on 16 February 2010. Another two were detained in Aurangabad.

The Maharashtra Anti-Terrorism Squad (ATS) identified Yasin Bhatkal, believed to be a relative of Indian Mujahideen founder Riyaz Bhatkal, as one of the main conspirators of the blast in a preliminary report submitted to the State Government on 7 April 2010. The investigating agency, in its report, has identified four more suspects involved in the blast, including the planters of the bomb – laden bag which went off in the German Bakery. Maharashtra home minister R.R. Patil told the Legislative Council that the suspects would be arrested in a few days and more details would be disclosed at a later stage.

On 24 May 2010, Maharashtra ATS arrested Abdul Samad Bhatkal, younger brother of Yaseen Bhatkal, as he got off Air India flight 812 at Mangalore International Airport for his alleged involvement in a little-known murder case. However, Home Minister P. Chidambaramlater identified him as the prime suspect in the German Bakery blast. Bhatkal had left for Dubai shortly after the blast and was returning after his visa expired. He was arrested using a Lookout Notice that was issued by the Mumbai police. Samad was trying to slip into the country through the Bajpe Airport by taking advantage of the situation that prevailed following the 22 May 2010 crash at Mangalore of flight Air India Express Flight 812. Bhatkal was apprehended based on investigation of CCTV footage from the German Bakery.

In September 2010, the ATS arrested Mirza Himayat Baig (29) for his involvement in the attack, as well as his aide Shaikh Lalbaba Mohammed Hussain alias Bilal (27), both believed to be members of Islamist militant terrorist organisation LeT. Baig was said to have taken bomb-making training in Colombo in 2008.

On 30 November 2011, the Delhi Police arrested six suspected Indian Mujahideen operatives whom they claimed to be the perpetrators of the 2010 Pune bombing, the Chinnaswamy stadium blast and the 2010 Jama Masjid attack. One Pakistani national was also reported to have been arrested. Two of the seven people were arrested in Chennai and were identified by the Delhi Police as Mohammad Irshad Khan (age 50) and Abdul Rahman (age 19), hailing from Madhubani district of Bihar. Another individual – Ghayur Jamil – a student at amadarsa in Darbhanga was also arrested from Madhubani on the charge of recruiting youths from near the Indo-Nepal border for terrorist activities, Abdul Rahman being one of such recruits. This charge was disputed by Jamil's father who billed him as a good orator and an honest, religious man who had lost a bag containing his belongings – including his PAN card, residential proof and photos – a few days back.

A Pune court on 18 April 2013 awarded death sentence to Indian Mujahideen operative Himayat Baig, who was earlier in the week convicted for his involvement in the blasts. Baig's lawyer A Rahman had said that though they respected the verdict, they would appeal against it in the Bombay High Court.

2010 JAMA MASJID ATTACK

The 2010 Jama Masjid attack occurred on 19 September 2010 when two gunmen on a motorcycle fired at a tourist bus near Gate 3 of the Jama Masjid in Old Delhi, India and injured two Taiwanese tourists. The incident provoked fears about security for the upcoming Commonwealth Games in Delhi. About three hours later a car parked approximately 150 meters from the spot caught fire, apparently due to a minor blast.

Two bike-borne gunmen opened fire at a stationary tourist bus purportedly carrying a TV crew from Taiwan at 11:24 pm, near Gate 3 of Jama Masjid. An explosive-laden device was planted in a Maruti 800 car, parked near a transformer near the mosque. The car had approximately 20 litres of fuel in its tank, which would have caused considerable damage if it had exploded successfully, but bomb timers failed and it did not go off. There were two victims of the shootout, Zeseweiu (27) and Chiang (28), both Taiwanese citizens. Zeseweiu head was grazed by a bullet while trying to escape, while Chiang was shot in the abdomen and had to be operated on. Both were declared to be out of danger the next day when the state CM and Union Home Minister paid them a visit.

Batla House encounter link

"In the name of Allah we dedicate this attack of retribution to martyrs, Shaheed Atif Amin and Shaheed Mohammad Sajid who proudly laid down their lives valiantly fighting the idol worshippers Delhi police on this day. Surely each and every drop of their blood brought a new life in the Muslim community and this is confirmed from the fact that Indian Mujahideen have swelled unexpectedly manifold.."

Email sent to media

The attack is significant because it took place on the second anniversary of the Batla House encounteron 19 September 2008, in which Atif Amin, suspected member of the Indian Mujahideen was killed. The Indian Mujahideen had been blamed earlier for a number of terror attacks, in Delhi, Ahmedabad, Jaipur Surat and Faizabad, between 2007 and 2009. According to investigating agencies, the revival of the group was announced in an email to the media, which also elaborated on the outfits intention of avenging the death of their former members.

Investigation

Subsequent police investigations revealed that one of the timers of the cooker bomb was timed to go off exactly at 11:37 am, approximately the time when the Batla House encounter was reported to have taken place two years before on the same day.

The terror attack took place barely 200 meters away from the Jama Masjid police station, and at the time of the shooting, the cops from PCR van stationed at gate number 3 had gone to settle a family brawl nearby in the Khankhana street, in the Machli Bazar area, allowing the bikers to flee. The Guide (Vikrant K.Sharma) accompanying the T.V team took the injured inside the bus and called the police immediately, the 20 CCTVs which were installed near the Masjid, were found to be lying defunct. The cameras had been installed on 14 April 2006, after the twin blasts at the Masjid. According to the police, the terrorists were divided in two groups; the first reached the spot on a motorcycle and the second group followed them in a Maruti car, which later caught fire due to the "crudely assembled" pressure cooker bomb in it. Police detained 30 people for questioning.

Subsequent investigations revealed that the revelatory email was sent through a SIM card connection whose location was traced toBorivali. It was purchased by a man in his 20s, from a shop in the Dadar Truck Terminus area in Mumbai, and the police were looking for a man from Beed in Maharashtra, who had furnished a driver's license and a pan card under the name "Purva Shinde".

On 30 November 2011, the Delhi Police arrested six suspected Indian Mujahideen operatives whom they claimed to be the perpetrators of the 2010 Pune bombing, the Chinnaswamy stadium blast and the 2010 Jama Masjid attack. One Pakistani national was also reported to have been arrested. Two of the seven people were arrested in Chennai and were identified by the Delhi Police as Mohammad Irshad Khan (age 50) and Abdul Rahman (age 19), hailing from the Madhubani district of Bihar. Another individual – Ghayur Jamil – a student at a madarsa in Darbhanga was also arrested from Madhubani on the charge of recruiting youths from near the Indo-Nepal border for terrorist activities, Abdul Rahman was said to one such recruit. Jamil's father disputed his son's arrest and billed him as a good orator and an honest, religious man who had lost a bag containing his belongings – including his PAN card, residential proof and photos – a few days back.

In August 2013, Yasin Bhatkal co-founder of the Indian Mujahidin and his close aid Assadullah Akhtar alias Haddi were arrested byNational Investigation Agency and as per NIA, in the in interrogations they accepted that they had carried out the attack at the Masjid. As per NIA, Yasin said that he was instructed by Karachi-based IM head Riyaz Bhatkal to target the mosque as the group was upset with Imam Ahmed Bukhari for allowing *"semi-naked"* foreigners inside it.

On 19 April 2014, a special cell of Delhi Police filed its final report before a local court in Delhi against the two under various sections of the IPC including 307 (attempt to murder), 120B (criminal conspiracy) and under the provisions of Unlawful Activities (Prevention) Act and the Arms Act. The police claimed in the charge sheet that Bhatkal was instructed by Pakistan-based handlers to carry out terror attacks just before the beginning of 2010 Commonwealth Games which were held in Delhi.

2010 VARANASI BOMBING

The 2010 Varanasi bombing was a blast that occurred on 7 December 2010, in one of the holiest Hindu cities, Varanasi. The explosion occurred at Sheetla Ghat, adjacent to the mainDashashwamedh Ghat, where the sunset *aarti*, the evening prayer ritual to the holy river,Ganges had commenced, on these stone steps leading to it, where thousands of worshipers and tourists had gathered. It killed a two-year old girl, sitting on her mother's lap, the mother was one of three critically injured, more than 38 other people were injured. In the ensuing panic after the blast, a railing broke causing a stampede leading to an increase in the number of injuries. The bomb was hidden inside a milk container on the Sheetla Ghat. The blast occurred a day after the anniversary of the 1992 Babri Masjid demolition, in which a mosque was demolished at Ayodhya leading to nationwide religious riots killing over 2,000 people. Subsequently, the Islamist millitant group, Indian Mujahideen, claimed responsibility of the blast, via email to Indian media. This is also the second terrorism-related incident in the city which was rocked by the serial blasts of 2006, in which 28 people were killed, it included an explosion at the Sankatmochan Temple, some two kilometres away.

Sitala Ghat is the southern extension of the Dashashwamedh Ghat, and its stone steps lead to Sitala Mata Temple. Also close by is the historic Kashi Vishwanath Temple, the Shiva temple which has one of the 12 Jyotirlinga of India. The present ghat was re-furbished in c. 1740 by Pt. Narayana Diksit the preceptor of Peshwa Baji Rao I, the Prime Minister of the Maratha Empire.

Aftermath

After the incident 20 injured were admitted to BHU Hospital, 13 in Kabir Chaura Hospital, while 4 were sent to Heritage Hospital in the city. Six foreigners tourist were also injured including an Italian, Alexandeo Mantello, who was later said to be out of danger, French national Rachael, Ki Taro from Japan, South Korean Wan

Sen Kim, Italian Lydia de Mayo and a German citizen, Ozel. The death of the Italian tourist was wrongly reported in some media agencies, while he was recuperating in a city hospital.

The responsibility for the attack was claimed by the Pakistan-based Islamist millitant group, Indian Mujahideen, via email. In an email, dated 6 December, which was traced to WiFiconnections in the Vashi suburb in Navi Mumbai by the Mumbai Police, the Indian Mujahideen claimed that had carried out the blast as a revenge for the supposedly "biased" Babri Masjid verdict of 30 September 2010.

The bomb blast occurred at one of the steps of the Sitala ghat leading to the famous Sheetla Devi temple, which was surrounded by devotees and foreigner tourists. After the incident the Chief Minister of Uttar Pradesh Mayawati and Union Minister of Home Affairs P. Chidambaram visited the site, and appealed for peace. A national security alert was sounded and police intensified patrols in major cities like New Delhi, Mumbai, and Bangalore.

Elsewhere in hyderbad and Cyberabad the intelligence alerted local police on possible attacks on Dutch nationals in the city, after intercepting SMSs opposing the anti-Islam Dutch film *Fitna* (Devilry) by Dutch politician Geert Wilders.

On 11 December, a 50-year-old woman, visiting the town to watch the *Ganga Aarti* on the Dasashwamedh Ghat, succumbed to her injuries at a local hospital.

Investigations

The following day, Mumbai Police investigations showed that Pakistan-based Bhatkal brothers, Riyaz and Iqbal, the chiefs of the Indian Mujahideen (IM) being the brains behind the explosion, which was carried out by Dr Shahnawaz presently based both in Dubai and Pakistan.

He is the brother of IM foot soldier Mohammed Saif, who was arrested in the Batla House encounter on 19 September 2008 in which IM commander Atiq Amin was killed, while Dr Shahnawaz along with Khalid, Abu Rashid and Bada Sajid or Mohammed Sajid had fled to Nepal and now hold Nepalese passports.

On 8 December, three people, two amongst them identified as Shahnawaz and Assadullah (arrested by NIA August 2010 in Indo-Nepal Border), were arrested by the Uttar Pradesh state Anti Terror squad (ATS), and as per ATS sources they are linked to the 2008 Delhi serial blasts and also the Batla House encounter, which also occurred in 2008. The arrests suggested the revival of the Indian Mujahiddin terror outfit, which was dormant after the last encounter in 2008, a fact that is worrisome both for the state as well as the central government. The group however was previously suspected to be involved in the September 2010 Jama Masjid attack, in which two tourists were wounded in a machine gun attack, just before the 2010 Commonwealth Games in Delhi.

In the subsequent investigations at the site, which was cordoned off soon after the incident and screened by the investigating agencies,improvised explosive device (IED) was recovered from a metal dustbin, though no residue of the explosives, remains of any circuit or detonator were found, the device did not have shrapnel in it, thus there were no burn or shrapnel injuries, and all the injured were hit by pieces of wall that broke following the explosion, all suggesting the use of plastique explosive, PETN, TNT or C4. Early results revealed used of Semtex, a general-purpose plastic explosive containing RDX and pentaerythritol tetranitrate (PETN), however the final report of the Forensic Science Institute, Gujarat is awaited.

A writer for *The Diplomat* suggested that the blast not having occurred on the anniversary of Babri Mosque destruction on 6 December, and the shoddy design of the attack, were indicative of the weakening of the Indian Mujahideen due to police action.

MUMBAI 7/11 TRAIN BLASTS

This is one of the few attacks in the past few years that the IM did not lay claim to. In fact, days after the 11 July 2006 bombing of Mumbai's suburban train system, the Prime Minister went on national television to assert that he was "certain that the terrorist modules responsible for the blasts are instigated from across the border." More recently, in 2009, however, TV audiences were feted to a videotaped police interrogation that was leaked to the media in which Mumbai resident Mohammed sadiq sheikh confessed that he and four other men had carried out the bombings on behalf of an organisation that has since become well known as the IM. Yet, in November 2006, a 10,667-page chargesheet filed by Maharashtra prosecutors, alleged that seven Pakistani LeT operatives, each paired with an Indian partner, had planted the bombs. Sheikh's testimony leaves room for the possibility that the unidentified Pakistan perpetrators were, in fact, five Indians and more disturbing, that the Indians now being tried for planting the bombs may have had a peripheral role in the attacks or none at all. "Although both the Government of India and Mumbai Police appear convinced that an unassailable case has been built up, serious questions remain on both the integrity and content of the evidence." The question marks over the role of the LeT or the IM or both remain, with Mohdammed sheikh being discharged in May 2009 for his alleged role in the July 2006 Mumbai train blasts, after the Mumbai anti-Terrorism squad (aTs) stated that "there was no prima-facie evidence to prove his involvement but added that he was deeply involved."

In fact, in September 2008, doubts over the real perpetrators had started when the Mumbai Police crime branch arrested five IM operatives and held them responsible for the ahmedabad, Delhi, Mumbai 7/11 and all other blasts since 2005. Sheikh's release indicates the finesse with which IM terrorists operate, in that they leave very few (identifiable) signatures behind. Contradictory claims being made by police officials on different occasions cast serious doubts on investigations and whether the police is getting hold of the right people and is in possession of any evidence to convict or even charge them.

JAIPUR SERIAL BLASTS

On 13 May 2008, nine blasts rocked the Pink City within a span of 20 minutes, starting at 7.25 pm. The tenth bomb was found and defused. This was the first time that the city of Jaipur was subjected to terrorist attacks. Nine bombs in seven locations exploded between 7.25 to 7.45 pm. The blasts were synchronised to inflict maximum casualties. The first two blasts occurred at

Manak Chowk and as the crowd ran towards Johri Bazar, another two blasts at the national handloom Centre blocked the exit point, pushing the panicked crowd towards Tripolia Bazaar and Chandpol area, where subsequent blasts caused severe casualties. One of the blasts occurred in the vicinity of hawa Mahal, a popular tourist attraction, while two others occurred outside Hindu temples at sanganeri Gate and Chandpole. The bombs were of low intensity, but by meticulously placing them in highly crowded areas, the terrorists ensured a high death toll. Most of the bombs were planted on locally purchased bicycles in tiffin boxes, containing ammonium nitrate, tightly packed with metal pellets, shrapnel and ball bearings. The bombs were shaped to blast the pellets and shrapnel in a 60 degree arc, for maximum damage, with minimum explosives.

The Indian operational commander of HUJI-B, Mohammed Jalaluddin, arrested in Lucknow in 2007, had revealed during investigations that Jaipur was the prime target in the sights of HUJI-B. Police found credible evidence linking the Jaipur terror suspects to Bangladeshi militants. During interrogations, the bicycle sellers confirmed that the suspected terrorists who bought bicycles spoke Bengali. Two days after the blasts, the IM claimed responsibility for the attacks by sending an e-mail (containing a video) to a private TV channel. The e-mail address used was 'guru_alhindi_ jaipur@yahoo.co.uk'. The video showed a bicycle (serial number 129489) containing a parcel. Police officials confirmed that the bicycle used in Choti Choupad blast had the same serial number. Through the e-mail, the IM sought to caution the nation and threatened to "demolish the faith of the infidels of India". The e-mail was later traced by the police to a Ghaziabad cyber café.

The blasts followed patterns similar to the bomb blasts in hyderabad and Varanasi.

Police and intelligence sources suspect a collaborative effort of HUJI-B, LeT, SIMI and IM. The tactics of attaching bombs onto bicycles bears a resemblance to the November 2007 bombings in Uttar Pradesh by HUJI-B. The responsibility claimed by the IM for the blasts establishes the nexus between HuJI-B and the Indian outfit. In the first week of August 2008, the police made arrests and detained seven persons for questioning. One of the shopkeepers questioned had allegedly sold nine bicycles to a single individual, two days before the blasts took place.

Bengaluru Serial Blasts: On 25 July 2008, a series of nine low intensity bombs went off between 1.20 to 2.35 pm. The bombs were believed to have been planted around hosur and Mysore road, three days prior to the blasts. One unexploded bomb was found on 26 July 2008 and was defused by the bomb disposal squad. The bombs were rudimentary devices, composed of ammonium nitrate and urea, but for the first time, a high-tech micro chip was used that was programmed to go off at a set date and time. Mobile phones were used to trigger the bombs.

The blasts were oriented for maximum psychological impact and the motive was to target and terrorise the IT capital of India. On 29 July 2008, the Bengaluru Police ATS arrested sameer sadiq, a SIMI activist from Bengaluru.

BODH GAYA BOMBINGS

On 7 July 2013 a series of ten bombs exploded in and around the Mahabodhi Templecomplex, a UNESCO World Heritage Site in Bodh Gaya, India. Five people, including two Buddhist monks, were injured by the blasts. Three other devices were defused by bomb-disposal squads at a number of locations in Gaya.

The temple itself and the Bodhi Tree (where Gautama Buddha is believed to have attained enlightenment) were undamaged. However, the Archaeological Survey of India confirmed damage to new structures in the temple complex. International figures, including the Dalai Lama, Sri Lankan President Mahinda Rajapaksa and Myanmar Opposition leader Aung San Suu Kyi, condemned the attacks. On 4 November 2013, the National Investigation Agencyannounced that the Indian Mujahideen was responsible for the bombings.

Bombings

The Mahabodhi Mahavihara is an important temple for Buddhists worldwide. The bombs exploded between 05:30 and

06:00 IST (00:30–01:00 UTC), concurrently with the Sutta chanting and meditation which begin the daily routine of the *mahavihara*.

Four of the blasts occurred within the Mahabodhi Temple complex:

- The first bomb exploded at 5:30 IST, during prayers in the temple sanctuary.
- About two minutes later a bomb exploded on the east side of the complex, at the Animesh Lochna Temple. Wooden bookshelves, stacked with Buddhist scriptures, were damaged by this blast.
- A third bomb exploded on the south side of the complex, at the Butter Lamp House. This blast damaged the Bodhgaya Temple Management Committee (BTMC) ambulance parked there.
- A fourth bomb exploded on the north side of the complex, inside a small shrine; however, an image of the Buddha in the shrine was unaffected by the blast.

Five blasts occurred in Gaya, within a 500-metre radius of the Mahabodhi Temple complex:

- A small bomb exploded at an 80-foot (24 m) statue of the Buddha.
- Three bombs exploded at the Tergar (Tibetan) Monastery. One bomb was placed behind the door of a classroom where children study Buddhism. The windows and classroom doors were damaged; there were no injuries, since the children were on holiday.
- One bomb exploded on a bus parked at the Sujata bypass.

Indian Home Minister Sushilkumar Shinde said on 8 July that there were ten blasts, not nine as earlier reported; it was unclear where the tenth bomb detonated. Despite the blasts, BTMC monks opened the main sanctuary of the temple for routine prayer and rituals.

Bomb-disposal squads defused three more bombs, which did not explode because the analog timers in them failed. The bomb-detection team separated the detonator from the power source to defuse these bombs:

- A cylinder bomb at the Tergar monastery
- Another bomb near the 80-foot statue of the Buddha
- A third bomb was found during the afternoon, near the Royal Residence Hotel in the village of Baiju Bigaha.

Three pamphlets, handwritten in Urdu, were reportedly found with the defused bombs. Code words in two of the pamphlets seemed to describe the locations where the bombs would be planted, while the third pamphlet included the phrase "Revenge for Iraq".

Investigation

On 8 July the Bihar Police released CCTV footage of the blast sites at the Mahabodhi Temple and, based on an analysis of the footage, sketches of the suspected attackers. Sahidur and Saifur Rehman, brothers from Scotland and Saudi Arabia respectively, were identified from the sketches; both are alleged Indian Mujahideen (IM) operatives.

Another man, Vinod Mistri, was also arrested since his identity card was found at the blast site. However, Mistri claimed to have lost his card days before the blasts.

National Investigation Agency (NIA) released Mistri on 10 July for lack of evidence after taking his statement. An alleged IM tweet claimed responsibility for the Bodh Gaya bombings on the day of the blasts, warning that Mumbai would be the next target. The IP address was traced to Pakistan, and NIA investigated the claim.

On 16 July, NIA released the sketches and a video clip of a suspect in the bombings. According to the agency, the suspect (in Bhikkhuclothing) planted four bombs in the Mahabodhi complex. Witnesses noticed that the suspect performed Parikrama incorrectly. NIA reported that the suspected bomber intended to blow up the main statue of the Buddha, but did not enter the sanctuary because prayers had already begun.

Investigators discovered that the 13 Lotus timers used in the bombings were bought at a shop in Guwahati. They also ascertained that the clocks attached to the unexploded bombs were manufactured at a factory in Rajkot, Gujarat. The cylinders attached to the bombs were obtained in Bihar, so NIA suspected local involvement.

Investigators also confirmed that the bombs used in Patna and Bodh Gaya were nearly identical; one of the many similarities investigated was in the way the bombs were planted. On 4 November 2013 NIA raided a lodge in Ranchi, finding evidence of a plot to bomb pilgrimage sites. The evidence included a map of planned bombings and the coded names of the terrorists. An NIA agent confirmed that "the charts they recovered matched precisely".

The evidence confirmed that the Ranchi cell of the IM was responsible for the blasts. According to reports, Imtiaz Ansari placed a bomb near the Thai Monastery and Ainul (a.k.a. Tariq) placed one at the Tergar Monastery.

Mujib placed bombs at four locations in Bodh Gaya. The six-person attacking squad allegedly worked in pairs, and was assigned to place three bombs each.

NIA named the five bomb planters, who planned the attack over a year ago: Hyder Ali, Imtiaz Ansari, Tariq (a.k.a. Ainul) and Taufeeq and Mujibal Ansari. The agency suspects that Ali masterminded the plot with guidance from Tehseen Akhtar, a Ranchi-based IM operative. Investigators suspect that Riyaz Bhatkal, a Pakistani IM leader, commanded the attack.

Alleged warnings

Some members of the media blamed the Bihar Police, saying the blasts resulted from a lack of security at the management and operational levels. The metal detectors at the Mahabodhi Temple were not calibrated to detect bombs, and there were only four guards on duty when the blasts occurred.

A security expert said, "The decision to let the Bodh Gaya Management Committee man security inside the premises is preposterous and immature". Questioned by NIA in the US in June 2010 about the 2008 Mumbai attacks, David Headley claimed that Lashkar-e-Taiba prepared a video on the Mahabodhi Temple and was planning to trigger blasts there. The IM, responsible for the 2012 Pune bombings, revealed plans to attack the Mahabodhi Temple in Bodh Gaya in October 2012. In April 2013 the NIA issued a list of alleged IM operatives, including Gaya-born Amir Reza Khan (alias Parvez, alias Rizwan, alias Muttaki), a resident of the village of Maheyan in Mohanpur, Gaya who was the sixth wanted member of the list.

Reza, perpetrator of the Bangalore and Pune blasts, is suspected to have provided reconnaissance on the Mahabodhi Temple site. TheIntelligence Bureau (IB) issued several warnings, one in 2012 and two in 2013. The Bihar Police were alerted in June 2013 about the targets by the IB, and on 2 July the IB alerted them about the entry of two suspects into Gaya.

The Ministry of Home Affairs warned on 3 July that the temple was a target. The warnings caused a Bihar Police meeting the same day about security at the Mahabodhi Temple, but the blasts occurred within 100 hours.

The treasurer of All India Bhiku Sangha, Pragya Deep, said: "The administration had prior information. There was a report of the IB. A series of security review meetings have been conducted. There have been at least five to six meetings. It's shameful that despite this, the blasts have taken place. This is a mistake on the part of the administration".

After the blast, Chief Minister of Bihar Nitish Kumar said: "The government had always been on the alert and taken steps to ensure the security of the Mahabodhi temple and Bodh Gaya in general". A senior official of the IB said, "The Bodh Gaya temple was a long standing target and we had been reminding the Bihar state agencies about it. But our warnings were not taken seriously".

Perpetrators

As of 9 July 2013 no group had yet claimed responsibility for the attacks, and there was considerable media speculation about who might be to blame. The possibility was raised that the blasts might have been revenge attacks by Pakistan-based groups in response to the persecution of Muslim minorities in Myanmar by Buddhists. Similar Muslim-Buddhist tensions in Sri Lanka and

Thailand were also raised as possible motives for the bombings. A Myanmar-based Al-Qaeda affiliate, *Jamatal Tahawid Jihad*, was mentioned as a possible culprit (although the Indian Ministry of Home Affairs ruled that out).

The IM was also mentioned in connection with the blasts: an IM operative, Sayeed Maqbool, reportedly confessed during interrogation by the Delhi Police that he carried out the attacks. Prime Minister of Sri Lanka D. M. Jayaratne speculated that it might have been perpetrated by supporters of the Liberation Tigers of Tamil Eelam. The Bihar Police suspected Maoist connections to the bombings, but the Maoists denied their involvement.

Reactions

Indian President Pranab Mukherjee called the blasts a "senseless act of violence targeting innocent pilgrims and monks who had gathered to worship at this temple dedicated to the great apostle of peace—Gautama Buddha". Prime Minister of India Manmohan Singh condemned the incident, saying that India's "composite culture and traditions teach us respect for all religions and such attacks on religious places will never be tolerated". A national organisation of Buddhist monks, the All India Bhiku Sangha, also reacted to the attacks.

Its chairperson, Bhante Sadanand Mahasthaver, said: "Buddhist monks all over the country feel saddened by the attack. The international community is also shaken. We try to put people on the right path and we have been made the target of an attack. The All India Bhiku Sangha condemns this attack. This should not have happened. We spread the message of peace across the world. This is an attempt to spread terror and create discord among the messengers of peace". The Rajya Sabha condemned the attacks on Mahabodhi Temple; Chairman Mohammad Hamid Ansari described the attacks as "senseless act of violence" and "a cause of anguish and deep concern to all". The Government of Bihar proposed to establish an Anti Terrorist Squad unit in the state after the bombings.

The 14th Dalai Lama called the attack "unfortunate". Lobsang Sangay, Prime Minister of the Tibetan government-in-exile, said:

"I am deeply saddened to learn about the series of bomb blasts at Mahabodhi Temple. My prayers [are] for the injured and their family members". Karmapa Ogyen Trinley Dorje said he was "saddened to hear of the senseless violence" and asked Buddhists "to remain calm and refrain from any further escalation of the violence". Karmapa Trinley Thaye Dorje said he was "deeply saddened to hear of the bomb attacks", and prayed "that we are all able to respond with compassion to all those affected by this tragic event".

Sri Lankan President Mahinda Rajapaksa was shocked by the news of the explosions: "[i]t is with deep sadness that I condemn the explosions within the hallowed precincts of the most venerated and sacred Bodh Gaya shrine in Bihar in India. Undoubtedly, it is one of the holiest shrines highly respected and venerated not only by Buddhists throughout the world, but by all peace-loving human beings".

Burmese government and opposition leader Aung San Suu Kyi expressed her unhappiness over the blasts.

The Government of Thailand was "deeply disturbed by the bomb explosions", voicing security concerns.

Delegates from a number of Buddhist traditions at the Eighth Global Conference on Buddhism in Singapore passed a resolution on the bombings: "We are deeply saddened, but we forgive those responsible for bombing the Mahabodhi Temple in Bodhgaya. You may damage the most important temple in Buddhism but you will not destroy our faith in forgiveness and compassion".

The Northeast Indian Bhikkhu Sangha and Buddhists submitted a memorandum to the Prime Minister of India: "It is indeed a sad incident that miscreants tried to cause damage to one of the holiest Buddhist shrines which is not only the place of Buddha's enlightenment but from where the message of love and compassion pervaded the entire universe. The Mahabodhi Mahavihara, also being a World Heritage Site, is venerated by the world Buddhist community and such acts of vandalism deserve our strongest words of disapproval. We condemn the dastardly act and request the Government to deal with such anti social elements with a strong hand so that such acts of mindless violence do not occur again in any place of worship of any religious denomination".

In Nagpur during a protest, Buddhist monk Bodhi Priya Vinay tried to immolate himself but was stopped by police. Buddhist monks from Thailand, Laos, Myanmar, Bangladesh, Vietnam and Sri Lanka, including the World Fellowship of Buddhists, condemned the Gaya attacks. Throughout India, protestors led peace rallies and bandhs against the Bodh Gaya bombings.

World Council of Churches general secretary Olav Fykse Tveit expressed "heartfelt sorrow and solidarity" over the bombings. In a letter to the Buddhist community, he said: "We wish and hope that this incident, despite its traumatic and tragic dimensions, may be transformed into an opportunity to offer the world a glimpse of the best of your morality and spirituality".

6

Threat of Indian Mujahideen

INTRODUCTION

The origin and growth of the Indian Mujahideen (IM) have been linked to a host of issues including communal riots, perceived alienation among the Muslims, and even India's diplomatic relations with Israel. Some organisations and personalities have, on the other hand, termed it a mere conception of the intelligence agencies and an imagination of the media. Such speculations and presumptions notwithstanding, the evolution of the IM and its growth dynamics continue to be baffling. In the context of 18 episodes of explosions in 14 Indian cities since 2005, which accounted for hundreds of deaths, and despite the arrests and capture of several cadres, the group's violent campaign appears interminable and its capacities seem unassailable. The success of the IM could inspire terrorist outfits elsewhere to emulate, revitalise and challenge the state in a unique way.

Home-Grown and Expanding

The IM's aims and objectives, loosely defined as 'a war on a Hindu India on behalf of the persecuted Muslims' have constantly shifted. The first-ever 'manifesto' of the group released in 2007, after the bombings of court complexes in Lucknow, Varanasi and Faizabad, claimed that the blasts were intended to "punish local lawyers" who had attacked suspects held for an abortive kidnap plot by the terrorist group Jaish-e-Mohammad (JeM). Two other 'manifestos', released after the 2008 blasts in Delhi and the 2010 explosions in Varanasi, faulted "the Supreme Court, the high courts, the lower courts and all the commissions" for failing the Muslims in India. The focus on the judiciary has since shifted and in fact has become more mysterious, with the outfit discontinuing the practice of mailing its 'manifesto' following each attack, compelling the state agencies to depend upon the interrogation of arrested cadres to unravel the intentions behind the explosions.

As per such interrogation reports, the explosions in Pune in the state of Maharashtra in August 2012 were intended to avenge the killing of its imprisoned cadre Qateel Siddique by his cell mates. Blasts targeting the Buddhist shrine in Bodhgaya in the state of Bihar in July 2013 were said to have been in response to the attacks on the Rohingyas in Myanmar. The 27 October 2013 explosions in Patna, Bihar were reportedly carried out to protest against the communal riots in Muzaffarnagar in the neighbouring state of Uttar Pradesh. The recovery of a large amount of explosives at Ranchi in the state of Jharkhand on 4 November demonstrated the outfit's plan of maintaining the momentum in its violent campaign. Similarly, the recovery of other documents has further pointed to the possibility of the IM carrying out more violent attacks on Buddhist shrines, on foreign tourists, and public installations in the state of Chhattisgarh. The choice of such a wide array of unconnected objectives underscores the fact that, instead of remaining a purely ideology-based organisation with both local as well as global aspirations, the IM could be willing to carry out attacks by invoking almost any cause that might suit its convenience. Believed to be controlled by external forces and to nurture the aspiration of making common cause with the Al Qaeda, the IM's image could be transcending way beyond the metaphors of a traditional outfit that was triggering explosions only on behalf of the 'wronged Indian Muslims'. Largely defined as an indigenous or home-grown terror organisation within India, the IM leadership does not appear to be averse to the idea of transforming the outfit into a pan-Islamist terrorist formation in the long run.

Shadowy Network

The IM inherited a band of highly radicalised individuals from the Students Islamic Movement of India (SIMI), the proscribed

Islamist outfit, which served as a contact group and service provider for Pakistan-based outfits like the Lashkar-e-Toiba (LeT), Harkat-ul-Jihad-al Islami (HuJI) and JeM. Along with these outfits, SIMI was involved in a spate of attacks in India's urban centres. Towards the late-1990s and early-2000, however, SIMI underwent a vertical split, with a hyper-radical group separating from the parent organisation and forming the IM. Since then, meticulous planning combined with external support from its sponsors in Pakistan has shaped the IM into a formidable group.

Its success as a terror group rests primarily on the secrecy surrounding its operations. Information on the process of recruitment of cadres, assembly of weapons, funding pattern and internal sharing of vital information largely remain in the realm of unknown. In fact, its organisational fluidity and operational secrecy have turned out to be its greatest strength. Since its first attack in 2005, the outfit has managed to carefully create a highly fluid structure, capable of withstanding losses resulting from arrests of its cadres and pressures from the state agencies, and to continue with its bombing campaigns. While its top leadership is believed to be based outside the country, the middle-level and low-rank functionaries are primarily based in India, dispersed throughout the country and operating as 'shadowy networks' of small modules. A belief in the ideology of the group binds the modules together, whereas knowledge and operational plans to orchestrate attacks remain module-specific and localised. As a result, full knowledge of the group's operational dynamics and overall strategy is not available with a single module. The possibility that the IM could have undergone multiple splits itself, with each faction reporting to various leaders based in India and outside, has further complicated an understanding of the organisation's changing character and mode of operation.

The adoption of an amorphous decentralised structure and *modus operandi* contributes to the outfit's success and prevents an outflow of complete information in case a cadre falls into the hands of the state agencies. This explains the reason why so little is known about the operational aspects of the outfit, even after the arrest of hundreds of its cadres involved in the previous episodes of explosions. One important addition to this long list of arrests was Yasin Bhatkal, a senior leader of the outfit who was picked up from a village on the Indo-Nepal border in August 2013. Each such arrest has led to revelations of interesting bits of information about the cadres' personal history within the organisation but almost nothing about the organisation's future targets and activities. Not surprisingly, the arrest of Yasin Bhatkal did not yield much indication about the explosions in Patna, which were to occur less than two months after his arrest.

The IM tasks its modules to function as focal points of contact for recruitment drives. Educated, computer-and tech-savvy youths are the usual targets. However, young men who do not fall into the broad description of tech-savvy have also been recruited to be used to plant explosives, function as couriers and to assist in logistics. As the Patna blasts revealed, the haste in using the newly-recruited cadres in planting explosives has contributed to failures in the organisation's plans. In recent times, a young woman, students preparing for competitive examinations, shop-and hotel-owners, and even a former retired police officer have come under the scanner of the intelligence outfits for being active cadres of the outfit. Yet, the neutralisation of the IM's fully expendable cadres is not expected to impact the outfit in a significant manner.

The IM has used locally-procured materials to manufacture improvised explosive devices (IEDs), a tactic which not only makes the manufacturing process cost-effective but averts the danger of interception. At the same time, the IM also has worked to create depots of centrally-manufactured IEDs, to be supplied to individual modules when required. The outfit retains the services of few explosives experts, which include a couple of Pakistani citizens. Over the years, some Indian cadres have also been trained in assembling the IEDs, although their level of perfection may not have reached the highest levels. Some of the IEDs used in Patna and Pune failed to explode because of manufacturing faults.

In spite of some recent operational failures, the IM remains an extremely tricky outfit to neutralise. Indian official assessments of the IM's strength have varied significantly. In 2011, based on the interrogation of an IM cadre, Danish Riyaz, the agencies concluded that the arrests of a large number of cadres have severely dented the group's operational capabilities and badly affected its recruitment-and fund-raising drives. Recent official assessments, however, portray the picture of the IM as not just regaining its strength within India, but having spread into Pakistan as well as Afghanistan.

The success of the IM could indeed provide important pointers to the possible recovery of some of the groups in Southeast Asia from their current state of weakness and to how they might be able to recalibrate their strategies. The IM's unique personalised recruitment campaign, operational dynamics, localised mode of operations, harnessing of local grievances and global issues for eliciting support, and seamless switching between prominent cities and lesser-known locations for its bombing campaigns, could impart lessons to radical Islamists in countries like Indonesia, Thailand and the Philippines. Within the operating environments and constraints imposed upon their activities by the state agencies in Southeast Asia, these groups can attempt to seek a turn-around in their anti-state campaigns by using the IM model. While the IM's linkages with the Al Qaeda still belong to realm of speculation, the Southeast Asian groups, especially those belonging to Indonesia and the Philippines, already have a head-start in this regard, which could make them even more lethal.

On the other hand, the three key problems affecting the Indian response to the IM's violent campaign have several lessons for the counter-terror practitioners in the region. First, the presence of external support and India's sense of non-cooperation from Pakistan, where the top leadership of the IM is based, are critical elements for the survival of the top echelons of the outfit's leadership. Second, the lack of coordination between the centre and the states (provinces) in India inhibits the framing of a unified and effective counter-terrorism response. And third, knowledge gap regarding the changing character of the group prevents a fair assessment of its strength and effective responses to thwart future attacks.

Accordingly, the preparedness among the Southeast Asian countries to deal with any such evolving threat from the local groups would be critically linked not just to inter-state cooperation and intelligence-sharing, but also to the capacity to collect ground-level and operational intelligence regarding terrorist recruitment, dynamics and plans to take advantage of local grievances. Apart from expecting the directly-affected countries to share intelligence with their unaffected neighbours, the latter have an obligation to work closely with and, to an extent, show solidarity by offering resources and expertise to the less-resourceful countries so that they could effectively deal with the threat.

INDIAN MUJAHIDEEN: AFTER YASIN BHATKAL'S ARREST

When Yasin Bhatkal, cofounder of Indian Mujahideen (IM) was arrested on 29 August 2013 at India-Nepal border, there was more of disbelief than relief. The incredulity was because he operated with different aliases – Ahmed Siddibappa, Imran, Asif, and Shahrukh – at different places across India. He was also careful not to overly use mobile phones or emails for communication; did not stay in a particular place in India for more than a couple of weeks; even so, he preferred outskirts of towns or rural areas that are Muslim-dominated. Though wanted by counter-terrorism units of 12 states of India — Uttar Pradesh, Bihar, Delhi, Maharashtra, Rajasthan, Gujarat, Madhya Pradesh, Andhra Pradesh, Karnataka, Kerala, Tamil Nadu and West Bengal — Yasin Bhatkal evaded them for several years.

In fact, he was lucky at least three times from being nearly caught by the police. Surprisingly, he was once arrested in Kolkatta, but was given bail because the West Bengal police did not realise that he was indeed the IM kingpin Yasin Bhatkal. Yet, Yasin has managed to successfully plant bombs in Delhi, Pune, Bangalore, Mumbai, Ahmedabad, Surat, Jaipur, Hyderabad and Varanasi. No wonder, he has been dubbed as "the ghost who bombs". He is so hardened that his remark on bomb blasts was without any remorse: "these things (bomb blasts) happen; there is nothing new about them." The present arrest was possible only after a solid and continuous trail for over six months.

Now, the crucial question is: what is the significance of Yasin's arrest from India's counter-terrorism point of view? The importance of the arrest should be seen from the role and importance of Yasin to the Indian Mujahideen's objectives and functions. He has been the terror group's chief recruiter and bomb-maker for quite some time.

He personally built a network of sleeper cells and modules in places like Aurangabad, Jalna, Beed, Nagpur, Pune, Hyderabad and later at Darbhanga in Bihar. These places were preferred for indoctrinating Muslim youth due to the high density of Muslim population; and, in the case of Darbhanga, its proximity to the porous Indo-Nepal border. Minus Yasin, sustenance of present modules is in big question; also new ones are bound to suffer.

Having liaised with actors based in Pakistan, Yasin should be in a position to explain in detail the extent of Pakistan's involvement in terror attacks in India, especially the role of Pakistan's intelligence agency, ISI. He could help find answers to the many unanswered questions. Are the Pakistani claims that it really is not in a position to control anti-Indian militant groups based in its soil, valid? Or, is Pakistan controlling all activities, from planning to execution of terror attacks against India? Are other IM leaders – Iqbal and Riaz Bhatkal – hiding in Pakistan? If so, where are they? Who have been helping them? What are their plans for the future?

Also Yasin may have information about the various Pakistan-based militant groups that are linked to IM: their leadership, motivations, FUNDING, recruitment, training, bases (both political and military), logistical support, their linkages with state and non-state actors in Pakistan, other internal and external networks, their modules and 'sleeper cells' in India, process of selection of targets, plans for future attacks, and extent of their connections with Indian terror groups such as SIMI and IM. Not to mention, the IM leader's interrogation would throw a deep insight into the working of the IM: its leadership, organisational structure, recruitment pattern, funding sources and network, existing modules and sleeper cells, their future targets, local and external accomplices and so on.

Most importantly, Yasin Bhatkal's case would help the Indian authorities to understand the various causes for radicalisation of Indian Muslim youth, those groups involved in radicalizing them, on how the youth graduate to indulge in terror attacks against their own people, and, in the process, how they get their lives and ambitions trapped and finally destroyed.

From the prosecution point of view, Yasin Bhatkal could clear air in few cases like the Mumbai train blasts case of 2007 and the German Bakery blast case of 2010 where there is some confusion as to the real perpetrators. From law enforcement point of view, information from the IM leader would help the internal security mechanism to review the present counter-terrorism strategy and plug loopholes. Two lessons come out clearly in Yasin Bhatkal's case. One is the absence of a national database on criminals or terror suspects and network of all police stations. Such a database would have nailed Yasin long back. The second lesson is lack of coordination between central and state agencies and among various state police forces. Such deficiencies helped Yasin to stay free for long.

YASIN BHATKAL: THE MAKING OF THE INDIAN MUJAHIDEEN

Yasin Bhatkal, accused of being part of the Indian Mujahideen, is now in custody, but does the group face an uncertain future, or does it still hold lethal potential?

The origins of Ahmed Yasin Siddibappa, the man we know as Yasin Bhatkal, is in a prosperous enclave along the Mangalore coast at Bhatkal. At the family home, Yasin's father told us a familiar narrative of confusion and denial, that their son would do no wrong.

The school Yasin went to, run by the Anjuman Trust, is the legacy of progressive educational institutions of Bhatkal.

But Bhatkal, for all its progressive nature, and prosperity, is no stranger to communal tension that had swept the country. The Mangalore coast was one of the earliest points of entry for the BJP into the South, sparking a wave of violence.

Bhatkal witnessed deadly riots in 1993, in the aftermath of the Babri demolition in which 20 were killed followed by the killing of two BJP politicians in 1996 and 2004.

Through those turbulent years, as Yasin was coming of age, a parallel radicalism was taking effect amongst the Muslim community, with the growing influence of the ultra-conservative sect, the Tabhlighi Jamaat, drawing young men like him.

His father says that he called Yasin to Dubai, to work with him, but Yasin wanted to start a sports shop, over which they had an argument. After which they claim Yasin dropped out of sight.

The answers to those lost years could lie not far away from Yasin's home, in the home of Riyaz and Iqbal Bhatkal, accused of being founders of Indian Mujahideen, under whom Yasin would eventually serve-and who intelligence agencies claim are in Pakistan.

But their parents, too, claim innocence, saying their sons didn't even know Yasin.

It is true that Iqbal and Riyaz grew up in Mumbai in Kurla, where their father had set up a small business.

The parents say after their degrees, they returned to work in and around Mangalore.

But when asked about where their sons have been for the past five years, the family has no clear answers.

But investigating agencies say they have a fairly clear idea what the young men from Bhatkal were upto during the lost years, mainly after the arrest in 2008 of someone who lived near them in Mumbai, and who admitted to being part of the core team of the group that would evolve into the Indian Mujahideen.

That man is Sadiq Sheikh, a native of Azamgarh was living in the Cheetah Camp slum, abutting Kurla.

Sadiq claims he met Riyaz and Iqbal at SIMI gatherings in early 2000, just before the organisation was banned for adopting a violent path.

Sadiq was already on a violent path. He owned upto plotting, along with Amir Raza Khan, the Calcutta based criminal and Jihadist, the attack on the American Embassy in Calcutta in 2002.

He's also admitted to his role in the Shramjeevi train blasts in 2005, for which he claimed he was assisted by Atif Amin, another Azamgarh based native, killed in the Batla House encounter.

And Sadiq also admitted to one of the most devastating terrorist strikes in India's history-Mumbai serial train blasts of 2006.

When I met Sadiq recently, as he was being taken back to prison after a court hearing, he says he has retracted his admissions, saying they have been forced from him but police say subsequent events bore out what he told them.

The meeting of Sadiq and the Bhatkals would form the nucleus of the Indian Mujahideen.

Amir Raza Khan, from Kolkata, who had escaped to Karachi, would supply FUNDS and instructions. Riyaz and Iqbal Bhatkal, along with their lieutenant Yasin, would provide explosives from sand quarrying mines of Bhatkal.

Sadiq recruited young men from Azamgarh, amongst whom their main bomb maker, Arif Badr and the rising force in the group Atif Amin.

According to Sadiq's confession, the name Indian Mujahideen was decided at a meeting between him, the Bhatkals and Atif, at a McDonalds in the Mumbai suburb of Andheri, part of a strategy for an even more spectacular series of attacks, with emails prior to each blast.

The first of those emails signalling the Indian Mujahideen arrived two days after the Jaipur blasts, followed by blasts in Ahmedabad, Hyderabad and Delhi.

The attacks may have brought the higher profile the group intended, but it would also prove to be their undoing. A week after the Delhi blasts, both the Mumbai and Delhi police had breakthroughs. In Mumbai, more than 20 arrests made of key members of the Indian Mujahideen. In Delhi, the Batla House encounter had fatal consequences for Atif Amin, another alleged co-founder of the Indian Mujahideen.

During that wave of arrests, Iqbal, Riyaz and Yasin are believed to have fled to Karnataka. Based on leads from other arrests, a team from Mumbai police raided their hideouts, at Ullal, about 10 km from Mangalore. But the local police, not wanting to risk a communal provocation, had arrived with a huge presence, including the media. This alerted them and they could slip away.

The Bhatkals are believed to have travelled to Delhi onwards to Darbhanga in Bihar, and into Nepal, from where Iqbal and Riyaz fled to Pakistan.

Yasin, investigators say, stayed back in Darbhanga, signalling a new chapter in the Indian Mujahideen story. Here, he is alleged to have recruited local youth for fresh wave of blasts.

Yasin's first major strike on his own was the German Bakery blasts in 2010 after two years of silence of the Indian Mujahideen.

In a rare instance of luck for investigators, he was identified in the CCTV footage.

Despite this, he would figure as the main accused in the Bangalore blasts, also in the same year, bombs that went off two hours before an IPL match in Chinnaswamy stadium.

The Bombay serial blasts in 2011, was also, according to the Maharashtra police, the handiwork of Yasin Bhatkal.

By late 2011, the investigating agencies claimed they were alerted to the Indian Mujahideen's Bihar connection, making a series of arrests from in and around, the Darbhanga region.

Despite these setbacks to his group, Yasin, it is believed carried out the twin blasts in Hyderabad's Dilsukhnagar as recently as February this year, an indication that the Indian Mujahideen might still have active recruits.

And it is to trace them, that the NIA have been conducting raids. Looking, amongst others, for those like Tehseen Akhtar, a young man from Darbhanga, they believe has succeeded Yasin, and who like Yasin has a Rs.10 lakh bounty on his head. His distraught father says that his son has been missing for 2 years, and is innocent.

While the arrest of Yasin Bhatkal could lead to fresh arrests, as investigators try to crack down on the Indian Mujahideen network it has also intensified the demands for justice of those who believe they are being blamed for blasts carried out by Yasin.

Like Himayat Baig who has been convicted for his role in the German Bakery blasts.

The evidence on the basis of which Himayat was convicted had raised serious questions. He was arrested, standing at a bus stop in Pune, by the ATS, who claimed he was a Lashkar trained operative. The ATS took him to his house the same day and miraculously found RDX at his house. Now with Yasin Bhatkal's arrest, Himayat's lawyers hope he will get justice.

There is an even older backlog of accused, who say they have been wrongly blamed for crimes committed by the Indian Mujahideen.

Indian Mujahideen founder Sadiq Sheikh's confession-that he carried out the train blasts-has raised serious questions over the men arrested by the Maharashtra ATS for the same attack.

And while Yasin's arrest may be crucial in cracking down on the Indian Mujahideen's networks, equally crucial is to ensure that those wrongly accused of the same crime are given justice.

INDIAN MUJAHIDEEN AND ITS DUBIOUS ORIGIN

For all the claims, the probing and prosecuting agencies have not come out with one individual who has a proven association with this so-called nationwide organization supposedly working at the behest of Lashkar e Toiba, Hizbul Mujahideen, Taliban and you name who, so how do we know IM really exists or is merely the figment of imagination of the IB/Saffron brigade happily lapped up by an already biased media?

But let us just glean through the official explanation. Wikipedia says, "Investigators believe that Indian Mujahideen is one of many groups composed of lower-tier SIMI members. According to the Indian Intelligence Bureau, SIMI took new titles because the top leadership of SIMI have been detained and would be available for interrogation. The change in name is believed to signal a change in tactics as SIMI affiliated militants attempt to garner more support from India's Muslim community rather than be seen as a group consisting of foreigners. Two days after the 13 May 2008 Jaipur bombings, the extremist group sent an e-mail to Indian media in which they claimed responsibility for the attacks and said they would "demolish the faiths (all religions apart from Islam) of the infidels of India". The biggest and boldest attack to date by the group was the 2008 Ahmedabad serial blasts, where it gained national notoriety with a casualty count towards 50."

Now who banned SIMI and when was it banned and on what grounds? First came the terror attack on the Indian Parliament on December 13, 2001, which is a grey area because of the apprehension of the whole exercise sponsored by the then NDA-led government and specifically the Union Home ministry under the then Home Minister LK Advani. Soon thereafter Narendra Modi led Gujarat government patronized the pogrom of Muslims ostensibly to avenge the burning down of kar sevaks in coach number S-6, in the Sabarmati Express on February 27, 2002, just two months after the Parliament attack. Those who don't suffer from a memory loss remember the whole charged atmosphere created by Advani-Modi and Jaitley combine against the Muslim youth in preparation of bringing in POTA and to justify POTA SIMI was banned just a little before POTA was conceived. While announcing the ban Advani held a press conference in North Block and distributed to the media some SIMI posters in Urdu, none of which carried any seditious material. All these were expressions of anger and frustration over the Gujarat pogrom and the inability of anyone to counter Modi.

So what is wrong in saying that IM is an outcome of Gujarat pogrom? When did IM come into prominence and how? The official version says, "Two days after the 13 May 2008 Jaipur bombings, IM sent an e-mail to the Indian media in which they claimed responsibility for the attacks and said they would "demolish the faiths of the infidels of India". The biggest and boldest attack to date by the group was the 2008 Ahmedabad serial blasts, where it gained national notoriety when 56 people were killed in those serial blasts." This is the official version.

Who according to the official version are prominent leaders of IM:

1. Abdus Subhan Qureshi, alias Ali Tauqeeer a Gujarati software engineer from Mumbai

2. Safdar Nagori from Indore
3. Qayamuddin Kapadia, a TRADER from Vadodra
4. Usman Agarbattiwala, a PG diploma holder from Vadodra
5. Alazeb Afridi, a jobless youth from Ahmedabad
6. Abdul Razzzak Mansuri, an embroidery unit owner from Gujarat
7. Mujib Shaikh, a stone polishing artisan from Gujarat
8. Zahid Sheikh, a mobile repair owner from Ahmedabad
9. Amil Parvaiz, a native of Ujjain. These were the original IM men according to the IB along with just one Mufti Abu Bashir from Azamgarh. Later after the Batla House incident of Delhi, according to the investigative agencies it had also spread its tentacles in UP as well, and in particular in Azamgarh district.

But then stating the obvious becomes a crime and the BJP cries hoarse attacking poor Shakeel Ahmad while the Congress always lacking spunk, hurriedly withdraws what with the Heir Apparent in the ruling party advising everyone not to irritate BJP/Modi too much and so poor Shakeel has to shut up.

RIYAZ BHATKAL AND THE ORIGINS OF THE INDIAN MUJAHIDIN

Today, the Indian Mujahidin has been implicated in a number of attacks in India, and there are signs that the group could become increasingly dangerous due to its growing collaboration with Lashkar-i-Tayyiba (LT, or LeT) in Pakistan. The expansion of this network could pose a serious challenge to regional stability in South Asia.

Prosecutors in New Delhi charge that the principal organizers of the Jolly Beach gathering were Riyaz Ismail Shahbandri (also known as Riyaz Bhatkal) and his brother Iqbal. Most of the men at Jolly Beach knew each other only by aliases, but Indian intelligence officials believe that the gathering included the Bhatkal brothers, Abdul Subhan Qureshi, and the key figures responsible for the physical execution of bombings in northern India, Mohammad Sadiq Israr Sheikh and Atif Amin. Documents filed in Indian courts allege that the men played a key role in recruiting operatives, sourcing bomb components and organizing attacks. Furthermore, according to recent statements attributed to Pakistani-American jihadist David Coleman Headley (also known as Daood Gilani), the Shahbandri brothers now lead the "Karachi Project," an alleged LT operation to train and equip Indian jihadists for attacks in India. The bombing of the German Bakery in Pune on February 13, 2010, for example, may have been part of this project; one of the suspected bombers was Riyaz Shahbandri's lieutenant, Mohammad Zarar Siddi Bawa, known as Yasin Bhatkal, who was also present at Jolly Beach.

This chapter provides an overview of Riyaz Shahbandri's journey into India's nascent jihadist movement, while also providing insight into the origins of the Indian Mujahidin and how its collaboration with the LT is a growing threat to the region.

RIYAZ SHAHBANDRI'S EARLY LIFE

Riyaz Shahbandri's father, Ismail Shahbandri, left Bhatkal approximately three decades ago, hoping to make his fortune in Mumbai. He established a successful leather-tanning business in Mumbai's Kurla area, and eventually purchased an apartment in Kardar Building off the busy Pipe Road—an impossible dream for most city migrants. Ismail Shahbandri's prosperity ensured that his son, Riyaz, who was born in 1976, was able to study at local English-medium schools, and later civil engineering at Mumbai's Saboo Siddiqui Engineering College. In 2002, Riyaz married a Bhatkal-area woman, Nashua Ismail, the daughter of an electronics store owner. By this time, however, Riyaz's story had begun to diverge significantly from the trajectory his businessman father had likely mapped for him.

Shafiq Ahmad, Riyaz's brother-in-law to be, lived in the family's apartment as he pursued his studies in Mumbai. Shafiq, however, was also an activist in the Students Islamic Movement of India (SIMI), an Islamic youth organization, and eventually rose to become the head of the group's Mumbai chapter. Set up in 1977 by the Jamaat-i-Islami Hind organization, the Indian branch of the largest Islamist grouping in South Asia, SIMI was the group's student wing. SIMI, however, was disowned by its founders five years later due to its increasingly inflammatory rhetoric, which was viewed as pushing Jamaat-i-Islami Hind into confrontation with the Indian government. SIMI sought to re-establish the caliphate, without which it felt the practice of Islam would remain incomplete. Muslims comfortable living in secular societies, its pamphlets warned, were destined for hell. Ideologies other than Islam were condemned as false and sinful. After Hindu fundamentalists demolished a mosque in the north Indian town of Ayodhya in 1992, SIMI began to call for direct action. SIMI President Shahid Badr Falahi demanded that "Muslims organize themselves and stand up to defend the community."

Later in the decade, SIMI's polemic became increasing venomous. In a 1996 statement, SIMI declared that since democracy and secularism had failed to protect Muslims, the sole option was to struggle for the caliphate. Soon after, it put up posters calling on Muslims to follow the path of the 11th century conqueror Mahmood Ghaznavi, and appealed to God to send down a latter-day avatar to avenge the destruction of mosques in India. The organization was finally proscribed after the 9/11 attacks in the United States when SIMI activists organized demonstrations in support of al-Qaeda chief Usama bin Ladin, hailing him as a "true mujahid."

Due to Shafiq's SIMI activism, Riyaz began to spend time at SIMI's offices in Mumbai around 2001 at the peak of the organization's radical phase, associating with men who would play key roles in the development of the jihadist movement in India. Among them were: Abdul Subhan Qureshi and Mohammad Sadiq Israr Sheikh, who would co-found the Indian Mujahidin along with Riyaz Shahbandri; Ehtesham Siddiqi, who is now being tried for his alleged role in the bombings of Mumbai's suburban train system in July 2006; and Rahil Sheikh, who recruited dozens of Maharashtra jihadists, most notably for an abortive 2006 terrorist strike in Gujarat to avenge the anti-Muslim violence that had taken place there four years earlier.

In addition to his role in SIMI, Riyaz's worldview also appears to have been shaped by his brother, Iqbal. Iqbal's adult life took a rather different course from that of his brother. He studied Unani medicine, a form of traditional healing based on Greek, Arab and Indian practices that has some currency across South Asia. Yet Iqbal's primary interests were religious. Although it does not appear he received a formal education in theology, Iqbal was an enthusiastic participant in the activities of Tablighi Jama'at, a neo-fundamentalist Islamic proselytizing order whose annual gatherings at Raiwind in Pakistan are reputed to draw more followers than any Muslim congregation other than the Hajj pilgrimage.

Later in his life, Iqbal appears to have been drawn to the work of the controversial neo-fundamentalist Mumbai-based doctor-turned-televangelist, Zakir Naik. Naik has never been found to be involved in violence, but his words have lit up the imagination of diverse jihadists—among them New York taxi driver Najibullah Zazi, who pleaded guilty in the United States in February 2010 for plotting to attack New York City's Grand Central Station, among other targets. Zazi reportedly "became enchanted" with Naik's preaching.

Naik's Islamic Research Foundation (IRF), which was listed as an approved theological resource on the LT-affiliated Jama'at-ud-Da'wa website, has proved a magnet for LT operatives and many rank-and-file SIMI members. Rahil Sheikh, a key LT organizer who allegedly assembled a jihadist network that sought to execute terrorist strikes in the state of Gujarat, recruited cadre at the 2003 Srinagar convention of the Salafi Jamaat Ahl-e-Hadis, where Naik was a speaker. Sheikh's associate, Feroze Deshmukh, who is being tried on multiple terrorism-related charges in Mumbai, worked as a librarian at the IRF.

Naik has made various speeches that could result in radicalization. In one speech, he said, "If he [Bin Ladin] is fighting the enemies of Islam, I am for him. If he is terrorizing America the terrorist—the biggest terrorist—I am with him." Naik concluded, "Every Muslim should be a terrorist. The thing is, if he is terrorizing a terrorist, he is following Islam." When interviewed by reporters after Najibullah Zazi's arrest, Naik insisted, "I have always condemned terrorism, because according to the glorious Koran, if you kill one innocent person, then you have killed the whole of humanity." Nevertheless, ideas such as these were profoundly attractive to angry young Muslim men in the years after the anti-Muslim violence that tore apart the state of Gujarat in 2002. For Riyaz and the men who would form the Indian Mujahidin, their anti-India jihadist project represented a response to the political challenges confronting their communities, not an abstract global cause.

In 2001, Riyaz's SIMI links to ganglord Aftab Ansari brought him into contact with well-known organized crime figure Asif Raza Khan, a year before Khan was killed in a shootout with the Gujarat police. Authorities believe that Riyaz looked to Khan to use crime to fund jihadist operations. Following Asif Khan's death in 2002, his brother, Amir Raza Khan, set up the Asif Raza Commando Force, a jihadist group dedicated to the memory of his brother. Amir Khan, who is linked to a welter of jihadist operations including an attack on the U.S. Consulate in Kolkata, allegedly provided passports and funds to facilitate the training of several Indian Mujahidin members in Pakistan. In May 2003, Mumbai police investigators say that Riyaz and Ehtesham Siddiqi held the first of a series of meetings, some involving Khan, to discuss the prospect of using Nepal as a base to train jihadists. Nothing came of this plan, but Riyaz is alleged to have used Khan's funds to send several operatives for training in Pakistan.

By 2004, Riyaz had succeeded in tapping diverse sources to put together an organization committed to jihadist violence within India. The Jolly Beach meeting would serve as a key planning gathering before the group executed a series of increasingly lethal bombings.

THE ORIGINS AND FORMATION OF THE INDIAN MUJAHIDIN

Information on the early years of the Indian Mujahidin has been drawn from Sadiq Israr Sheikh, the only founding member of the group in custody. Like Riyaz and Iqbal, Sheikh was born in a family that had migrated to Mumbai. Beginning in 1996, he began attending SIMI meetings near his home in Mumbai's Cheeta

Camp area. Perhaps drawn by the sense of purpose, SIMI appeared to provide many young Muslims in Mumbai a calling when the relationship between Hindus and Muslims became increasingly strained due to communal violence. According to police, Sheikh grew tired of SIMI's polemics and was in search of a more effective medium to turn his beliefs into action.

In April 2001, a relative of Sheikh set forth a process where Sheikh would eventually meet Asif Raza Khan. Riyaz and Sheikh had known each other from their days as SIMI activists in Mumbai; however, they came together as partners in the Indian Mujahidin project through Asif Khan. After reportedly receiving training at an LT camp in Pakistan, Sheikh, on instruction from Amir Raza Khan, began to recruit cadre in Azamgarh, starting in late 2002. Key among them were Atif Amin, who was killed in an October 2008 shootout with New Delhi police, Arif Badar, and Mohammad Shahnawaz.

By 2005, after the gathering at Jolly Beach, the multiple Indian Mujahidin network components had fallen into place. Prosecution documentation filed in New Delhi suggests Atif Amin's Azamgarh cell was responsible for providing manpower for the attacks. Sadiq Sheikh liaised between the Azamgarh cell and the Indian Mujahidin's Mumbai-based senior leadership.

Iqbal Shahbandri raised operatives for a specialist computer-services cell. Riyaz Shahbandri and his cell sourced explosives and bomb components that were assembled into usable devices. Abdul Subhan Qureshi traveled nationwide, finding SIMI sympathizers to assist with cells.

During this period, parallel jihadist groups led by figures who knew the Indian Mujahidin leadership from their time in SIMI proliferated as well.

For example, Rahil Sheikh formed cadre who attempted to stage an abortive attack on Gujarat in 2006—an operation the Maharashtra police claim involved assault rifles and grenades packed into computer cases and shipped across the Indian Ocean by the LT. Nevertheless, the leadership of each separate jihadist network appears to have maintained operational secrecy, despite their common political past.

Little is known about the precise state of play between the Indian Mujahidin and the Karachi Project, but it is clear that the Indian Mujahidin network itself is just part of a larger jihadist project across India. The 2008 bombings in Bangalore, for example, were carried out by a jihadist cell that had supplied explosives to Riyaz, but had no knowledge of his operations. In the Bangalore case, LT-linked SIMI operative Sarfaraz Nawaz funded a Kerala-based jihadist cell run by long-time Islamist activist Tandiyantavide Nasir that trained recruits to carry out bombings on a ginger plantation in the forests around Kodagu, in southern India. Nawaz, who had worked closely with Qureshi in SIMI, does not appear to have known of his role in the Indian Mujahidin.

The central point is that the jihadist networks in India remain extremely fluid and consist of small groups of individuals who are loosely allied together. In this sense, they bear little resemblance to the large, hierarchically-structured Pakistan-based jihadist groups such as the LT or Jaysh-i-Muhammad—although even in the Pakistani cases there appear to have been some recent splintering.

Conclusion

Riyaz Shahbandri's story is evidence that substantial political problems are driving jihadist mobilization within India. It also makes clear, however, that the LT's infrastructure in Pakistan is critical to these networks' reach and lethality. Key leaders such as Riyaz Shahbandri and Sadiq Israr Sheikh trained in Pakistan. Indian investigations into the Indian Mujahidin's bombings have not reached closure because figures central to the network's functioning have sought safe haven in Pakistan.

Many in India's intelligence services fear that the recent bombings in Pune in February 2010, Bangalore in April 2010, as well as the abortive attack in Deloitte in Hyderabad in May 2010 herald the coming of a renewed wave of jihadist violence intended to undermine the country's economic progress and status in the run-up to the high-profile Commonwealth Games, which will be held in New Delhi in October 2010. Whether or not Riyaz Shahbandri's so-called Karachi Project is a new endeavor or simply a name for ongoing jihadist activity directed at India, the country clearly faces a growing problem from Indian Muslims who have become radicalized and are able to seek assistance from Pakistan-based militants.

Praveen Swami is Associate Editor of the Hindu, one of India's largest English-language newspapers, and reports on terrorism and low intensity conflicts in India. His most recent book, India, Pakistan and the Secret Jihad: The Covert War in Jammu and Kashmir, 1947-2002, was published by Routledge in 2007. The book was written while he was a Jennings Randolph senior fellow at the United States Institute of Peace in Washington, D.C., in 2004-2005. His scholarly work includes a 1999 book, The Kargil War, chapters in several edited volumes, and papers in journals including The India Review and Faultlines. Mr. Swami has won several major awards for his work, including the Indian Express-Ramnath Goenka Print Journalist of the Year prize, 2006.

7

Pakistan, the Radicalization of the Jihadist Progress and the Challenge to China

IDEOLOGICAL ROOTS AND STRATEGIC CIRCUMSTANCES

Political Islam has always been a reality in Pakistan since its birth in 1947. It is likely that political Islam exhibits a greater influence on the country's overall Muslim population than the myriad of extremist groups combined. The clearest manifestation of political Islam is within the creation of the *Jama'at al-Islami* (JI), Pakistan's first and largest political party founded by the late Maulana Mawdudi (1903-79), a Sunni Pakistani theologian, political philosopher, and influential 20th century Islamic revivalist whose work on Islamic resurgence and doctrine defines the group's activities and membership.

When he speaks of "Islamic nationality," Mawdudi means allegiance to the *umma,* which he envisaged as a sort of Islamic super-nation uniting all Muslims in the world into a single, indivisible community. He asserted a bi-polar worldview that juxtaposed the Islamic sphere with all else and insisted that Muslims should completely isolate themselves from those he deemed not to be Muslims. The struggle to make this change is known as Jihad.

For Mawdudi, Jihad was akin to a war of liberation for the establishment of politically independent Muslim states. He significantly changed the concept of Jihad in Islam and began its association with anti-colonialism and "national liberation movements."

Mawdudi was certain that the Islamic state would be "the very antithesis of secular Western democracy." He had written about the need for a "revolution" to create an Islamic state, but he believed this revolution had to be prepared by a long campaign of persuasion. Mawdudi himself never had a sufficient following to make a concerted bid for power in Pakistan.

Mawdudi's ideas set the agenda for Islamic movements from Morocco to Malaysia. From his revivalist efforts came the inspiration to re-achieve the glory that is Islam.

His ideas were carried to their ultimate conclusion by an Egyptian Muslim Brother, Sayyid Qutb (1906-66), who borrowed heavily from Mawdudi's vision of an Islamic state, but was far more impatient and urged that a believing vanguard organize itself, retreat from impious society, denounce lax Muslims as nonbelievers, and battle to overturn the political order. Qutb thus transformed what had been a tendency toward violence into an explicit logic of revolution and thus became the spiritual father of al-Qaeda.

Zia-ul-Haq, the military ruler who came to power in Pakistan through a *coup d'état* in 1977, strengthened the Islamic Ideology Council, revitalized the religious ministry, appointed the leaders of *Jamaat-e-Islami* (JI) as his advisors and declared himself the "soldier of Islam." The legacy left by Zia-ul-Haq during the late 1970s further solidified the government's ties to extremist groups.

RADICAL MADRASAS IN PAKISTAN

Madrasas are Islamic religious seminaries, usually established by a cleric of some importance. Madrasas owe their allegiance to various Sunni and Shia Islamic schools. Sunni madrasas adhere to different doctrines, such as those of the Deobandi, Ahle Hadith and Brelvi schools of thought. Depending on their doctrinal leanings, individual madrasas are aligned with different federations, the most prominent of which are *Wafaq-ul-Madaris al-Arabia, Tanzeem-ul-Madaris Ahle Sunnat, Wafaq-ul-Madaris Shia,* and

Rabiat-ul-Madaris al-Islamia. Wafaq-ul-Madaris represents the Deobandi school of thought, and has the largest number of followers.

The vast majority of madrasas pursue highly political activities that set them apart from non-religious schools. The madrasas' role in issuing *Darul Iftas* – religious edicts for individuals and organizations seeking legal opinion or Islamic legitimacy for their actions – also fuels sectarian tension. The poisonous books, pamphlets, audio and videocassettes published by sectarian organizations are widely distributed in madrasas.

Pakistan has seen a phenomenal 2745 % increase in Islamic madrasas since its independence in 1947 until 2001. In 2002 some 10,000 private madrasas with 1.5 million students representing 33 percent of total enrolment in Pakistan operated with very little monitoring by the government.

The convergence of the Iranian revolution, Soviet intervention in Afghanistan, the CIA-ISI (the Pakistani Inter-Services Intelligence) nexus to create a band of militant Islamists, the Islamisation program of the military regime of Zia-ul-Haq and the unremitting flow of external funding for ideology-based religious education, mainly from Saudi Arabia, have accelerated the process.

The message of Jihad in the madrasas was originally targeted against communism, to ensure a continued supply of recruits for the Afghan holy war against the former Soviet Union.

International patrons supplied arms and religious literature that flooded Pakistani madrasas, including special textbooks in Dari and Pashtu designed by the Centre for Afghanistan Studies at the University of Nebraska-Omaha under a USAID grant.

The end of the war against the Soviets in Afghanistan "removed the *cause célèbre*," but by then the Pakistani political system "had become hostage to this tendency."

The Taliban were the products of this type of Islamic education during the civil war in Afghanistan. By 1996, when the Taliban came to power in Afghanistan, the Islamist Pakistani organizations with the active support of the Pakistani government became the warehouse of militant supplies for the Kashmir conflict.

In 2000, the Khudamudeen madrasa trained students from Burma, Nepal, Chechnya, Bangladesh, Afghanistan, Yemen, Mongolia, and Kuwait. Out of the 700 students at the madrasa, 127 were foreigners. Darul Uloom Haqqania, the madrasa that created the Taliban, also trained students from Uzbekistan, Tajikistan, Russia, and Turkey. Pakistani groups and individuals help finance and train the Islamic Movement of Uzbekistan, a terrorist organization that aims to overthrow secular governments in Central Asia.

More than five years after Pakistani President Pervez Musharraf declared his intention to crack down on violent sectarian and jihadi groups and to regulate the network of madrasas, banned sectarian and jihadi groups, supported by networks of mosques and madrasas, continue to operate openly. The new Pakistani government elected democratically in February 2008 does not seem to have changed this trend.

The madrasas' role was highlighted in July 2007, after the female students of *Jamia Hafsa* and male students of *Jamia Faridia* madrasas – both controlled by Islamabad's Red Mosque clerics Maulana Abdul Aziz and Maulana Abdul Rashid Ghazi–occupied a government building for several months in Islamabad, challenging the authority of the Pakistani government. The stand-off led to a military operation in which Maulana Abdul Rashid Ghazi and dozens of madrasa students were killed.

The madrasas in the North West Frontier Province (NWFP) and in the federally administered tribal areas (FATAs) have been blamed also for the growth of Taliban-led militancy and a series of suicide attacks in Afghanistan and Pakistan in the last year.

The government of the Punjab province declared in July 2008 that 80 madrasas in the province are dangerous and ordered regular monitoring of their extremist activities. In the NWFP's Swat district, at least 26 madrasa students disappeared recently, and are believed to have been taken by the Taliban to train as suicide bombers.

TALIBAN — CREATURE OF PAKISTAN

During the 1980s, the United States and Saudi Arabia poured $7.2 billion of covert aid into the Jihad against the Soviets, the vast majority of which was channeled by the ISI to the most radical religious elements. After the Soviets withdrew, returning commanders, mujahideen groups and common criminals fought over the carcass of Afghanistan.

When it became evident to Islamabad and the ISI that the anarchy in Afghanistan was counter-productive to a policy of strategic depth as well as potentially destabilizing for Pakistan, they formed the Taliban. Beginning from a minor local movement in Kandahar Province in 1994 with few weapons and money, with massive covert Pakistani financial and military support, the Taliban rose to power and took over Kabul in 1996.

The Taliban, by hosting bin Laden's al-Qaeda, became an integral part of Sunni fundamentalist mythology and its international networks, and Afghanistan became a place where extremists from around the world could meet safely, share ideas, develop strategies, and receive training-a physical base of terror. Moreover, Pakistani extremist groups have functioned as umbrella organizations for other international terror groups that sought shelter in Afghanistan.

Ehsan Ahrari called this phenomenon the "Taliban syndrome"-the movement to create an Islamic order in Afghanistan based on a blend of strict observance of Islam from Saudi Arabia's *salafiyya* (puritanical) tradition. Islamic forces of Pakistan have created and nurtured this syndrome in the *madrasas* where the Taliban ("students" in Farsi) from Afghanistan received their education. Since the chief thrust of this education is on Islam and the need for *Jihad* (holy war) to establish an Islamic government, the Taliban members become firm believers and fervent practitioners of this training.

The "Taliban syndrome" also refers to the role of radical Islamists in the domestic and foreign policy of Pakistan and other contiguous states. Since this syndrome recognizes no borders it zealously seeks to establish an Islamic form of government anywhere in the region.

In July 2001, the Bush administration decided to isolate the Taliban leadership, eliminate the threat of their guest, Osama bin Laden, and put pressure on Pakistan to stop military and financial support. After the September 11, 2001 terrorist attacks in the United States, the American forces occupied Afghanistan. After the demise of the Taliban the world was made to believe that the movement ceased to exist. In fact, an accommodative approach towards the Taliban was adopted soon after US victory in Afghanistan. President Musharraf, addressing a news conference in October 2001 in Islamabad, said that "moderate Taliban" should be part of any coalition government in Afghanistan in order to achieve "national integration." Addressing the same press conference, US Secretary of State Colin Powell echoed the same opinion.

TERRORIST ACTIVITIES

The Jammu & Kashmir Conflict

This chapter will not look at the 60 years old conflict between Pakistan and India. There is already a huge amount of information and analysis by Indian, Pakistani and Western researchers, on this subject.

However, it should be stressed that various Pakistani governments have used the Kashmir issue for populist ends. General Zia-ul-Haq's efforts to Islamize the Pakistani state in the 1980s, by providing a religious basis for opposition to the Soviet presence in Afghanistan, and for his personal rule in the country, later found his expression in support for the Islamist insurgency against Indian rule in Kashmir.

The al-Qaeda pre-9/11 terrorist activities

It should be stressed that contrary to the impression given by the media and some analysts in the West concerning its so called diffuse independent networking character, al-Qaeda began life and continued its operations with the support of states: During the 1980s it began its activity against the Soviets in Afghanistan as the Mujahedeen movement with support from Pakistan, Saudi Arabia, and the US.

From 1990 to 1996 it worked alongside the Islamist revolutionary regime in Sudan to export revolution to Egypt, Algeria, Saudi Arabia and Eritrea. During the last phase of state support, 1996-2001, it was allied with the Taliban, and Afghanistan and Pakistan were used as an operational base.

Thus, Pakistan was involved directly or indirectly for two decades in the emergence and spread of global jihadist terrorism, including during the critical years for the preparation and execution of the 9/11 attacks on US soil.

Pakistan has been host since the 1980s to thousands of foreign jihadis who feared persecution if they returned to Egypt, Jordan, Yemen or Algeria. Some moved to Pakistan and others fought alongside the Taliban. The inflow of Arabs continued even during the 1990s with an estimated 35,000 foreign students in Pakistani seminaries or working with Islamic charities or NGOs. Half were Arabs, 16,000 were Afghans and the rest came from Central Asia, Burma, Bangladesh and elsewhere.

Under pressure from Egypt, Algeria, and others, Pakistan deported the Arab mujahedeen from Peshawar in 1991. Osama bin Laden financed the travel and false passports of 300 of them and shifted them to Sudan to continue their guerrilla training.

During the FBI investigation of the February 26, 1993 bomb beneath the two towers of the World Trade Centre (WTC), evidence was put forward showing that the plot was hatched at a terrorist training camp on the Afghanistan-Pakistan border. The mastermind of the attack, Ramzi Yousef, had resided in the bin-Laden-funded Bayt al-Shuhada hostel in Peshawar for the majority of the three years before his arrest. and was captured in Pakistan in 1995.

On 22 February, 1998 Osama bin Laden announced in Pakistan the creation of the World Islamic Front for Jihad against the Jews and Crusaders (WIF), in association with radical groups from Egypt, Pakistan and Bangladesh. Two main signatories of the statement were Mir Hamza, Secretary-General of Pakistan's Ulema Society (Jamaat-ul-Ulema-i-Pakistan) and Fazlur Rahman Khalil, Chief of Harkat-ul-Ansar (HuA) in Pakistan. The establishment of WIF was accompanied by two Islamic decrees (*fatwas*) by bin Laden and The Association of Islamic Clerics in Afghanistan (Ittihad al-Ulama' fi Afghanistan), declaring a religious war against the US. Critical to the formation of the coalition and its subsequent terrorist activity was the moral, political and logistical support provided by the Taliban in Afghanistan as well as Islamist movements in Pakistan.

The simultaneous truck bombings of the US embassies in Nairobi, Kenya and Dar-es-Salam, Tanzania on August 7, 1998, which killed some 250 people and injured thousands, the great majority of them Africans, was the first attack by al-Qaeda after the formation of the WIF and the major one before 9/11.

Bin Laden and terrorism proliferation issues had become an important benchmark in US-Pakistan relations. Pakistan strengthened its co-operation with the US through the arrest and extradition to the US of Ramzi Yousef, and an Arab follower of Osama bin Laden allegedly involved in the Nairobi blasts of 1998.37 However, this cooperation came quite late and under serious American pressure.

In October 1999, Pakistani Prime Minister Nawaz Sharif was deposed by General Pervez Musharraf. The Clinton administration hoped that Musharraf's coup might create an opening for action on bin Laden and influence the Pakistani military intelligence service, which supported the Taliban. By late 1999 diplomacy with Pakistan, like the efforts with the Taliban, had, according to Under Secretary of State Thomas Pickering, "borne little fruit."

Terrorism in Pakistan after 9/11

Osama bin Laden and "his crew" are most likely today in the FATA, in what is called the Bajaur agency. In 2003, Khalid Sheikh Mohammed, al-Qaeda's chief of operations, was arrested at the home of Ahmed Abdul Quboos, a member of *Jammat-e-Islami*. In August 2003, three Pakistani army officers, including Lt. Col. Khalid Abbassi and one Major Atta, were arrested on charges of helping Khalid Mohammed.

The al-Qaeda strategist Mustafa bin Abd al-Qadir Setmariam Nasar (aka. Abu Mus'Ab Al-Suri), who played an important role in international jihadist terrorism providing practical training, and theoretical foundation for the violent campaigns was reportedly arrested in Quetta in the Pakistani province of Baluchistan in late autumn 2005.

The Pakistan government has handed over to the US al-Qaeda leaders like Abu Zabaydah (March 2002), Ramzi Binalahibh (September 2002), Khalid Sheikh Mohammad (March 2003) and Walid B'Attash (April 2003).

The Taliban leadership (the "Kandahari clique") who are directing the attacks against the NATO coalition forces in southern Afghanistan resides in the city of Quetta, Pakistan. It is almost certain that the Pakistani intelligence agencies know the location of these individuals and actually have some kind of a liaison with them.

Lately, the creation of the so-called Pakistani Taliban, the radicalized tribal groups in the FATA have created new alliances under the name Tehrik-i-Taliban (TTP) and target the Pakistani state often using suicide attacks. Their best known leader is Baitullah Mehsud who was probably responsible for the assassination of former Prime Minister Benazir Bhutto on 27 December 2007.

Pakistan's counterterrorism effort thus remained intense but selective-with significant consequences for the overall success of the war on terror. The core members of the Taliban and al-Qaeda leadership have survived and remain active antagonists in the war against Afghanistan and the United States. Also surviving is the terrorist infrastructure supporting violence in Kashmir, which increasingly assists the Taliban and al-Qaeda.

The greatest challenge to Pakistan is arguably the rise of local militant Islam, both as an ideology and political force. The number of organized and ad hoc groups in Pakistan today that represent a radical form of "political Islam" is unknown, but arguably have a mass following from various quarters of society, including some elites, members of the armed forces, a booming madrasa population, and women members of right-wing women groups.

Pakistan's Taliban made outstanding progress in 2008 by controlling the tribal areas and undermining America's strongest ally in the region, former President Pervez Musharraf. Al-Qaeda expected improved relations with Pakistani authorities as the military command has been separated from the presidency.

The November 2008 Islamist attacks in Mumbai, India, highlighted the possible involvement in this major terrorist operation of Pakistani based terrorists with support from rogue Pakistani intelligence or military elements. The extremists behind the strikes "planned, trained and launched their attacks from Pakistan, and the organizers were and remain clients and creations of the ISI (Inter-Services Intelligence)," Indian Foreign Secretary Shiv Shankar Menon said.

Pakistani-born Ajmal Amir Kasab, 21, is the only gunman captured alive during the terrifying three days in Mumbai where 10 sites were attacked, including two five-star hotels and a Jewish centre, killing more than 170 people. His trial, on charges of terrorism, criminal conspiracy and waging war against the state, began in May 2009.

Pakistan has outlawed Lashkar-e-Toiba (LET), the organization behind the Mumbai attacks and arrested five conspirators who, according to Indian investigators, were involved in planning the terrorist strike and having it carried out, but they have not yet been prosecuted. However, Hafeez Mohammad Sayeed, the Amir of the Jamaat-ud-Dawa (JuD) a front organization for the outlawed LET, has been released by the Lahore High Court before which he had challenged the legality of his detention.

THE CHALLENGE TO CHINA-ETIM AND OTHER JIHADISTS

The special strategic defense, political and economic relationships between the People's Republic of China and Pakistan did not make it immune from growing Uighur terrorist and political Islamist and separatist activities based in Pakistan and Afghanistan under Taliban rule.

The Afghanistan/Taliban period

During the 1980s, Hizbul Islam Li-Turkistan, the first Islamist separatist movement in Xinjiang, was founded by Abdul Hakeem. One of his pupils was Hasan Mahsum, who left China in the early 1990s and settled in Afghanistan, where he established the East Turkistan Islamic Movement (ETIM). From 1995 to 1997, the struggle in Xinjiang reached its peak, with increasingly frequent attacks by militants in Xinjiang. Until the US invasion of Afghanistan in 2001, ETIM focused on recruiting and training Uighur militants at a camp run by Mahsum.

East Turkistan terrorist forces were responsible for over 200 terrorist incidents in Xinjiang between 1990 and 2001 that claimed the lives of 162 people and injured 440. These terrorist activities included explosions, assassinations, attacks on police and government officials, crimes of poison and arson, and establishing secret training bases in order to create an atmosphere of terror in Xinjiang.

In February and December 1998, dozens of members of ETIM who had received special training in Afghanistan sneaked into Xinjiang and inland provinces and cities, and established 15 secret cells to offer technical training in explosives to 150 terrorists from various regions. The Xinjiang police uncovered many of these underground training stations and confiscated large numbers of antitank grenades, hand-grenades, detonators, guns and ammunition.

In early 1999, bin Laden met with the leader of the ETIM, asking him to coordinate every move with the Uzbekistan Islamic Liberation Movement (IMU) and the Taliban, while promising financial aid. In February 2001, bin Laden and Taliban leaders decided to allocate an important sum of money for training the ETIM terrorists and offered them weapons and ammunition. After the training, some of the key ETIM members were secretly sent back to China to set up terrorist organizations and carry out terrorist activities and some joined the Taliban armed forces in Afghanistan.

Just several weeks before the 9/11 attacks, Ahrari made an interesting evaluation: "even if the Taliban are defeated in Afghanistan the attempted Islamization of Pakistan and its neighboring areas would only slow down or be postponed. Islamization is a politico-religious phenomenon that is based on Islamic internationalism. Whether a moderate or a hard-line version of Islamization materializes in Pakistan and elsewhere in Central Asia will depend on how the existing governments treat political dissent within their borders."

He noted that the People's Republic of China has special reasons for concern over the potential effects of the "Taliban syndrome" and the growing radicalization of Islamic parties in the region on the political stability of its Xinjiang Province, where the Uighur Muslims are seeking to win independence.

The effects of 9/11 and the demise of the Taliban

With the U.S. attack on Afghanistan in October 2001, ETIM was routed and its remnants fled to Central Asia and Pakistan. In September 2002, the United States declared ETIM a terrorist organization. Twenty-two Uighurs were captured in Afghanistan and Pakistan late in 2001 and transferred by US military authorities at the Guantanamo prison. M's leader, Hasan Mahsum was among eight persons killed when Pakistan Army commandoes raided a suspected al-Qaeda hideout at Angoor Adda in the tribal area of South Waziristan on October 2, 2003.

Following Mahsum's death, a leaderless ETIM continued to interact with the Taliban and various Central Asian militants, particularly Uzbeks, and slowly reformed into a more coherent core in the Pakistan/Afghanistan frontier. In 2005, there were stirrings of this new Uighur Islamist militant group, the Turkistan Islamic Party (TIP), which established a robust presence on the Internet. In 2006 a new video surfaced calling for Jihad in Xinjiang, and later that year there were reports that remnants of ETIM had begun re-forming and moving back into Xinjiang.

The growth of the Pakistani Taliban and the links to ETIM

According to police sources in the North-West Frontier Province (NWFP), the Mir Ali area of North Waziristan in the Federally-Administered Tribal Areas (FATA) of Pakistan is under the effective control of the Islamic Movement of Uzbekistan (IMU). Small groups of Chechens and Uighurs are also present in the area. They work under the over-all command of Qari Tahir and are helped by Maulana Sadiq Noor, a local tribal leader close to the Neo Taliban.

On November 17, 2008, Mohammad Uyghuri, speaking from his base in the tribal areas of Pakistan, announced that Al-Qaeda leader Osama bin Laden issued a directive appointing Abdul Haq Turkestani, a resident of Xinjiang, as the organization's leader in China. Uyghuri added that some 300 Chinese Muslims were currently living in the border areas of Pakistan and Afghanistan, and that these Chinese Muslims have training camps in the tribal areas from which they are sent to China to join the armed resistance.

A man named Abu Suleiman, who claims to be a member of Al-Qaeda' media team in the region, said that the Islamic militant group in China is called Hizb-e-Islami Turkestan (Turkistan Islamic Party-TIP) and is funded by al-Qaeda. Chinese Muslims in the tribal areas are also publishing a magazine called *Al-Turkestan ul Islamia* (The Islamic Turkestan).

The three issues of this magazine published until May 2009 are similar to other jihadist journals such as Sawt al-Jihad (Voice of Jihad), published by al-Qaeda. They show that either the TIP is trying to associate itself with al-Qaeda and allied Salafi-Jihadi groups or al-Qaeda is aiming to attract "Turkistanis" to their global jihadi movement.

The TIP was unknown before it emerged in 2008 to make claims of responsibility for various terrorist attacks across China and also issued threats of attacks on the 2008 Beijing Olympics.

According to a reliable Pakistani newspaper, 172 of the 917 foreign students in the International Islamic University in Islamabad are from China. The most popular faculty among foreign students is Usuluddin (principles of Islam).

W.O., a French recruit of al-Qaeda, stated that the Arab camp was the smallest grouping of foreign fighters in FATA with about 300 to 400 recruits, mostly from Saudi Arabia but some from other parts of the Middle East and North Africa. According to him the largest group of foreign fighters in FATA was from East Turkestan.

Pakistan – China relations and the Uighur problem

In September 2003, Lequan Wang, Communist Party secretary for Xinjiang Automomous Region, and member of the party's top-level Politburo, stated that the Islamist separatists in China are trained and are securing assistance from international terrorists, including instruction in "several training camps in Pakistan." He also said that the Taliban had helped train many of the Xinjiang separatists.

In May 2004, Chinese Deputy Director of Public Security, Ma Mingyue, stated that some terrorists from Xinjiang are hiding in Lahore and Rawalpindi and have mixed up with the Chinese community in the two Pakistani cities.

In June 2006, Chinese diplomats in Pakistan declared that members of ETIM were planning to kidnap senior Chinese diplomats in the country.

In May 2007, the Chinese government requested Pakistan to hand over more than 20 Chinese activists of ETIM hiding in the tribal areas bordering Afghanistan.

The Chinese concern is due to three reasons: first, the threats to the lives of Chinese nationals. There have already been five attacks with four fatalities on Chinese nationals between 2003-2007 in Balochistan, in the North-West Frontier Province (NWFP) and the Federally-Administered Tribal Areas (FATA). Two of these incidents took place after the commando action in the Lal Masjid in Islamabad between July 10 and 13, 2007.66 Secondly, the failure of the Pakistani police to make any progress in the investigation into these incidents and arrest and prosecute those responsible. Thirdly, the failure of the Pakistani intelligence agencies to locate and neutralize about 20 Uighur terrorists belonging to ETIM who, according to the Chinese authorities, have taken sanctuary in Pakistan. The Chinese authorities were greatly worried that these Uighurs might organize a major terrorist strike in Xinjiang coinciding with the Beijing Olympics.

Hu Shisheng, a Chinese specialist in South Asian politics at the China Institute for Contemporary International Relations in Beijing, sums up the Chinese-Pakistani common strategic interests by stressing that a stable Pakistan is essential for building a stable Xinjiang. A disintegrated or dismantled Pakistan will be a disaster for China. Without close cooperation with Pakistan, how can China ensure stability in the huge tribal areas where Uygurs are active, he asks? Therefore China will contribute to its stabilization.

In this context, the moves of the Pakistani government in recent years to clamp down on Uighur settlements and on religious schools used as training grounds for militant Islamists are relevant. When tensions over Islamic extremism developed between China and Pakistan after Islamic vigilantes kidnapped several Chinese citizens, President Musharraf responded quickly and many believe that his decision to use military force against the extremists at the Red Mosque in Islamabad stemmed largely from the incident with the Chinese citizens, which had greatly embarrassed his regime.

In June 2009, Pakistan has extradited to China 10 of the over two-dozen arrested Chinese terrorists belonging to ETIM. The ETIM militants had actually been arrested after they attacked Pakistani Security Forces in the tribal areas.

All those extradited to Beijing were involved in terrorist activities both in China and in Pakistan and had also developed links with al-Qaeda network in the tribal areas of Pakistan. Moreover, ETIM threatened to kidnap Chinese diplomats in the Pakistani federal capital with a view to highlighting their cause.

The July 2009 sectarian riots between Muslims and Han Chinese in the city of Urumqi, Xiniang's capital, the worst ethnic violence in decades, when an Uighur mob took to the streets burning cars and buses, smashing shops and provoking tit-for-tat reprisals by the government, have left 183 dead, 137 Han Chinese and 46 minority Uighurs.70 Calm has been superficially restored to the Xinjiang Autonomous Region, but the internal and regional consequences of these grave events are not yet clear.

However, it can be already noted an escalation in the threats from jihadist circles and militants in Central Asia, Middle East and North Africa. On the jihadi Internet forums surfers remind readers that Xinjiang has a border with Pakistan, and call the Taliban and al-Qaeda to take revenge. Others threaten the thousands of Chinese workers in Mecca building train tracks, or suggest that al-Qaeda members in the Maghreb kidnap Chinese people and execute them.71 The most extreme responses were of surfers who demanded global Jihad leaders to put China in the Jihadi equation and to start supporting the "Turkistan Islamic Party" financially and morally.

Conclusion

According to a senior Pakistani nuclear scientist, "[ten years after the bomb], Pakistan has turned out to be a country that is badly insecure and frightened of its future... The most significant reality was that the bomb promoted a culture of violence which, in those circumstances, acquired the form of a monster with innumerable heads of terror; and today Pakistan is badly in its grip... In the near future, Pakistan faces real danger, not from India but from terrorism and fundamentalism.

The near-term policy consequences of the ongoing radicalization in Pakistan, and the failure of the Pakistani government to prohibit refuge for the Taliban as well as foreign jihadis in the FATA, are the continued destabilization of southern Afghanistan, the spread of the Taliban insurgency, and the further subversion of democracy in Pakistan.

Globally, there are fears that the collapse of the current Pakistani regime could lead to an implosion of the state itself, with grave repercussions on regional and international security. Pakistanis themselves are very much concerned about a disaster of national proportions.

On this background, less than a month after the newly elected democratic Pakistan government approved a military-devised accord with the Swat-based extremists on 13 April, 2009, the *sharia* (Islamic law) was established in this territory, and Taliban militants advanced to within 100km. of the capital, Islamabad, raising concerns about increased terrorist threats. Ahmed Rashid, the well known Pakistani journalist called it "galloping Talibanization."

As the tribal militants openly defied the writ of the state and under significant international pressure, the Pakistani military at last launched a campaign to eradicate Pakistani Taliban groups from their strong-holds in the Malakand region, including Swat.

After the Swat military offensive, Pakistan's army launched a military operation into South Waziristan – the stronghold of Baitullah Mahsud and the TTP network, potentially the toughest battle Pakistan's military has fought against the Taliban. The military's mandate, according to Prime Minister Yousaf Raza Gilani, was "to eliminate the Taliban once and for all".

It's hoped that the new resolute and tough strategy of the Pakistani government and army will eradicate or at least weaken significantly the radical Islamist movements, militias and terrorist groups and thus bring security and economic and social development to this beleaguered country and defuse threats of terrorism and subversion against its neighbors.

8

The Indian Mujahideen and the Islamist Terror Matrix

Following a series of urban terror attacks in 2008, including the three-day long Mumbai siege, terrorist groups maintained a low profile throughout 2009. Jihadi groups like Lashkar-e-Taiba (LeT), Harkat-ul-Jihad-al-Islami (HuJI) and the homegrown Indian Mujahideen (IM) remained surprisingly inactive as they regrouped in the face of a continuous crackdown on terror infrastructure across the country. Investigating agencies have managed to arrest a number of IM, LeT and HuJI operatives and have neutralized their support structures, mostly comprised of outlawed Student Islamic Movement of India (SIMI) cadres.

However, in a twist of events, the intelligence agencies issued an alert this January about a novel threat emanating from the supposedly weakened Indian Mujahideen. According to intelligence inputs, the IM have been planning to carry out major terror strikes using hijacked airliners. India's Intelligence Bureau (IB) has identified a pair of IM militants who have undergone pilot training in recent years, namely Shahzad Ahmed (a.k.a. Pappu) and Mirza Shadab Baig, a senior IM operative. Both are suspected of spearheading a planned 9/11-style terror event on Indian soil.

Shahzad, who hails from Uttar Pradesh, has been on the run since the September 2008 Batla House encounter in the national capital of Delhi. Shahzad's online profile and activities on a social-networking website (Orkut) exposed IM's future designs. (India Today, January 6).

THE INTELLIGENCE BUREAU DISCOVERS A MASSIVE PLOT

IB officials achieved a breakthrough on January 17 when they arrested a self-styled HuJI commander identified as Mohammad Abdul Khwaja (a.k.a. Amjad) from Chennai, in Tamil Nadu. The 27-year-old native of Andhra Pradesh had intended to strike major installations in South India during the forthcoming Republic Day (January 26) celebrations. According to his confessional statements he planned to target the Indian Oil Corporation (IOC) depot on the outskirts of Hyderabad city as well as refineries in Visakhapatnam and Chennai. Besides these installations, he also plotted to carry out assassinations in Hyderabad, mostly targeting police officials involved in past terror investigations. For these activities, Khwaja scouted at least 25 other Muslim youths from south India and reportedly sent them for terror training in Pakistan (Daily News and Analysis [Mumbai], January 19).

The most disturbing aspect of Khwaja's activities is the transnational linkages he has established over the years. Khwaja was found to be operating in and out of India, Sri Lanka and Bangladesh in the past few years, coordinating with the LeT, Jaish-e Muhammed (JeM) and IM leadership and establishing close ties with IM's elusive mastermind, Riaz Bhatkal (a.k.a. Ismail Shahbandri). Khwaja, who had worked closely with HUJI's slain operative Shahid Bilal and underwent terrorist training in Pakistan, was found to be using three passports—Indian, Bangladeshi and Pakistani—in three different names (Times Now TV, January 20).

Transnational Ties of the Indian Mujahideen

Though IM, a relative newcomer to the South Asian jihadi landscape, claims to be an indigenous terror group, IM's working relations with transnational terror groups (primarily Pakistan and Bangladesh-based) calls for close scrutiny. Even if the indigenous tag of IM is well suited, it is becoming clearer by the day that IM is a hybrid terrorist group with militants from a number of other terrorist outfits (including SIMI, LeT and HuJI) comprising the group's core. Recent Gujarat police investigations established the existence of this lethal combination when they concluded that IM operatives had carried out blasts under the direction, guidance and assistance of Pakistan-based HUJI operative, Amir Raza Khan (Ahmadabad Mirror, January 12). Khwaja's confession has now substantiated that assertion.

Following the countrywide crackdowns and the well-executed September 2008 Batla House encounter in Delhi (in which two IM members were killed by police), many IM militants are in custody while others are still evading arrest. A number of IM operatives with obvious SIMI backgrounds were arrested from Gujarat, Maharashtra, Madhya Pradesh, Rajasthan, Delhi and Uttar Pradesh. Others, including Zahid Shaikh, Yunus Mansuri, Abu Bashar Kazmi, Qayamuddin Kapadia, Abdul Raziq, and Asghar Peerbhoy, were arrested in the southern states of Karnataka and Kerala. However, the top leadership and the masterminds of the attacks, Iqbal Bhatkal, Riyaz Bhatkal, Abdul Subhan Qureshi (a.k.a. Taqueer), are still at large, with as many as 29 others who have been identified by the investigating agencies (Indian Express, January 9).

A Record of Terrorist Attacks

IM has claimed responsibility for a number of terrorist acts across India between 2006 and 2008, including the Mumbai commuter train blasts (July 2006); the serial blasts in Uttar Pradesh (November 2007); serial explosions in northeast India's Assam and Tripura states, (October 2008); and attacks in Jaipur city (May 2008), Bengaluru (July 2008); Ahmadabad (July 2008); and Delhi (September 2008). The Assam and Tripura (Agartala) attacks were claimed by the previously unknown Islamic Security Force-Indian Mujahideen (ISF-IM), which appeared to be IM's northeastern franchise. Lastly, investigations into the November 2008 Mumbai episode reveal tell-tale signs of IM's footprint, though the evidence is not yet conclusive. According to intelligence sources, a huge amount of money was sent from the Gulf through IM's Riyaz Bhatkal to execute the Mumbai carnage. The recent probe into LeT's Chicago conspiracy (which is directly linked to the Mumbai terror events) revealed that prime suspect David Headley and Tahawwur Rana received logistical support from IM operatives while they were in India. IB believes that Bhatkal knew about the

Mumbai attack plan and helped arrange local logistics through his underworld links in the city.

CONNECTIONS TO LASHKAR-E-TAIBA

IM's LeT connection is much deeper than previously thought. IM-LeT operations in South India (mainly in Kerala state) were looked after by Tadiyandavede Nasir (a.k.a. Ummer Haji) and his brother-in-law Shafaz Samsuddin, with direction from Pakistan-based Amir Raza. Both IM operatives hail from the Kannur district of Kerala and masterminded the July, 2008 Bengaluru serial blasts with funding and instructions from the LeT. Both Nasir and Shafaz were believed to be part of IM's Shahbuddin Gohuri Brigade as well.

Nasir's arrest in late 2009 also revealed IM's recruitment tactics and operational secrets. According to his disclosure, SIMI/IM and LeT operate under the guise of a Sufi sect known as Noorisa Tariqat, which has branches in many parts of southern India, including Kerala and Andhra Pradesh. Nasir and his fellow cadres reportedly indoctrinated many Muslim youths in the jihadi ideology with anti-Hindu diatribes and by focusing on alleged atrocities against Muslims in Afghanistan, Lebanon and Palestine.

Al-Qaeda Infiltration?

The threat from this hybrid but loosely knit terror group called IM now seems to be going in a more lethal direction. Recent reports suggest that SIMI/IM will give way to al-Qaeda, Harkat-ul-Mujahideen (HuM) and the anti-Shi'a Lashkar-e-Jhangvi (LeJ) of Pakistan as these groups set up bases on Indian soil. Intelligence Bureau officials suspect that international terror groups are thinking seriously about revamping IM, which is now in a state of disarray. There are terrorist sleeper cells across South India and a well entrenched SIMI network, primarily in Kerala, Karnataka and Andhra Pradesh. It has been reported that SIMI has at least 12 front organizations in the above-mentioned states which not only facilitate the establishment of an al-Qaeda led conglomerate, but also provide ample operational advantages (Rediff.com, January 12).

The IB believes that al-Qaeda and its affiliates have already started their operations with IM/SIMI by setting up sleeper cells, giving a breather to LeT and JeM, whose activities came under international scrutiny following the 26/11 Mumbai events.

Though al-Qaeda's foray into the region's Islamist terror scene came as a bit of surprise to many, the recent capture of Afghan national Ghulam Rasool Khan (a.k.a. Mirza Khan) has cleared the picture. Ghulam Khan, associated with the Hyderabad-based Indian Muslim Mohammadi Mujahideen (IMMM), has admitted to associating with al-Qaeda and the Taliban in the past. He also revealed his activities in Pakistan's Swat Valley and Afghanistan's Kandahar province during 2004-05. He was arrested while attempting to sneak into Bangladesh through the India-Bangladesh border at Purnia, Bihar state (Press Trust of India, January 19; Hindustan Times, January 20). The IMMM in question seems to be the same group headed by the LeT's Azam Ghauri prior to his April 2000 death in Andhra Pradesh. However, there are still lots of dots to be connected before the police figure out the actual extent of the activities of Ghulam Khan's organization and its purported ties with al-Qaeda and the Taliban.

Conclusion

Undoubtedly, the terror trajectory in India perhaps will take a sharp turn with al-Qaeda's formal entry into the region by bringing the existing terror groups under one umbrella. However, the most pressing threat to India in the long term comes from none other than the hybrid and homegrown Indian Mujahideen, as the IM/SIMI combined will provide the necessary space and foot soldiers to the sub-continental terror strategy of the larger LeT and al-Qaeda organizations.

TERROR AND THE INDIAN MUJAHIDEEN

There is something disquieting in what Ashish Khetan has written and said recently on terror in India (in The Hindu and on Tehelka.tv), and centrally within it, the Indian Mujahideen. More so, because it comes from one of the most credible journalist's today, who has done some commendable work over the years. A journalist I personally respect. But there are several reasons which compel this response. And yet, this is not just a response, but also an attempt to elucidate the many complex processes within which 'terror' is located today, and the way the discourse has transformed, and has implications for a people's negotiated relationship with their state.

Over the last one year, through Gulail.com , Ashish Khetan has exposed several cases which have been fabricated against individuals and groups, all of them Muslims. This expose, through the revelation of classified Interrogation Reports in the public realm-using the police's own documents to challenge their own story-has been, till now, the most brilliant and effective way to challenge the cases, which many, suspected to be fabricated from the very start. And this expose was, and remains, a brave and mammoth task requiring extensive contacts, sources, and credibility, as anyone working in the fiercely guarded territories of national security and 'terror' would know.

It is this body of work that constitutes the historical background and legitimating authority of his recent op-ed in The Hindu on terror in India , and forms its silent and silencing basis. And yet, the work itself is neither the point of the article, nor forms the basis of what Mr. Khetan is trying to say, while the article exists primarily in the realm of speculation and an authoritative *khutba* meant for the country's muslims. The larger argument in the opinion piece-the first one in which Mr. Khetan has made sense of his one year long research on terror cases in India-is not based on facts, beyond the jurisdiction of journalistic inquiry, unwarranted, un-necessary, laced with presumptions, and even possibly incorrect. But what makes it dangerous, so much so that the article seemingly overturns the very idea that Mr. Khetan has been challenging in the past, is the way it is implicated, and plays to, an extremely communal politics and narrative within which terror today has been a central rallying point. The ideological framework within which the fabricated terror cases have been expounded-neither supported by facts, nor seeking in any way to serve the struggle for human rights of the citizen-, sits comfortably with particular political agendas today. Let's take it piece by piece.

I am compelled to state that I do not write here as a Muslim. I am neither trying to contest a narrative of terror that has been associated with Muslims, nor am I speaking from the location of a Muslim in whatever else I am trying to say. I write here, today, as a citizen contesting and challenging the infringement of human rights of its citizens by the state-whether minorities or tribals, or any of those peoples, communities, religious groups who have been expendable in the state's slow and gradual weakening of democratic institutions. All in a political game of power and control over peoples and dissent.

Mr. Khetan's central argument is this: the Indian Mujahideen is a reality, a terrible spectre responsible for many of the blasts that have taken place in the last decade, and that Muslims should come to terms with it, develop a political understanding, move out of narrow narratives of victimization, stop defending all and any who have been accused of terrorism, and demand that all should be brought to justice-including the IM who are Muslims. Tactfully arranged within it is a secondary argument: that before the IM was busted in 2008, many innocent Muslims were wrongly prosecuted-as he has shown-and that the police and the judiciary has been complicit in producing and convicting them, making a mockery of the criminal justice system.

The stakes are high. To claim that the IM exists and that it is responsible for the many bomb blasts has huge implications, something that will be discussed later. But it is a claim that cannot be lightly made. What proof is offered behind the claim? None. Only Mr. Khetan's own reading and privileged access to Interrogation Reports(IR), none of which he deigns to share with his readers. Ironically, the only Interrogation Reports that have been revealed are those which have helped prove that the cases against some have been fabricated. It is based on this credibility that Mr Khetan argues that the Interrogation reports reveal a sinister reality of the IM that we as a people, or rather, muslims, have to come to terms with. But there appears to be a misplaced sense of value put on the Interrogation Reports', as well as limited understanding of how they can help prove that the accused in the 7/11 blast, or the others that Mr Khetan has revealed, were innocent.

There are three questions that need to be asked here:

1. Whether such a claim can be made based on IRs
2. Mr Khetan's authority or legitimacy to make such a claim
3. The possible, factual incorrectness of the claim.

The IRs are classified documents and are not meant to be shared publicly. They are prepared by the police for their own use. Though, that in no way raises its credibility, it does make them crucial if these internal reports stand in stark contradiction to another official case made by the same agency on the same matter. At the same time, IRs in themselves are of no evidentiary value in any court of law, nor do they have any inherent truth value as they could be lacking in any material basis as the information obtained by the police could be through the use of third degree and the person may be compelled to state what the agency *wants* to hear rather than the truth. Even in the realm of the commonsensical, the IRs are just that-reports prepared by the police of a suspect's interrogation, with no value whatsoever but as investigative leads. Since Mr. Khetan does not reveal the source and content of these IRs, one has to largely and only accept his word about there being anything in the IR's about the IM, if at all.

However, it is inconsequetial if there is anything in the IR's about the IM or not. The credibility of the previous work by Mr. Khetan, stems not from any inherent truth value of the IR's, but from something entirely different-the fact that these reports, prepared by the police themselves, *were contradictory* to the official case. And hence, a crucial part of the defence case against the official prosecution. The plea for the innocence of those prosecuted by the revelation of the IRs, has nothing to do with whether the IRs are true or not, but rests on contradictory evidence being available and the conscious and deliberate suppression of the same by the police. To put it simply while it is the job of the court to weigh the evidence and make a value judgment as to the truth or otherwise of the prosecution's case, the prosecution itself cannot act knowing that its case is false. In these cases, the IRs revealed that not only did the prosecution itself not believe in its own case, it infact had reason to believe that it was false. The good faith of the prosecution was hence absent and the prosecution was proved to have acted in bad faith. The IRs, in themselves are in no way any proof of the guilt of Sadiq sheikh or any others who have been clubbed together with the overarching term of the Indian Mujahideen. It would be enlightening to look at what Justice A.M Thipsey of the Bombay High Court who dealt with this issue in the 7/11 case had to say regarding this very point.

Much before the revelation by Mr. Khetan, the defence council of the 13 accused in the 7/11 train blast case wanted to tender as part of the evidence the confession of Sadiq Sheikh who claimed to have done the blast. The prosecution objected to the confession being tendered as evidence in this case by arguing, among other things, that the confession if admitted here would be:

"inconsistent with the guilt of the accused in this case…[and that]it would prejudice the accused in that case(Crime Branch IM case-MCOCA Special case no.4 of 2009) and would not afford them the chance." (Pg 37.)

The trial Court accepted the prosecution's argument. When the defense took it to the High court, Justice A.M. Thipsey setting aside the order explicitly pointed out:

" It is not possible to accept the view of the learned judge. In the first place, the appellants had not claimed-and could not have claimed that the confessions of those accused 'were true'. They were not expecting to 'prove' those confessions against those accused. What they were saying is that someone else has confessed of having committed the offense with which they are charged…and it is the court that decides whether the fact of a confession having been made is true and also whether the facts stated in the confession are true. Confessions are treated as circumstantial evidence of the truth of the facts stated therein and it is the court that decides whether the facts stated in a confession are to be believed or not in a given case. It is a matter of evaluation of evidence to be done by the court after it is tendered."(Pg 26,29)

It is important to note that a confession is immeasurably more valuable when compared to an Interrogation report. It can be tendered as evidence in court. Despite this, as the High court points out and rightly so, that even then there is no presumption to their inherent truth value, and, it is the job of the court of law to evaluate if they do and can be believed and relief upon. For, the court remains the final arbitrator of guilt or innocence.

How is it possible, then, to proclaim the guilt of the IM based on Interrogation reports, even when the cases of Sadiq Sheikh and the rest, under the rubric of the IM, are still sub-judice? Can a claim be made even on the basis of certain facts which journalistic research might have brought to light, when those facts are yet to be tested in court?

Mr Khetan offers us neither proofs nor explanations. What is offered instead is a narrative of how 5 people-Sadiq Sheikh, Mujahid Saleem, Asif and Amir Reza Khan, and Riaz Bhatkal-fired by ideas of Jihad and retributive justice, bankrolled by forces across the border, went about bombing places one after the other.

The preposterousness of the claim, in the sheer absence of any proof offered, even when all these cases are sub-judice, do not warrant a rebuttal. If anything, it warrants the forceful disciplining of the clause of 'contempt of court'-for the sheer damage that the claim could possible wreck for all the cases that are presently under trial at a time when the 'collective conscience of the people' has assumed legal weight.

And yet, as the narrative has been expounded by Mr. Khetan, I shall take it seriously within the bounds of this chapter, as, unfortunately the entire fabric of the discourse of terror has been created by such unsubstantiated and baseless allegations. Allegations which have assumed the status of commonsense-and through repetition-gained legitimacy and have become the "truth". And it needs to be said that this narrative is thoroughly contested-factually.

For the last one year, as a Research Fellow at the Tata Institute of Social Sciences, I have been researching on terror cases across the 4 cities-Hyderabad, Mumbai, Bangalore and Kolkata. Over this period, I have gone through all relevant documents-legal and otherwise-, met lawyers (both prosecution and defense) as well as accused and their families, of almost all the cases of bomb blasts and attacks in these four cities. This research has encompassed the criminal and social history of two of the 5 people that Mr. Khetan authoritatively mentions as the original member who started the Indian Mujahideen-Mujahid Saleem, and Asif Reza Khan. And the picture that emerges is completely different from what Mr Khetan has attributed to them without proofs or explanations.

Mujahid Saleem: A study of the 4 bomb blast cases of Hyderabad (*forthcoming in EPW*), as well as my meeting with the lawyer associated with his encounter case, his friends, as well as his father Aleem Islahi (whose provocative writing on Jihad and Babri Masjid is the sudden and only explanation offered by Mr. Khetan of Mujahid's crime) makes a story worth telling.

But, it is Maulana Naseeruddin, a cleric who has been a friend of Aleem Islahi as well as his son, whose story of prosecution is directly linked to that of Mujahid. The families of both Maulana Naseeruddin and Aleem Islahi live next to each other in Saidabad-a densely populated Muslim pocket of Hyderabad. Maulana Naseeruddin was first arrested in 1992 when he organized public prayer for the 'martyrship' of the Babri Masjid. He was arrested along with 62 other young men under TADA. Since then Maulana Naseeruddin has been accused in several cases of terror in Hyderabad, including the famous case of the murder of the Haren Pandya. Last year Maulana Naseeruddin, after spending almost 2 decades in prison, was acquitted of *all* charges in*all* the cases. A minor case is still pending against him. In 2004, when Naseerudin was first accused in the Haren Pandya murder case, there were protests and people had gathered when the Gujarat contingent came to arrest him. The Gujarat contingent was led by IPS officer Narendra Amin who is presently an accused in the Ishrat Jahan fake encounter case. Mujahid Saleem, then a 20 year old boy, was standing the closest to Naseeruddin, protesting with the others. He was shot at point blank range by Narendra Amin. At the time of his death, there was not a single case against him.

Md Rayeesuddin, a friend of Mujahid, was also there that day. He is the prime witness in the case of encounter against Narendra Amin. The case is presently lying dormant. Since the time time Md Rayeesuddin listed as a witness, he has been arrested and interrogated, in every single case of bomb blast in Hyderabad. He was Accused no 16 in the case no 198/2007, one of the 4 Mecca

Masjid Blast cases. In that case, his name was included in the chargesheet after he refused to step down as a witness. Even after receiving compensation for the false framing, he has been picked up and tortured after the recent 2013 Dilsukhnagar blast. Ironically, previously listed in the chargesheet as a member of Huji, Rayeesuddin was picked up and interrogated even as the police claimed that it was the Indian Mujahideen. He still refuses to step down as a witness in the day-light encounter of his friend Mujahid Saleem.

Aleem Islahi: The mere holding of an opinion, irrespective of its nature, does not constitute crime, unless an overtly violent act has been done. Though it is difficult to understand the link with the opinions of Aleem Islahi with the guilt of his son Mujahid, it remains a fact that Aleem Islahi has not been accused in a single case of crime or terror in Hyderabad. His name was in the FIR in case no 198/2007, it was however not included in the chargesheet.

Asif Reza Khan: Asif Reza Khan, a resident of Kolkata, was 22 years old when he was first arrested in 1994 under TADA. A student at Aligarh Muslim University then, Asif had just finished his graduation from the well known Maulana Azad College in Calcutta. At AMU, Asif had Kashmiri friends with whom he lived in the hostel. The arrest was among the hundreds of arrests of Muslims across the country for alleged 'Jihadi' links and disruptive activities pertaining to Kashmir. Also arrested under TADA at the same time was ShahidAzmi-the lawyer who was later killed defending those who were falsely accused in terror cases.

Asif Reza and Shahid Azmi spent 5 years in Delhi's Tihar Jail. Released in 1999, after the Supreme Court acquitted them of all charges, both Asif and Shahid, like most others who were released, were re-arrested in several cases, especially in the many hi-profile cases of kidnapping of businessman in the country. After their release, all three of them-Shahid and Asif and Aftab-were accused in the kidnapping of Partha Roy Burman, the 'Khadim's' shoe baron from Kolkata. Shahid and Asif were taken in custody and interrogated. Asif was also accused in the kidnapping of a Gujarat diamond merchant, Bhaskar Parekh. *(Gathered from my conversation with Abdul Azeez, JamiluddinNasir, Aftab Ansari. Abdul Azeez is friend of the Asif Reza family and knew Asif well. The facts are corroborated in the deposition of Ali Reza Khan, the brother of Asif.)*

In 2001, immidietly after SIMI was banned, the Gujarat police took Asif into police custody, and took him to Rajkot where they shot him on December 7 -one and half months before the American Centre attack. The police said, officially, that Asif, a member of SIMI, in a bid to escape, fired upon them by snatching the AK-47 of one of the policemen. They shot him in retaliation. None of the policemen were hurt.

The entire case of the Calcutta attack is built on the assumption that Asif Reza Khan was a terrorist with links with 'Jihadi organisations'. An assumption which is not substantiated by any proof or corroboration.

According to the official case, the American Centre attack which was a ride by shooting of the guards stationed outside the United States Information Service which lasted 40s, was carried out by friends of Asif (one of the two shooters was Sadiq Sheikh according to the police) who wanted to avenge his death. Strangely, the attack took place in Kolkata, even though Asif was killed in Gujarat, as Asif was initially in custody of the Kolkata police according to a confession in the case. Out of the total of 9 accused, 7 were sentence to death by the trial court. The High court acquitted two of them and reduced the punishment of 3 others to 5 years of imprisonment. Two of the accused who presently stand between the complete collapse of the case, face the death penalty in a case which is laced with irregularities, and where the possibility of fabricated evidence cannot be ruled out, as I have concluded after studying the records of the case and speaking to people concerned.. The appeal by the two accused against their convictions is up for hearing in the Supreme Court the next month, where the entire narrative of Asif as well as the attacks by his friends, including Sadiq Sheikh, will be put to test. Strangely, in this case where the accused have veered between two judicial extremes-from death penalty to acquittal-Sadiq Sheikh, the prime accused who was shown as absconding till 2008, is yet to be tried even though the final appeal of the other two who only have minor conspiratorial roles is being heard.

The reality of the IM is sub-judice in many courts of the country with the allegations against them yet to be evaluated and appraised by examination to the level of evidence. For, along with allegations, are also irregularities, severe contestations and allegation of possible fabrication as well as violence-as the legal and extra legal stories of two out of the five named by Mr. Khetan reveal. And this, here, is the crucial point: this is not a contestation of facts. The above facts about the individuals who have been condemned unheard by Mr. Khetan, have not been narrated here to proclaim the innocence of Asif Reza Khan or Mujahid Saleem, but rather, to reveal the falsity of the innuendos which form the basis of Mr. Khetan's proclamation of their guilt.

This chapter is also not a proclamation of the innocence of the Indian Mujahideen. What is intended here is to raise a crucial question: On what basis can the Indian Mujahideen be declared as a reality responsible for many blasts across the country – without evidence-when the matter is sub-judice and also deeply riven with contestation and stories of state violence?

Purely on the basis of a personal, closeted reading of Interrogation reports whose validity is less reliable than the facts pointed out above or the testimonies of all those who are willing to testify in court against it?

IMPLICATIONS, TERRROR AND PEOPLE'S RIGHTS

Terror today is neither limited to cases of bomb blasts and attacks and questions of justice therein, nor is it about the guilt or innocence of individual/individuals and groups. Terror-whether in the jungles or urban centres, or in the iniquitousness of security cameras-today, is a narrative. A narrative informing a politics, informing relations between the state and its citizens, informing our very ideas of lives negotiated as a people.

And it is this political centrality of terror as a narrative that has made cases of attacks and bomb blasts-the episteme of that narrative-not mere question of crime and justice alone. Put together, terror has taken a heavy toll on lives of the people. And yet, this number is insignificant if compared to, lets say, deaths due to hunger, poverty, diseases, or even traffic accidents. However, the centrality of this narrative today is undisputed-inexplicably. For, there is something in this narrative that offers enormous potential for the state and the powers that be, to assume an authoritarian, overriding, exception-making, dissent-quelling, posture, which commands unquestionable powers and obedience-all in the name of security of the state and its people. What this narrative allows is the people's collective acquiescence in the withdrawal of their own rights, or other's rights and permits the creation of a security state which seemingly only exists to protect people from each other.

Let's take the direct association or causal relationship between the two central terror attacks when this narrative of terror, as well as one of Muslims as terrorist, was being born-the parliament and the Kolkata attacks and the passing of POTA three months later-an act whose extraordinary provisions have been proved to have been used against the minorities for a communal politics.

Or, let's say, in the enormous ability of the narrative of terror to declare an unspoken state of exception. The most powerful example being the Mecca Masjid blast case, where the very evocation of the name, a blast, levied a state of exception on the city's Muslims so powerfully that the police could round up 200 Muslims after the blast, even when the place bombed was the community's own mosque and the people killed were the Muslims themselves. And no questions were asked.

These narratives of terror-that Muslims are jihadists spreading terror, or on the other hand, Muslims believe that all Muslims are innocent and ask for justice only for them (as also assumed in Mr. Khetan's asticle)-have been the basis of politics, political mobilization over the last decade. And this is the most crucial point here. That these narratives and its ideological counterpart-the question of security-have been the central rallying point of decade long politics, and the terror cases their site, the building block.

Hence, the falling apart of any case, is not an isolated incidence of wrong prosecution, but rather the collapse of a narrative which puts to question the very basis of the politics and the ideological formulation which has manifested itself into history post 2001.

These are the fissures that help us expose the myth that is being narrated to through our governments, media and war machines.

It needs to be said that Mr Khetan's previous contribution-the publishing of Swamy Aseemanand's confession, as well as the expose of the case, has helped dent this narrative. Yet, in the present formulation Mr Khetan has first tried to prove that some individuals are innocent, and then, used that credibility, to add weight to an extremely communal narrative-completely unsupported by evidence. This sleight of hand is subversive of the very struggle for rights and justice in its raising, or lending force, to the terrible spectre of the Indian Mujahideen-a new narrative to be used by both communal and authoritarian forces.

By implicating the Indian Mujahideen after giving SIMI a clean chit, Mr. Khetan seeks to demolish the argument built by an entire body of evidence of fabrication of cases against Muslims by the state-by stating that this is not a case of political targeting of a community, but of mistaken identity. A corollary of the argument : that the state has not acted communo-politically and targeted Muslims, and hence not implicated in the fabrication, but as much a victim of the fabrication as those wrongly accused by it. Mr. Khetan also seeks to subvert the other challenges to the state's blatant violation of human rights of its citizens-as the new data of fabrication proves-, the real spectre of Hindu terror especially after the Asseemanand confession, and most importantly the imputations that the state acted communally and in bad faith. And here comes the most lethal and dangerous aspect of Mr. Khetan's argument: it reinforces the belief that though not all Muslims are terrorists, all terrorists are indeed Muslims.

Bibliography

Allana, G.: *Pakistan Movement: Historic Documents*, Karachi, Department of International Relations, University of Karachi, 1967.

Arif. S.M.: *Islamic Fundamentalism and Jihad*, MD Pub, Delhi, 2010.

Das. P.K.: *Jihad : Terrorist Strategies Against the West*, Sumit Enterprises, Delhi, 2009.

Dilip H. Mohite : *Rise of Islamic Fundamentalism and the Grand American Strategy* : Kalinga, Delhi, 2002.

Gupta, J.B. Das : *Islamic Fundamentalism and India* : Hope India Publications, Delhi, 2002.

Hoffman, Bruce: *Inside Terrorism and Internet Crime*, New York: Columbia University Press, 1998.

John O. Voll : *Islam: Continuity and Change in the Modern World*, Syracuse, New York: Syracuse University Press, 1994.

Laquer, Walter: *Terrorism Attack from Computer Hacking*, Oxford: Oxford University Press, 1999.

Levitas, D.: *The terrorist next door: The militia movement and the radical right*, New York: Thomas Dunne Books, 2002.

Noorani, A.G.: *Islam and Jihad*, Leftword, Delhi, 2002.

Qureshi, A. Iqbal : *Islam and the Theory of Interest*, Kitab Bhavan, New Delhi, 1994.

Rizvi, Hassan Askari: *The Military and Politics in Pakistan: 1947 - 86*, Progressive Publishers 1986.

Sharma, Rajeev: *Global Jihad : Current Patterns and Future Trends*, Kaveri Books, Delhi, 2006.

Spindlove, J. R.: *Terrorism today: The past, the players, the future*, Upper Saddle Creek, NJ: Prentice Hall, 2000.

Thomas Arnold: *The Spread of Islam in the World, A History of Peaceful Preaching*, Goodword Books, 2001.

Whitaker, D. J.: *The Terrorism Reader*, New York: Routledge, 2001.

Index

A

Afghan Operations, 62, 63, 70.

C

Counterfeit Currency, 76.

D

Drug Smuggling, 76.

G

Global Terror, 78.

I

Indian Mujahideen, 123, 124, 126, 127, 128, 129, 130, 131, 133, 182, 183, 185, 187, 194, 195, 196, 200, 206, 208, 209, 211, 214, 215, 216, 217, 218, 219, 220, 221, 222, 223, 224, 226, 232, 237, 239, 240, 241, 242, 243, 270, 271, 272, 274, 276, 278, 280, 281, 283, 285.

Intelligence Agencies, 2, 13, 19, 27, 33, 40, 57, 58, 80, 81, 83, 85, 86, 88, 90, 91, 92, 93, 94, 95, 96, 97, 98, 105, 108, 109, 110, 111, 112, 113, 114, 115, 116, 117, 118, 119, 121, 122, 183, 184, 188, 205, 232, 240, 261, 266, 270.

Inter-Services Intelligence, 11, 13, 15, 17, 19, 22, 34, 36, 37, 38, 40, 189, 213, 255, 262.

International Community, 41, 42, 46, 48, 49, 50, 51, 52, 53, 55, 56, 58, 113, 114, 116, 117, 118, 229.

ISI, 1, 2, 3, 4, 5, 6, 7, 8, 9, 10, 11, 13, 14, 15, 16, 17, 18, 19, 20, 21, 22, 23, 24, 25, 26, 27, 28, 29, 30, 31, 32, 33, 34, 35, 36, 37, 38, 39, 40, 41, 42, 43, 44, 45, 46, 47, 48, 49, 50, 51, 52, 53, 54, 55, 56, 57, 58, 59, 60, 61, 62, 63, 64, 65, 66, 67, 68, 69, 70, 71, 72, 73, 74, 75, 76, 77, 78, 79, 114, 115, 116, 117, 118, 119, 120, 121, 122, 132, 135, 239, 256, 264, 270.

Islamic Terror Networks, 14.

Islamist Terror, 270.

J

Jihadist Progress, 253.

L

Lashkar-e-Taiba, 5, 8, 28, 48, 123, 183, 193, 206, 211, 213, 227, 270, 273.

N

Nuclear Security, 52.

O

Operations, 9, 11, 13, 15, 17, 21, 25, 26, 29, 33, 35, 36, 41, 42, 46, 47, 48, 49, 50, 51, 52, 55, 58, 62, 63, 65, 66, 67, 68, 70, 71, 75, 76, 77, 84, 95, 129, 134, 135, 137, 138, 141, 147, 148, 152, 158, 165, 167, 191, 234, 236, 249, 251, 258, 260, 273, 274.

P

Political Executive, 68, 73.

R

Radical Madrasas, 254.
Replication in Kashmir, 63.
Riyaz Bhatkal, 215, 218, 227, 245, 272.

T

Taliban, 4, 5, 6, 7, 8, 9, 10, 14, 18, 19, 20, 21, 23, 24, 26, 27, 28, 29, 33, 39, 40, 47, 48, 50, 52, 55, 56, 57, 58, 63, 64, 77, 116, 243, 255, 256, 257, 258, 259, 260, 261, 262, 263, 264, 266, 267, 268, 269, 274.
Terror Network, 11.
Terrorism, 1, 8, 9, 11, 16, 22, 23, 35, 38, 39, 40, 41, 42, 43, 46, 48, 50, 52, 53, 54, 55, 57, 58, 66, 78, 91, 92, 105, 109, 114, 115, 116, 119, 134, 135, 139, 184, 189, 193, 198, 204, 205, 209, 213, 214, 215, 219, 222, 236, 237, 239, 248, 252, 259, 260, 262, 268, 269, 276.
Terrorist Activities, 183, 216, 218, 258, 263, 267.
Threat, 42, 45, 52, 53, 54, 56, 58, 59, 82, 83, 92, 93, 105, 114, 134, 151, 201, 203, 232, 236, 237, 246, 257, 270, 273, 274.
Transitional Democracies, 80.

W

War, 1, 2, 3, 4, 5, 6, 7, 8, 9, 11, 12, 14, 17, 22, 23, 30, 32, 33, 36, 40, 41, 43, 44, 45, 46, 47, 49, 50, 52, 56, 58, 59, 70, 71, 73, 81, 82, 99, 120, 141, 142, 146, 148, 150, 163, 174, 177, 178, 183, 184, 189, 191, 192, 194, 196, 197, 201, 205, 208, 226, 236, 261, 281, 282, 284, 285.

Y

Yasin Bhatkal, 125, 127, 215, 218, 235, 237, 239, 242, 246.

❑❑❑